Peter White was brought up in Winchester, where he still lives with his wife Jo. They have four children. He travels widely for his broadcasting commitments, but is usually to be found on the terraces of the Dell when Southampton play at home.

See It My Way

PETER WHITE

WARNER BOOKS

A *Warner* Book

First published in Great Britain in 1999
by Little, Brown and Company

This edition published by Warner Books in 2000

Copyright © Peter White 1999

The moral right of the author has been asserted.

A CIP catalogue record for this book
is available from the British Library.

ISBN 0 7515 2547 2

Typeset in Imprint by M Rules
Printed and bound in Great Britain by
Clays Ltd, St Ives plc

Warner Books
A Division of
Little, Brown and Company (UK)
Brettenham House
Lancaster Place
London WC2E 7EN

To Mum who followed me to the shops and back,
but never let on.

Accept this book with love and gratitude.

Contents

	Prologue Signature Tune	1
1	Two Little Boys	7
2	Bristol Fashion	30
3	Train Stopped Play	66
4	The Blind Sons of Gentlemen	88
5	The Blind Misleading the Blind	104
6	Long, Tall Janet	127
7	All Dressed Up and Nowhere to Go	143
8	'Peter Goes Where the Action Is'	158
9	Radio Days	181
10	Taking Off	204
11	Family Fortunes	230
12	Have Stick, Will Travel	255
13	White's Last Stand	281
14	The Box Beckons	294

Prologue

Signature Tune

Thursday 20th November 1997 was a pretty hectic day for the ancient city of Winchester. Best known for its thousand-year-old cathedral and its round table of more doubtful date, on that day the city bore stoically a massive invasion of the media at its most manic. Six months earlier the country had been startled by Labour's landslide victory. Winchester had played its own small part in the drama, providing the last result after four recounts and almost twenty-four hours after polling had finished.

That result seemed to symbolise the nature of the disaster which had overtaken the Conservatives. Their representative fighting in one of the safest Tory seats in the country had managed to lose it by two votes, albeit not to Labour themselves but to the Liberal Democrats.

The sitting Winchester MP, Gerry Malone, would have done well to have accepted defeat as gracefully as he could and toddled off back to Scotland, but he chose to question the accuracy of the result in the courts. They ordered a re-run which was why we were all now back in Winchester to watch the election's belated death throes.

I arrived at Winchester Guildhall just after eleven in the evening. I'd been in London all day and had rushed down after doing a live feature on Radio 4's *Does He Take Sugar* programme about rumours of leaks and swingeing cuts to benefits for disabled people planned by the new government. Labour, it appeared, had now decided what to do with its huge one hundred and seventy parliamentary majority.

The Guildhall was seething with speculation. No result was expected until at least two in the morning but all the predictions were heading in one direction. The Lib Dem Mark Oaten was, the pundits said, about to cause a landslide of his own. Majorities of fourteen, fifteen, even sixteen thousand were being bandied about. I thought the prophesies sounded rather wild and said so on my election programme for BBC Radio Solent, the local station. I was one of those who believed that the inherently Conservative landowners, farmers, and nouveau riche of the countryside surrounding Winchester would blench at what they had done on 1st May and would return timidly to the fold. As a native of Winchester I reckoned I knew the people pretty well, and continued, long after the mounting evidence and the mounting piles of Lib Dem votes made it untenable, to share this theory with my listeners.

No matter! On nights like this atmosphere is far more important than accuracy for the broadcaster. We had a splendid position, perched high above the auditorium where the count was taking place and where the returning officer would eventually announce the result. It would also have provided an excellent view, had such a commodity been of the slightest relevance to a totally blind journalist like me.

As I sat up there ad libbing furiously into the microphone, receiving instructions about the next interview I was supposed to conduct in my left earphone, the next tape I would have to cue in my right, and whispered descriptions of what was going on in the hall from someone standing just behind me, I was in a seventh heaven. This was the hottest story of the day and I was covering it. A few yards to my right I could hear the output from BBC Television's Election Special, and the distinctive Canadian accent of Tony King, doyen of election pundits to whom I used to listen as a politically awakening teenager in the sixties. A few seconds later my producer tapped me on the shoulder. He said we could borrow Mr King for an interview. Eat your heart out, Robin Day!

As the excitement mounted the visual element in the story increased. Those tell-tale green boxes – or whatever colour they were – stuffed with votes were beginning to spell out the story all on their own. While a tape played and my microphone was closed the producer explained to me how Mark Oaten's boxes were stretching all the way along one side of a table then turning a right angle to extend halfway along the next edge. Meanwhile Gerry Malone's sad little huddle of boxes hardly made it to the middle, looking, the producer said, like a deserted village on the edges of a thriving town. It was a pleasing image, and as soon as my mike was live again, I stole it and claimed it for my own. I briefly wondered how many of the listeners, some of whom would be aware I couldn't see a thing, would ask themselves how I knew.

Then, at last, the result.

The realisation that those cocky experts had got it completely wrong. Far from romping home with a majority of 16,000 votes Mark Oaten had had to content himself with a victory margin of only just over 21,000 votes. Still, I was too busy to eat humble pie as we scrambled with all the other outlets to be the first to bring listeners the traditional crowing speeches of victory, and the not so penitent admissions of defeat. For me the result was pretty immaterial. What was important was that I had been there, in the centre of events covering it. Thirty years before this would for me have been a dream, and a seemingly impossible one, according to most people.

I got home at 4.00 am, had a winding down whisky or two, and went to bed. An hour later the phone rang. It was the *Today* programme. Did I know that the papers were full of leaks that Labour was proposing to slash benefits to disabled people? I told them wearily that as the BBC's first Disability Affairs Correspondent I did know this and had been warning them about it for weeks. We had broken the story on *Does He Take Sugar* the night before, a few hours before it was all over the newspapers.

They weren't interested in all that self-justification stuff.

Could I do a quick interview about it with the *Today* presenter Sue McGregor? In my back bedroom, sound-proofed by hundreds of Braille books, was a make-shift studio; or rather, one mike, one small mixing box and a high quality ISDN phone line. It's one of the perks of being a correspondent, that you can broadcast to programmes like *Today* in your dressing gown with a cup of tea at your elbow. My statutory two and half minutes over, I dressed hurriedly and went off to catch the train to London. It was going to be a busy day.

It was.

Every news outlet in the BBC, radio and television, wanted a piece of the action and I ricocheted from studio to studio like a ping-pong ball. I was at it until six in the evening. It would have gone on until later, but I had a long-standing engagement to talk to eighteen hundred further education students in Croydon. I had to talk to them about 'making the most of your opportunities'.

I got through that somehow, despite nodding off twice on the platform as the interminable prize giving which preceded my gig dragged on. Then, the condition of doing the job in the first place, a lift which got me home around midnight.

Signature Tune

The following day was a Saturday and anyone in their right mind and after the thirty-six hours I'd just had would have been enjoying a lie-in. But at seven-thirty I was back at Radio Solent preparing for a three-hour current affairs and phone-in show. I'm probably not in my right mind. A radio junkie, I'm still, after nearly three decades, celebrating the fact of being allowed to do the job I'd always dreamed of, but thought my blindness would prevent. How did it happen? Well, I'm not sure, but I'm about to try and explain it. To you and to myself.

1

Two Little Boys

'Not much sight in those, is there?' With these brief words, the eye specialist handed back to my mother her nine-week-old son and moved swiftly on to his next mission of mercy. No advice, no referral, no words of comfort were offered. The message was clear: go home and cope.

So she did!

In addition to the birth of a blind baby, my older brother Colin, she had plenty to deal with. It was 1943, and my five foot three father was a rather unlikely military policeman in North Africa. Mother was living at the time with her parents in Croydon. It was a toss-up whether Hitler's bombs or the lightning raids of my maternal grandmother's combative temperament were more troublesome. When the baby was born, my grandmother had only just begun talking to my mother again, after weeks of ignoring her for having the gall to get pregnant in the first place. Though she was a married woman, having babies during wartime was, apparently, an irresponsible activity, especially one suspects, when it must have involved sex. My grandfather did his best to be a tower of strength, but he had his own back to watch.

The first problem appears to have been what to tell my father. The truth, strangely, appears not to have been an option rationalised by the fact that he had enough on his plate already fighting the Hun. The reality, I suspect, was that the warm, funny, instinctively intelligent man I grew to love as my father was, at the age of twenty-six, still spiky, hot-tempered and very insecure. My mother's letters referred to 'a bit of a problem with Colin's eyes'.

The upshot was that Dad came home at the end of the war expecting to meet a two-and-a-half-year-old son with a bit of a squint. Instead he encountered a child who could just about see his hand in front of his face. As you can imagine, it came as something of a shock. An even ruder surprise followed swiftly. Colin, who was growing up in a household where his blindness was regarded as a fine excuse for smotherly love, was none too sure about the rough and ready ways of returning soldiers. Within twenty minutes he had taken a healthy bite out of Dad's forearm, a familiar tale after the war, I suspect. Their relationship got off to a shaky start.

Thanks to the war and aggravated by a dollop of parental interference, Don and Joan White's marriage had also experienced a shaky start, but fortunately it proved to be of stern, if combustible stuff. My parents moved into their own home – a grotty flat in Catford (with half the roof missing), but a place of their own. The flat belonged to Dad's Commanding Officer, a man bizarrely known as Polly Walters. As well as providing them with half a roof over their heads, he also gave Dad, who had been apprenticed as a carpenter before the war, a steady job. They fought and they frolicked, using their common sense rather than warmed-over theories to bring up Colin. They began to contemplate a second child, and in doing so, they asked the obvious question. Will a second child be blind? They received a supremely confident answer. 'Mr and Mrs White, that was a chance in a million. Don't worry.' On that basis they sailed ahead. I've always been indebted to the arrogance of the medical profession.

You would have done well to have had your money on a million to one shot running at 19 Tower Street, on 18 June 1947. The result was in doubt for an agonising few weeks, while both parents willed me to follow a sudden sound with my eyes, or grab for a shiny object. But when, after about six weeks, they were finally told that, if anything, I had slightly less sight than Colin, it was more of a disappointment than a shock. They had known all along really. And the dream of a sighted playmate for Colin, who could also eventually take responsibility for his care in an inevitable life of celibate basket-weaving, was at an end.

This may have been bad news for them, but I've always reckoned that, apart from the small matter of being totally blind, my luck in life's lottery has been remarkably good. Reasonable brain, rude health, combative temperament, looks which at least don't frighten the horses, and – if you like to take it a stage further – the mere chance of being born in a developed world, in the middle of the twentieth century, with two world wars neatly out of the way. But I maintain that my best bit of good fortune, if I was destined to be blind, was to have a blind brother, deftly knocking obstacles out of my way four years ahead of me. For many blind children, the brake on them is not their own low ability but the low expectations of others. In my case, Colin, who was bright, physically compe-tent, and remarkably confident at getting about, set a standard which I found hard to emulate. Instead of people saying, 'You can't expect Peter to do that!', they said, 'Colin can do that. Why can't Peter?' Crucially, right from the start, I had a role model I could look up to. For most blind children, by the time they meet anyone else blind, the damage about how they

regard blindness has been done. Blind Pew, ubiquitous collecting box and rattled tin, and the vague unstated
disappointment of their parents have achieved that. But I
didn't need to learn the politically correct mantra that 'Blind is
beautiful'. I just hero-worshipped my blind brother.

Mind you, I'm glad to say we would have presented a
nightmare for any psychologist or social worker trying to for-
mulate a theory on how blind children develop. We could not
have been more different. True, we walked and talked at about
the same ages but, in the reverse order. Perversely, in the light
of the people we were to become, I, the broadcaster, walked
first, and the more introverted Colin did the early talking –
both at about ten months. Colin was, and remains, the cautious
one, summing up the risks of any action carefully before
making a move. Although he was physically more competent
than me, I was the one who took the physical risks; it was said
of me that if someone told me to jump off a roof, I would do
so without hesitation, trusting that someone would be there to
catch me. Even at the age of four, Colin would have demanded
an undertaking to catch, signed in triplicate.

This fearless attitude extended to all living creatures.
Besotted from an early age by animals, I had the heart-stop-
ping attribute of embracing any dog, oblivious of the fact that
my affection might not be returned. Once, when I was about
three, we went into a shop which had an Alsatian with a fear-
some reputation and which was therefore usually kept shut
up. However, on this occasion, it had somehow escaped, and
the first the owner heard was a series of frenzied barks. She
ran aghast into the shop expecting to find a chewed customer
and a court order to destroy, only to discover her brave guard-
dog fighting for its breath with two skinny, three-year-old
arms around its neck. By contrast, on a family visit to the zoo,
Colin was invited to go up and see the camels and memorably
replied, 'They won't want to see me.' He was timid in personal

relationships. From a very young age, if I were crossed in my desires, I would argue. If I lost the argument, I would rage. If that did no good, I would proffer the charming apology. It was almost always the latter that did the trick, but the other two processes had to be ritually endured first. On the other hand, if Colin were thwarted, he would either acquiesce or sulk, depending on the matter's importance to him. He hated rows and didn't understand their dynamics. Rows seemed to be marriage-threatening, but in reality they followed clearly defined patterns and rules. Colin's failure to understand this was a considerable disadvantage for him. Though four years younger, I had to explain them to him but he never really caught on.

When it came to practicalities, he had me well and truly licked. At the risk of falling into the social worker's trap, I think it's true to say that children blind from birth have difficulties with spatial awareness. It's not so much the obvious fact that you can't see where you're going, more that you can't imagine where you're about to go. Raised lines on maps may be fine in theory, but they don't convert readily into complex configurations of pavements, hedges, lampposts, shin-high walls and spaghetti-like road intersections. Add to that the total inability of most people to give efficient directions, even to those who can see, and you can imagine that independent travel is a bit of a nightmare. It can be learnt, sure enough, but my childhood and adolescence was a constant battle between wanting to be free to go where I liked, but hating the embarrassment which inevitably resulted when I did. Colin, on the other hand appeared to have an in-built radar, enabling him, apparently instinctively, to go where he liked, first around the housing estate on which we lived, then the city, and finally anywhere he chose. This simultaneously excited and infuriated me. It meant it could be done. I just didn't see how I could do it.

The same went for almost any manual task. I could not, without the greatest difficulty, tie anything, join anything, or build anything. Only by precise repetition of what I had been endlessly shown could I perform the simplest chore involving my hands. One school holiday was totally ruined, because graduation from the infants to the juniors was dependent on one's ability to tie your own shoelaces. No matter that I could already recite the Kings and Queens of England from the Norman conquest up to the present day and, merely by being told a person's date of birth, could tell them within seconds the day of the week on which they were born. All that was of no consequence. If you couldn't tie your shoelaces, you must apparently stay in the infants for the rest of your life. As we wrestled for weeks with loops, double bows, and disappearing lace tags, there were tears and tantrums – and that was only Mother. Somehow, by endless repetition, I mastered the procedure and was allowed to continue my progress through the school. I wear slip-on shoes now, to avoid unnecessary trauma. Needless to say Colin laced his shoes at three, knotted his ties at four, and spent his childhood like some precocious Isambard Kingdom Brunel, constructing giant post office towers from Meccano and connecting miles and miles of model railway tracks. In short, we were chalk and cheese. We were living proof that generalisations about blind children are as doomed and dangerous as all other generalisations.

At the time of my birth my parents had none of the benefits of hindsight. All they knew was that after three years' separation caused by the war, aggravation from both sides of the family, barely adequate housing, and on money which had to be calculated down to the last penny, they now had to raise two blind children. Relatives and friends were at pains to tell them how difficult it was going to be. In fairness, what most people knew about blindness and blind people would not have been encouraging; many lived in institutions, few had jobs, and those that did wove baskets or made brushes. Only a handful rose to the dizzy heights of tuning pianos, and jazz pianist George Shearing was actually reported to be making a fortune in the States. It was difficult at the time, though, to imagine either Colin or I up in lights at Carnegie Hall. Conventional wisdom said that we would be jobless, wifeless, prospectless. It begged the question, whether we would be dependent on our parents for the rest of their lives. From that deeply discouraging perspective they proceeded to pull off one of those small miracles which so-called ordinary people consistently perform unnoticed. By ignoring the few professional experts available, and even more, the self-appointed experts in the family and down the street, they somehow contrived to give us a normal, stable, happy home life. If there was a trick in it at all, I think it was that they saw us as children who happened to be blind, rather than blind people who happened to be children.

Both of my parents were only a little over five feet tall, and both came from working-class backgrounds; that's where the similarities ended. Dad came from a large and boisterous Winchester family, where the arguments were loud and frequent, the language rich and earthy, and strong personalities contended for supremacy. Dad, the second youngest, was spoilt rotten by everyone, and emerged with his father's humour and skill with his hands, and his mother's filthy temper and possessive streak. Naturally clever – he was reading before he went to school – he had wide interests and random, unorganised knowledge. Leaving school at fourteen, he wanted to be a printer but, when an apprenticeship became available, the boy with the faster bicycle beat him to it. In the thirties you couldn't afford to wait for the next position to become available, so he turned to carpentry instead. He always professed to hate the job and steadfastly refused to mend chairs and put up shelves at home. Nevertheless he had an excellent reputation for good work. Witty, sociable and warm-hearted, he still always gave me the impression of knowing he could have done more with his life and regretting that he hadn't.

The Durhams, Mum's family, were a different kettle of fish. Her father, whom she idolised, was in the grocery trade. In the strange hierachy of working-class Britain of the time, this placed them a cut above the families of manual workers. Grandad Durham was one of nature's gentlemen, who dressed immaculately and had an eye for the ladies, which seems to have been quite warmly reciprocated. I dread to think what might have happened had he ever strayed and been found out. Nan Durham had cornered the market in disapproval. She believed the world was peopled with men who should have known better and women no better than they should be. She disapproved of them all! Mum assures me that she did possess a sense of fun once, but by the time I knew her she ruled the roost with a strategy based on mystery illnesses, dismissive looks and a very nasty tongue.

My mother, who was what used to be known as a spirited girl, emerged with her zest for life remarkably intact, although with an overdeveloped sense of what was fitting. When she met my father she was mounting the secretarial ladder of a major magazine publisher. It seems to have been love at first sight, although their marriage was hastened by the war, and the birth of Colin resulted from my mother's desperate desire to get out of the ATS (the Auxiliary Territorial Service) and my father's equally desperate desire to get her away from all those men. Their marriage was stormy and passionate, based on a mutual refusal to surrender on any point without a fight. His weapons were alternating temper and charm, hers a level head and an almost infinite capacity to maintain silent resistance when all else had failed. Not that she was incapable of flashes of inspiration – on one occasion not long after they were married my father had taken exception to

14

a meal she had cooked and thrown it out of the window, plate and all. With money tight, she wasn't going to put up with that kind of thing. The following night he came home to a piece of cheese. Dad, who had typically forgotten the incident of the night before, picked it up, puzzled, to discover it attached by a cord to the leg of the table. Mother's comment was succinct: 'Now throw that out of the window, you bugger!'

On the whole, though, he provided the fizz and the flair, while her contributions were those old-fashioned virtues of keeping an immaculate home, paying the bills on time and making everyone feel safe, often at the cost of her own pleasures. She displayed a stickability which, despite the loss of two husbands, survives today.

It may have been a great bonus for me to be raised in a family with two blind children, but my parents didn't quite see it that way. It wasn't too bad when I could be safely stowed away in a pram or cot. Problems started as soon as I began to crawl. Colin and I were like two unguided missiles in the house, set on a permanent collision course. Soon after I was born we moved out of an impossibly cramped house into one of the postwar prefabs for which my parents had been waiting. But they weren't exactly spacious either. It seemed that wherever mother put me down, Colin would unerringly come crashing over me, especially on the rare moments when I was not emitting raucous sound signals. Failing that, as soon as I began to walk, I would be forever careering over Colin, engaged in one of his eternal building or joining games, breezily scattering carefully assembled bricks, Meccano parts or Dinky toys. One of the other discernible differences between us was Colin's almost fanatical tidiness and my distinct preference for chaos. To Colin, possessions were precious; each Dinky toy had its box, each component of a game had its place. You couldn't join in his fun without disrupting some long-cherished plan. I was of a different

15

temperament. Things were not meant to be positioned carefully, but to be shaken, banged about, and eventually, when they had served their purpose, hurled away with as much force as I could muster. Mum became accustomed to the washing-up being punctuated by sporadic missiles winging their way past her head and thudding into the wall, if I was lucky, or the window, if I was not.

Occasionally people became the unintentional target of my aim. In one incident Dad was awakened from a post-prandial doze by a sharp pain. A misplaced ashtray, propelled with just the hint of spin, had struck him behind the left ear. The retribution was memorable, although not very effective. The next day his prized Busy Lizzie was neatly lopped off from the base of its stem by a toy brick which had temporarily lost its charm. There was more retribution, but I think Dad was beginning to acquire a grudging respect for my accuracy.

For the most part, Colin and I were firm friends as children, although my disruptive and his more stoical nature could be a combustible mixture, leading to a good deal of fraternal conflict. Colin would wind me up; I would lash out. These conflicts often ended with Colin pinned in a corner, being systematically kicked, fully knowing he dare not use his four-year advantage in height and weight. Two words, well beyond the vocabulary of my age group, dominated those early years: 'aggravate' and 'defiant'. But Mother's attempts to stop Colin deliberately rousing me to fury, and me from rising to every challenge, fell largely on deaf ears.

Despite our unruly natures, dire warnings from the self-appointed experts that we would be a permanent mass of cuts and bruises proved largely unfounded. True, I got my share, but then I was the kind of kid who always would. Hyperactive, as a toddler I would bounce up and down in my cot in the mornings to gain attention. One dawn Mum and Dad awoke to a bang and discovered my cot was empty. A frantic search revealed that I had catapulted myself over the edge, slid under the bed and promptly gone back to sleep. On one potentially more serious occasion, Grandad White had gone down into his cavernous cellar, inadvertently leaving the door ajar. Following him, doglike as usual, I plunged into the darkness. The first thing he heard were three bangs as I bounced down the stone steps on my head, cannoning into the back of his legs. I emerged largely unscathed with a shiner, a bump on the head and some damaged blood vessels, which for a while caused regular nosebleeds. These were satisfactorily cured a few months later when I wandered out of my bedroom early one morning, still half asleep, and plummeted straight down the stairs, striking my head on my toy car, standing in its normal place. Both parents shot out of bed and peered anxiously into the darkness to see me unconcerned, sitting at the foot of the stairs. Apparently, I apologised for having woken them up, and the nosebleeds were over.

In the event, the instinct to protect often caused us more trouble than allowing us free range. One day the well-meaning but hapless Grandad White removed a stick lying on the path at the bottom of the slope of his garden where Colin regularly rode his toy trolley at speed. Not long afterwards, Colin came in crying his eyes out and demanded to know who had removed the stick he had so carefully placed as a marker to prevent him crashing into the back gate.

Most attempts to interfere with our upbringing were doomed to failure, particularly those from the maternal grandparents. When Dad returned from the war, he felt Colin had been grossly mollycoddled and, like a lot of fathers at the time, he set about reasserting his authority. It's just possible that this process became exaggerated when the maternal grandparents came to stay. Coming home one evening, Dad asked Colin to go upstairs and fetch his slippers. After what was obviously a pretty perfunctory search, Colin returned, claiming the slippers were 'nowhere'. Dad, knowing full well that they were up there somewhere, promptly sent him back to look properly. The air was heavy with grandparental disapproval. Of course the poor little boy couldn't find the slippers – he was blind, wasn't he? Not long after, Colin, who could find every Dinky toy in the house at a moment's notice, returned with the slippers. A point had been made.

Neither of my parents were hard. They just seemed to have realised early on that wrapping us up in cotton wool would do neither of us any good in the long run. Colin in particular, with his small but useful vision, had licence to wander. Attempts were made to put him in the care of older children, with varying degrees of success. Returning home one day, in tears again and with another bump on the head, it was discovered that some of the children had been playing a game which involved whirling Colin round by his arms and telling him to jump at a critical moment (I don't know what had happened to Colin's legendary caution that day – I'm not sure even I would have signed up for that). Anyway, the inevitable happened. Geometry not yet on the four-year-old's syllabus, and sooner or later they misjudged the angle of trajectory and Colin embraced a passing lamppost. To their credit my parents refused to be panicked by such incidents. Colin did get into trouble on his sorties abroad, but mainly for crimes such as peeing in the local sandpit instead of coming home to use the proper facilities. Colin was always a bit lacking in the bladder department. Eventually one day Dad resorted to locking him in the loo to impress on him what it was for. Unfortunately, this incarceration happened after a Saturday lunchtime in the pub. Relieved of the cares of punishment, Dad promptly fell asleep. As time went by, Mum was faced with a dilemma. Father was not at his best when roused from an after-lunch nap. On the other hand, seven years' solitary in the bog seemed a bit steep for a relatively trivial offence. Eventually she roused him. 'Don, do you know that kid's still in the lav?' Not really a hard man, he was aghast. Colin was hastily released and the sanctity of the sandpit was guaranteed for the future.

My own desperate wish to explore posed more of a problem. The danger that I would be hurt rather than the certainty that I would get lost inhibited my progress. Blessed with the navigational skills of Columbus in search of the East, I could become hopelessly disorientated just crossing a room, let alone set free in the great outdoors. The map in my head somehow never corresponded with the ground beneath my feet. An all too familiar dilemma during my childhood was a choice of four directions without the faintest inkling of which one to take.

Our first change of home in 1951 went some way towards releasing me from house arrest. Our prefab was directly flanked by a through road, but the council house to which we moved when I was three-and-a-half was in a cul-de-sac. As one end was sealed up, the choice of directions open to me was effectively limited to three, immediately improving my navigational success rate by 25 per cent. Add to that the fact that it was bounded by kerbs and gardens, it meant that, wherever I found myself in 'the Square', I would eventually come back to where I started just by following the edge. And for me, this hundred square feet of dead-end meant untold freedom.

It must have inspired my parents with new-found confidence as well, because shortly afterwards I received my first bicycle at the age of four. Dad wheeled it into our back garden, proudly ringing the bell. This was a mistake, as for several minutes I was more enamoured with the bell than the bike. When I was finally persuaded to mount it, another disappointment lay in store. The bike was too large. My feet wouldn't reach the pedals, flailing ineffectually in mid-air instead, ignorant of what was expected of them. Frustration mounting, but clinging on doggedly to his surprise, Father fitted blocks on to the pedals. I could now reach them, which gave rise to disappointment number three. It quickly became clear that the concept of pedalling was one which was totally alien to me. Blessed with absolutely no sense of co-ordination, as one foot pressed down, the other stoutly resisted the progress of the pedal. When occasionally, more by luck than judgment, one foot persuaded the pedal to turn, the other one would unerringly miss its chance as it came up and around, causing me to crack my shins. Dad cajoled, and I continued to thrash about wildly, but we soon became thoroughly disenchanted by the *nice* surprise. The session ended with my being towed along, rather forlornly at the end of a rope to give me the concept of motion, and with a phrase ringing in my ears: 'This kid will never be able to ride a bike.' However, when Dad returned home the following lunchtime, a hunched shape hurtled towards him down the front path, almost cutting him off at the kneecaps. Unencumbered by adult expectations, I had spent the morning persuading my legs to act separately, but in co-operation with each other. My shins were like the craters of the moon, but this kid could now ride a bike.

It was a skill which was to introduce me simultaneously to the worlds of road safety and politics. I ran over a canvassing Labour councillor on my jet-propelled tricycle. I was supposed to confine my riding to the top quadrant of the Square, but a hundred square feet can feel pretty irksome, and I had decided to venture further down, just as far as the junction with the open road beyond. True to my word, I turned sharply at the bottom to ride back up again, only to come into smart contact with the forces of socialism.

She promptly transferred the harangue she had prepared for the docile and irretrievably Conservative burghers of

Winchester to me. She withered this four-year-old with an attack on the selfishness of a generation which thought only of itself, which rode roughshod over the needs of other people (I thought it was her feet, not her knees, but there you are, I supposed she knew best what I had ridden roughshod over), and which only thought of 'Me! Me! Me!' I was still trying to figure out what was wrong with that when I became aware that, amazingly, she had run out of steam and seemed to be distracted. In fact Mrs Green at No. 4, the Square's official busybody, had been stationed at her usual position beside her window and had seen what had happened. She was now leaning halfway out, gesticulating wildly at the other woman and mouthing in a stage whisper which could have been heard halfway across the city, 'He's er . . . without sight. Sightless. *Blind.*'

Having secured the other woman's attention thoroughly, No. 4 abandoned her stage whisper and reverted to her more usual stentorian bawl, delivering herself of a tirade she had been clearly longing to release for ages. 'Two of them, you know, both stone blind, and yet their mother lets them wander about all over the place. I just can't understand it. It's not safe, it's not right. They shouldn't be allowed out.'

At this point events took a strange turn. No. 4, it appeared, had made a serious tactical blunder. The accident victim, although chairman of the Winchester Road Safety Committee, was also the espouser of many good causes, especially those concerning 'handicapped children'. She believed such children should be given as much independence as possible and proceeded to give the astonished Mrs Green a firm lecture on the subject. She completed No. 4's discomfiture by marching me indoors and warmly congratulating my equally astonished mother on her foresight and common sense in giving us our heads. She then left, but two hours later she returned, completing a thoroughly confusing morning by presenting me with a box of chocolates. This, perhaps, was a gesture too far. A couple of days later, having once again ventured beyond the top of the Square, I narrowly missed mowing down a toddler even smaller than myself. 'Hard luck,' Colin yelled. 'You almost got another box of chocolates there.'

Despite these forays into the outside world, much of my life at this time was spent inside the house within my head, so deep inside at one point that my parents became quite worried about me. Whether or not endowed with common sense, the most level-headed of parents have a tendency to assume that any behaviour a little out of the ordinary from a blind child must stem from the disability. No matter that half the world's literature aimed at children is based on kids with imaginary friends, hearing imaginary voices or visiting imaginary planets. I just had an overdose of vivid imagination. Whereas most children would be content to play an imaginary role for half an hour, or even half a morning, I tended to belong to the Stanislavsky school of vivid imagination. A week was a short run for me.

One of my favourite tricks was to be 'out' when a slipperless foot or a snotty nose peeping from behind the sofa, indicated that I was quite palpably 'in'. Clearly, if I was out, I could not possibly talk to anyone – embarrassing for Mother, no doubt, but an admirable device for avoiding absurd questions about your extraordinary growth or your resemblance to one parent or another. 'Out' could mean almost anywhere. With the whole universe to choose from I had a peculiar penchant for the banal. I can remember spending the better half of one day travelling to Lincoln by train (two chairs pushed together with sofa cushions slung across them). I'm not sure why Lincoln got the nod over Jupiter or Mars, but it was a slow old journey, and proved an absolute godsend when both Aunty Glad and Aunty Edna (not really aunts, but friends of

Mother's) dropped in. Both could ask absurd questions for England, but had to be content with the fact that I was 'out'. However, the days when I was somewhere else were a complete doddle for Mother, in comparison with those when I became someone else. Once again I gave it the full method-acting treatment. The honour of my impersonation was not bestowed lightly, and apparently time and place were always chosen for maximum effect. Grandad White was a role which would have been irresistible to anyone, let alone a three-year-old child. He had a rich, gruff voice, with an asthmatic wheeze which seemed to rise all the way up from his boots; it rattled every time he breathed in, and whistled every time he breathed out. Grandad White's cough was a gem. It started deep in his throat, like a steam train gradually gathering speed, building up momentum, then exploding in a final flurry of phlegm and curses. Best of all, he could sneeze thirty-five times in a row never appearing to pause for breath. His language was splendidly colourful and studded with words and phrases I was not supposed to know, but playing his part gave me a licence to use them. Most of the time Granny and Grandad White, both pretty deaf, would converse with each other in a volley of exchanged insults, but I always caught the muttered undertones, definitely not intended for Granny's ears. Sometimes though, uttered in the piping tones of a three-year-old, they reached her all too clearly.

I always saved my performances for the days on which we visited their cottage. My mother recalls that mealtimes were worst. The clatter of knives and forks would frequently be interspersed with my commands: 'Pass the salt, Lil', and 'This bloody cabbage is underdone, Lil.' If she didn't call me Harry, in response, she could expect to be treated to a stony silence until she did.

But Mother's patience was finally exhausted when I spent most of one entire summer pretending to be Sally the

Alsatian. She could just about tolerate my constant barking, and crawling to the gate on all fours. She even managed to explain a rather nasty bite delivered to the baker's boy's forearm (he should have known better than to stick his hand through the gate to stroke a dog, however friendly it looked). But her hygienic soul was finally outraged by my insistence that I should eat my dinner off the floor from Sally's bowl.

At this point they took me to the doctor. Fortunately he was a man of plain common sense and told them it was perfectly normal for bright, rather lonely little boys to impersonate dogs, ignore adults and make unexplained journeys to Lincoln. It's interesting to speculate what kind of behaviour he would have considered abnormal.

He was right that I was very lonely and beginning to fret badly. Colin had gone off to boarding school and the spectre that was to haunt the whole of my childhood had loomed over the horizon. Back in the fifties, there was thought to be no alternative to educating *blind* children at *blind* schools. Such schools were thinly spread so, unless you were extremely lucky, this meant large chunks of the year spent away at boarding school, often starting at the age of five. My parents weren't really consulted about this, but told that this was what happened. I think they had convinced themselves that this was the best chance we had of being able to lead some kind of *normal* life. Nothing that occurred subsequently, or my total hatred of boarding school, has convinced me that, in the fifties at least, they were wrong.

At the time, though, I cared nothing for the nuances of the 'special' versus 'mainstream' argument. Colin had been packed off, first to what was known with a truly Orwellian paradox as a 'Sunshine Home' down in Newton Abbot, and then to a 'big school' in Bristol. He brought back truly horrific tales of boys immersed in water tanks and girls having their heads thrust down loos, all the while claiming to my parents that he was 'getting me used to the idea'. I was certainly getting used to the sure knowledge that, sooner rather than later, I was to be ripped from my secure, happy home and packed off to some dungeon miles and miles away, for periods of time which I already knew from Colin's absences were endless. After seeing Colin off at the beginning of one term, Mum discovered me in floods of tears. When quizzed, I said it was because Colin had gone. She was touched and vaguely encouraged, and assured me that soon I would be able to go with him. My tears redoubled.

I wasn't crying for Colin, I was crying because I knew I would be next.

The knowledge turned me from a happy if rather odd little boy into a paranoid basket-case. I became terrified of all change, fearing that it heralded the great betrayal I knew was to come. My first really clear memory of this is when we moved house from our cramped prefab to the three-bedroomed council house in the Square which was a great improvement in our circumstances. For the first time I would have my own bedroom. But right from the start I absolutely hated the house. It was a move Mum and Dad had longed for, inching their way agonisingly up the postwar housing waiting list. But I was determined to hate it right from the start.

My first memory of this house was of bare floors and a ponderously ticking clock, which seemed to be counting away my days of freedom. It was cold, the lavatory pan was cracked, and I couldn't find any of my toys. On the first evening Dad and my Uncle Pete, neither of them electricians by nature, managed to fuse all the lights. I wanted to go home, and said so constantly.

That was a Saturday. On the following Monday, I signalled my displeasure even more clearly by almost burning the place to the ground. Mum, in the way that only she could, had just cleaned the place from top to bottom. Then, most unusually for her, she popped across the road to borrow something or other, leaving me alone 'just for a minute'. I was eating a bag of sweets at the time; when I had finished them, I tossed the bag into the grate without bothering to screw it up. Then there was a pause. Then a very satisfying whoosh. A draught must have caught the bag. Mum came out from the neighbouring house and was immediately confronted by a pool of smoke billowing from our chimney. Dashing back, she found me still sitting serenely by the fire, and all of the freshly polished downstairs rooms covered in a thick layer of soot.

She cried. I knew she wanted to go home too.

As the house filled with furniture and other familiar objects, I grew to accept it, but now I wouldn't let Mum out of my presence, even for an instant, apparently convinced she was going to sneak off covertly, leaving the field clear for the school goblins to come and get me. I followed her doglike all around the house and garden, even standing guard outside the loo if she dared to retreat there for some peace and quiet.

Bedtimes became difficult for all of us. It was my suspicion that night was a time of maximum danger, when the goblins might slip through my bedroom window and carry me away to school. Mum never went out at night when we were small but, just in case, as soon as she had tucked me up and gone downstairs, I would start calling out for her to come back up again. Anything would do for an excuse – I was too hot, I was too cold, I needed a drink, I wanted my teddy. All I really wanted was the reassurance that she was still there. They made threats, I made promises, but the calling continued until I went to school.

By now Mum and Dad understood the problem. They realised I was engaged on a one-child terrorist campaign to avoid being shipped off. They realised that somehow they would have to get me used to going away without them. Great plans were laid with my favourite aunt and uncle, who also had two older children. I would stay with them for a few days and see how I managed. Mum and Dad did everything right; I was properly consulted. Would I go? Yes, I would. Would I make a fuss? No, I wouldn't.

Two days before the proposed visit my cousin Christine sent me an encouraging birthday card, doubtless under maternal orders, telling me how she was looking forward to my visit. On the day I had been rubbed, scrubbed, and generally made ready. I was still co-operating. Half an hour before the appointed time, Mum suggested I went out and waited in the road for them to arrive.

Uncle Will had a motorbike and sidecar. Part of the bribe to induce me to go was that I would get to ride in it, but at the sound of that motorbike approaching up our road, the dam of my resolve abruptly broke. By the time the bike had stopped, I was kicking, screaming, wailing.

They tried absolutely everything to cajole me into that sidecar: persuasion, bribery, guilt. I would be letting down my parents, disappointing my aunt and uncle and my cousin. Trips to the sea, favourite meals – I could even sleep with the new Corgi. It was all to no avail.

Mum and Dad finally suggested that they simply bundle me into the sidecar and Uncle and Aunt should leave, but Will was too soft-hearted for that. Eventually they gave up and regretfully rode away. The fact that Dad, usually very slow to anger with me, half booted, half carried me across the lawn and threw me on to my bed, was a small price to pay. I had won again – or so I thought.

On this occasion Mum and Dad showed they were made of sterner stuff. On the basis of my planned visit, they had arranged to go on a pub weekend outing, on their own, up the Thames. At first Mum was going to cancel, but in the end that golden rule of not allowing your children to run your lives prevailed. The following day was a Saturday and we went down to Granny White's. This was unusual but, as often happens after a stunning victory, a little complacency must have crept in and my usual antennae failed me.

Grandad White was demonstrating a slide he had made at one end of the garden. Meanwhile my treacherous parents did what I had sworn I would never allow them to do. They slunk off unnoticed, even managing to close Grandad's notoriously noisy gate without a sound. I had at last been successfully abandoned. Strangely, when I finally discovered their betrayal, I took it with remarkable calm. After all, Grandad's cottage was definitely not Bristol. They might have secured their weekend through subterfuge; what they had definitely not secured was my acquiescence.

A final incident brought the dreaded event even closer. One Monday afternoon we received a telegram which said that Colin, away at school at the time, had been rushed into hospital with appendicitis. Mum and Dad worked themselves into a state about this, and it was arranged that the following Saturday our social worker would take us all down to Bristol by car – we still had no transport at this point – to see him. I discovered two interesting things on that day. First, the expression 'as white as a maggot', used to describe Colin when they emerged from his ward. I wasn't allowed in. The second discovery was even more fascinating: I could be copiously car sick, apparently at will, and proximity to Bristol seemed to act as an emetic.

And so the die was cast. Bristol had become inevitable. We even had a date: 10 September 1952. My love/hate relationship with the calendar, counting off either terms or holidays, had begun.

I knew now that I had lost. I had run out of options, and the battle would have to be fought on another front nearly a hundred miles from home. On my last evening, as she tucked me in for the final time, I asked Mum if there was a god. She told me they would explain all that to me at school. The following day, I was to discover that if indeed there was a god, he regarded the Bristol Royal School of Industry for the Blind as a no-go area.

2

Bristol Fashion

Nurse Patricia Mapson was starched and fierce. She moved quickly and decisively, and you did what she said. She was from Chippenham and was twenty-two. For all I know she may have been desired by half the males in Wiltshire, but to me, comparing her with my mother, her voice sounded harsh and her hands felt hard.

Her first duty was to clean me up. The initial bout of roadside vomiting had hit me at Stockbridge, followed by metronomically regular puking stops at Salisbury, Warminster, Trowbridge, Bradford-on-Avon, and finally, and by now relatively unproductively, Bath. I suppose if I ever get to be *really* famous, visiting American tourists may make reverent halts at little patches of grass scattered along the A36 and the A4.

Why anyone would hesitate to be parted from me after this journey from hell is hard to imagine, but Mother, bless her, hung around miserably for a while, although clearly uninvited to participate in the businesslike administrations of Nurse Mapson. Eventually, while Nurse Mapson was thrusting me backwards and forwards on a tatty old rocking horse in a ferocious attempt to comfort me, Mother finally slunk away, wondering whether she could ever get used to this.

She never did. Even though I now have children of my own, I find it difficult to imagine how awful that first day at Bristol must have been for my mother. Having finally disentangled her hair from my clutching fingers, she had to go home; strip the bed I'd slept in; comfort the dog which kept whining at the gate; and then wonder how to spend those long evenings, freed from all those entreaties to 'just come upstairs for a minute'. All the while she was burdened with the knowledge of my extravagant grief, my desperate outburst to force her, someone, anyone to do something. They'd seen the place. They knew it was stark and tough. Colin coped, but he was self-contained, keeping his own counsel. How would this nervy, mouthy, emotional, manipulative little boy manage?

If I hadn't discussed it with contemporaries in later life, I would be tempted to wonder whether my image of Bristol had not become exaggerated by the pain it caused me at the time. But it really was the embodiment of every Dickensian, scholastic hell-hole conjured up by the great man's fertile imagination. Amazingly though, this was not 1822, but 1952. We were just eight years away from the swinging sixties, but the only things swinging at Bristol were the occasional door from its hinges and the unpolished toe-cap of a sadistic Scotsman's boot thudding into the backside of some unfortunate miscreant who had broken yet another unfathomable rule.

Many people would expect the most traumatic thing about taking a blind child from his home, transporting him eighty-three miles and dumping him down in another environment would be the loss of familiarity with place: not knowing where anything was, being unable to relate one location to another, feeling totally lost. Oddly I don't remember this sensation at all. My loss was purely of people, not place.

My first strong impression of Bristol was that it was damp, drab – and dark! It may be odd that my abiding memory should be a visual one, but when your only concept of vision is light perception you tend to make the most of what you have. I see long narrow corridors, the only light filtering in from high windows. The floors were wooden – usually full of splinters – and the furniture was sparse. When you reached the dormitories the beds were bare metal frames with protruding springs. The smell was that usual enticing boarding-school cocktail of chalk and polish, boiled cabbage and lingering urine. Bristol had a few pungent ingredients all of its own. A seemingly endless cycle of Dettol and vomit, vomit and Dettol, old farts, and the odour of stale hair-oil, which oddly hung in the air despite the only very occasional visits of Mr Hoskins the barber.

I quickly learnt to find the things I wanted: food, my bed, the bog! The rest didn't matter much, until I needed something else. Seduced first by a rocking horse, then by a mouth organ, I set about discovering exactly where I fitted into this very strange society, so different from the one I'd just left behind. Where, if I wanted anything, I yelled for Nurse instead of Mum. Where seven other people slept in my bedroom. Where I had to have jam on my bread instead of sugar, and where the tea tasted of sawdust. And where apparently, and most strangely of all, I wasn't always the most important person in the world. What irked was that people didn't know me: my likes, my dislikes and the fact that I wasn't really such a weed behind all the expansive weeping. There was no need to offer me a rubber sheet on my bed that first night, or to burst in and dress me the following morning as if I was just some sack of potatoes! And what if I couldn't tie my shoe laces yet. I had come to school to learn, hadn't I?

The food was unrelievedly but unremarkably bad: cold, lumpy porridge in huge tureens; bits of charred bacon, small enough to put in your ear – probably the safest place for them; and the inevitable, uncooked, inedible vegetables, apparently designed to put children off roughage for life. The food's only redeeming feature was a strange and exotic sausage. I still remember its peculiar taste. In the light of our knowledge of BSE, I dread to think what it was made of, but it certainly had . . . individuality.

The food was as scarce as it was horrible, which can be the only reason why so many of us have survived for so long. The minuscule breakfast, followed by uneatable lunch, was topped off each and every day by bread and jam at 5.30. Then, unless you had attained the unimaginable age of twelve and had supper at eight o'clock, you were forced to survive for fourteen hours until the whole merry-go-round of Bacchanalian gluttony began all over again. Still, you could perhaps forgive Spartan surroundings or meagre food. It was, after all, still quite soon after the war, and public funds were tight. What I find impossible to forgive is a moronic, pointlessly harsh regime, which took children as young as five from loving homes and proceeded to treat them as if they were in the army.

I developed an idea of my new pecking order that first night in the dormitory. You did not, for instance, muck around with six-year-old Roger, else he'd bash you. In any case, he could count up to a hundred, had once been run over by a car and could see a little bit! Tony, on the other hand, was a different kettle of fish. Although he was just as strong as Roger, he had even then what I thought of as a 'sensible' streak. He kept an eye out for the smaller ones. At seven, and by now a senior 'Tiny' (as the infants were known), he was clearly a good bloke to get on your side. So I did. The rest seemed to be grouped warily around either Roger or Tony, watching carefully the muted power struggle, making sure they would know which way to jump when the time came.

The process of being made to conform, Bristol fashion, began as soon as you first set foot in the place at the start of term. Firstly, they were totally obsessed about getting you out of your own clothes – your 'private' clothes, as they were known – into what passed for their uniform. I haven't a clue now what material these clothes were made of, except the school seemed to have a genius for finding garments harsh to the touch and unpleasant to the skin: rough, coarse trousers, thick woollen socks, scratchy, prickly shirts and heavy, zipper jerkins, which somehow contrived to leave you hotter in the summer and colder in the winter. Once you were seven the whole grisly outfit was topped off by great, galumphing boots with steel studs, which appeared to be intended to make you look more like an orphan than ever. Unless, that is, they were intended to ensure you wouldn't be able to move quickly enough to escape. They couldn't wait to thrust you into this garb, but only after one more ritual humiliation: the beginning-of-term shower.

No matter that you would almost certainly have had a bath on the last night of your holidays. No matter that school itself was stinking and unhygienic. The place ran on the willing, law-enforcing eagerness of gangs of older boys and on the first day of term they roamed the school like pig-sticking parties, hunting down smaller boys who had somehow managed to slip through the net, herding them into the shower rooms at the end of one of those long, dark corridors. The aim must have been to flush out the effete bugs of home in order to make room for the tougher, more robust Bristol variety. Holocaust symbolism may have been beyond my grasp at six, but it strikes a rather nasty chord now.

The effect of all this was that your own clothes, snatched from you at the very earliest opportunity, developed an almost spiritual significance. Their return, on the very last night of term, became a truly heart-wrenching experience. I still can't smell moth-balls without shedding a tear.

It was a fittingly bizarre initiation ceremony to prepare you for the undoubtedly strange world you were entering. Bristol it has to be said, was a very odd institution; it should have produced far more novelists that it has. It encompassed an enormous age range, taking pupils from four up to the age of sixteen, but it also had workshops where school leavers learnt to weave baskets and facilities for studying piano-tuning and certain clerical jobs. It was like a village for the blind, almost a sociological experiment, although with nobody apparently in control of the laboratory. Oh yes, just to add to the combustible mixture, it was co-educational.

The practical effect of this on younger kids like myself was that the lines between adults and children, staff and pupils, became hopelessly blurred. You would find people whom you thought were pupils teaching classes as part of their course. Dormitories of seven- and eight-year-olds were routinely run by prefects, boys and girls of no more than fifteen. Live-in care staff had a shadowy and illusive presence. You were far more likely to find yourself being looked after by someone who knew little about child development – not that I suspect that the care staff knew much about that either – but was rather better informed about absent-minded cruelty and juvenile sexual shenanigans!

It's not as if the children they were supposed to be looking after were an uncomplicated bunch. Forget for a moment that we were all blind. We usually did. But Bristol took the concept of mixed-ability teaching well beyond the scope of the most committed convert to the idea of comprehensive education. It tried to accommodate everyone from likely high-fliers such as me to children who nowadays would be described as having 'severe learning difficulties'. Not equipped at the time with the correct medical jargon, we thought they were 'bloody odd', or just plain 'mad'. No one ever tried to explain the condition of these children to us. They would come along, talk to themselves, have tantrums – and then disappear. Just like that. Sometimes it seemed they simply went in the night. It was not unusual to ask what had happened to Paul or John, only to be told, 'Oh, 'e's gone to Condover.' Condover was the place where children with 'additional handicaps' were sent at the time. Its name was feared, because it seemed to work as a kind of Burke and Hare operation, whereby anyone behaving strangely could be spirited away. Odd behaviour was therefore very carefully watched, and speedily commented on.

There was a lot of illness at Bristol, some of it well out of the normal run of coughs, colds and spots which children come to expect. Much of it, though I didn't understand this at the time, was connected with blindness. For example, reasons for absence from the average school rarely include, 'Oh, 'e's having a brain tumour, miss,' but brain tumours are not an uncommon cause of blindness. In my childhood they were almost as normal as chickenpox, and their effects were far more interesting. Rodney, for instance, if punched, would burst into song: 'I'll eat you for my supper, I'll eat you for my tea.' With an act like that he was punched quite a lot, which must have done his brain tumour the world of good. Henry, on the other hand, buzzed. I suppose he really had a stammer, but the noise he made was not the staccato 'putter-putter' motorboat effect you expect from a stammerer, but more of a continuous throbbing note, like that bagpipes make before they get up to speed, or perhaps, given his strong North Devon accent, that of a combine harvester with morning starter troubles. Many happy childhood hours were spent asking Henry short, sharp questions that required long and torturous answers, then running away long before the results were in.

Some of the effects of tumours were more sudden and dramatic. Children had 'episodes', which I associated with popular radio series like *The Archers* and *Journey into Space*, but which seemed to cause a great deal more consternation among the staff. We learnt to take it in our stride.

One morning I woke up to a collection of apparently unrelated sounds, unusual even for our dormitory. From a bed at one end came a long, braying monotone, presumably human. From a bed at the other end came a series of short grunts. Oscillating between them were brisk whooshing sounds, followed by concerned clucking. I was reassured to learn that all that was happening was that William and John were simultaneously ''aving a fit', and that Matron Bennet, a busy, shrewish dwarf of a woman, was dashing madly between the two of them, using a spoon to try to stop them from swallowing their tongues. Given the lack of food available, I couldn't see what was so bad about swallowing your tongue, but apparently it was yet another thing adults regarded as undesirable. By the end of the day the incident had been almost forgotten, but at some level it left a feeling of unease; ''aving a fit' seemed somehow to be an inevitable part of life, and I awaited mine with weary resignation.

Of those who weren't 'mad' or 'ill', many were just distinctly peculiar. Blind children seem to possess some very distinctive mannerisms. Some rock backwards and forwards, others wave their heads from side to side, or point their eyes skywards, apparently trying to see some distant plane. Others try to poke their fingers or thrust their fists into their eyes, even to the point where one boy had rings around his eye sockets from putting so much pressure on them. Some, including me, did all of these things. No one knows why for sure, although some pretty irritating theories have been proposed. 'The restless movements of their heads is caused by the absence of a visual point on which they can focus; the movement is a search for such a point.' Or 'the rapid backwards and forwards rocking motion of blind children is occasioned by an excess of physical energy, which sighted children expend in games of running, jumping, throwing,' and so on. Personally, I would have thought all those fits, plus punching out the lights of kids who sing when struck, would have used up a fair bit of energy, but then, who am I to know, I've only got the condition.

Relatively unaware of my own mannerisms, those of others afforded me a fair amount of harmless entertainment. John and Paul, for instance, were inseparable friends who would sit side by side on a bench in the day room, talking endlessly of their single passion, sport. As they talked, they rocked, and the doings of Bristol City and Bristol Rovers or Gloucestershire County Cricket Club would reach you in rising and fading bursts of sound, like two children on a swing. Occasionally their rocking would get out of sync, and this would dislocate their conversation as well (presumably they couldn't hear each other properly). While John would be hunched forward, like an air passenger preparing for a crash, continuing to extol the virtues of Tom Graveny as captain of England, Paul would be miles away from him, bent backwards like a sedentary limbo dancer, yet again bemoaning the failure of the England football selectors to see the merits of City striker John Ateyo. In the end, though, the law of averages would bring them back together again, and conversational harmony could be resumed.

Colin was also a rocker, but he was a solo artist. He would stand by a radiator, rocking backwards and forwards, singing popular songs. Every time he rocked backwards, the corner of the radiator would catch him a smart blow in the small of his back, causing a satisfying thud and a sharp intake of breath. The effect, made more musically pleasing by the fact that the radiator always hit him on the off-beat, was to equip him with the sound of the most popular rhythm section of the mid-fifties: double bass and washboard.

Set against this motley collection of invalids and eccentrics, bullies and bullied, the staff at Bristol were actually rather an anaemic bunch. Gauleiter Mapson and her storm-trooper nurses lauded it over the Tinies. They probably weren't that bad, but in my memory they all seemed to have attended the Mapson school of abruptness. Precious little was offered in the way of tender loving care. But one shining exception somehow seemed to slip through the net: Nurse Palmer. She was suddenly there like a healing balm, after I had been at Bristol for about a term. She was everything the others weren't: soft-voiced, gentle and prepared to touch you not simply when it was necessary to propel you in a certain direction. I know now that she was good-looking by the number of times my dad mentioned her when he came down to visit. And who could blame him? We all loved her dearly. For a time, it looked as if Robert Jones was winning in the battle for her affections, as he had to go to her room to wake her when she had to leave early one morning. But then I stilled all doubts. Feigning toothache, I spent the whole night in her bed. Jones and the rest were put to flight. Not long after that, she left. I assumed that it was a direct result of our affair. Part of the Bristol ethos seemed to be to take things away if you seemed to like them. Her replacement, Nurse Laughton, proved the importance of not letting down your guard. A tough North Country woman, she was known as Poof-bang for her habit of sweeping into a room, criticising everything and everyone in it, then sweeping out again. She out-Mapsoned Mapson for barking and biting.

It's hardly surprising that the nurses took things out on us. They were ruled with a rod of iron by Matron Bennet, the lady with the spoons. Short and tyrannical, she was a holy terror when bosom to nose with a six-year-old, but a simpering, sycophantic coward when confronted by your parents or when other influential visitors were around. She called me 'Peewee' when my parents visited, telling them what a good little boy I was. Once they had left, I was back to being 'a cheeky, argumentative little toe-rag; as different from your brother as chalk and cheese'.

In addition to supervising the nurses, she was also in charge of the medical well-being of the school. Whooping cough, chickenpox, German measles (twice) and various strains of flu all struck the school at different times. I went down with the lot. Frequent and virulent epidemics raged through Bristol like tornadoes. This was hardly surprising when I recall the communal towel-rolls in the washroom, caked with what seemed like centuries of snot. Reminiscent of the plague, a few weaklings would go down first, to be followed by around half a dozen the following day. By the third day the dribble transformed into a torrent as an endless tide swept towards the sick-bay. Then the sick-bays became too full, and you had to stay in your dormitories. By the end of my time at Bristol, I worked out that it was best to catch one of these diseases either early on, or not at all. If you caught it early, there was still enough interest to guarantee you a little care, and you also had access to a radio. I once managed to make a bout of German measles coincide with a test match, Wimbledon, and the 1958 World Cup. The alternative was not to get it at all. That meant (a) you were regarded as really tough and (b) teachers – if they had not succumbed themselves – for once took some notice of you.

On one occasion the school's laissez-faire attitude to treatment almost landed it in trouble. I went down with a particularly savage bout of flu. A couple of days before the Christmas holidays I emerged from sick-bay relatively unscathed, only half a stone lighter than the already skeletal frame with which I had gone in. When she met me at the station, my mother was horrified to see that I was covered from ear to ear with a patchwork of scabs and spots. No note of explanation had accompanied me. No treatment had taken place. She whisked me down to the doctor the following day, to be told that I had impetigo, caused by a combination of cross-infection and neglect. With the right treatment it could be cleared up in forty-eight hours. My parents were incensed, knowing from the lack of any communication that the condition had been completely ignored. I longed for them to complain. Even at the age of six I sensed that this might get Matron Bennet into as much trouble as she created for me. Sadly, as parents do, they weighed up our relative power to cause problems, and refrained.

It seems appropriate that I should describe the teaching staff last, as that's where they figured on the school's agenda as well. Learning, it seemed, was at best a distraction, at worst a positive hindrance to achieve the perfectly adequate activities which had been set aside for the blind: basket-weaving, piano-tuning, or even a bit of therapeutic typing (although maybe on reflection, such clerical activities were flying a bit high). Under the circumstances, it has to be to their credit that some of the teachers at least recognised that a few of us might want to extend ourselves beyond that regime. Mrs Miller, a large-sounding lady with a booming voice, watched over my faltering attempts to learn Braille and signed my application to join the National Library for the Blind, my passport to free-dom. Miss Chamberlain was bossy and pedantic, but another book lover. Blind herself, she provided early evidence that blind children, confronted with one of their own, will show no mercy. Sporty Mr Simmons, who thought I read too much and should get out more, paid the price with a strange, polio-like illness which laid him low for two terms. Busy Miss Kelly from Carlisle, who nursed me through the exam that led me out of the gates of that hell-hole, has my undying gratitude. Her other claim to fame was that she had a brother who read the weather forecast on the radio. Mr Lampard, studious and quiet, once caught us discussing, after lights out, which girls we would like to marry – I think that's what we had in mind – and as a result said we should form a junior debating society. And Mr Ray, the Scot with the well-aimed boot, umpired our cricket matches, so he couldn't have been all bad. These were the people with whom I was destined to spend the next six years. I had no concept why, but I knew I would do anything to get out. If that meant learning more than the teachers already knew, then so be it.

Teachers dithered about terribly before actually teaching you anything. After the first day's lessons, when it seemed to me we'd wasted a hell of a lot of time sitting around the piano singing, acting out *The Three Billy Goats Gruff*, drinking bottles of tepid milk and eating ABC biscuits, I asked Mrs Miller straight: When were we going to start to learn something useful, like how to read? Another difficult aspect of the first day was the number of things that everyone else seemed to understand and take for granted but which were totally new to me. Apart from my christening and the odd wedding, I had not spent time inside a church, so I found assembly a bit of a puzzle. I got into quite a heated argument with Mrs Miller over whether we'd had one hymn or two. I knew perfectly well that we'd sung for a bit, then some geezer had muttered something unintelligible for a while, and then we'd sung again: QED two hymns. And yet this supposed teacher was swearing black was white that we'd only had one hymn. Nothing would shift her. It was the first alarming indication that this woman might not know everything. Only after endless repetition of that monotonous dirge each morning did I discover we'd been singing the Lord's Prayer. So, why sing a prayer?

Just before bedtime on that first day, Colin sauntered over from the juniors. 'How are you making out?' he asked.

'All right,' I said. Satisfied, he sauntered back again. Poor Colin. Torn between his nine-year-old dignity, which might be tarnished by too close association with the Tinies, and his solemn promise to Mum to 'keep an eye on Pete', Colin, as usual, compromised. He did his duty – just.

That first day remains as clear in my mind as yesterday, the following day less so. A smell of fish in the dining room – but that could have been any Friday! A collision in the corridor; falling hard on my bum; wishing I was back home. And I remember the first Sunday service, which seemed interminable. I'd forgotten to go to the toilet beforehand, and the final humiliation occurred when I just couldn't wait any longer. After that the attempt to recapture individual days at school has to be abandoned. They merge into one another, losing their identity in a six-year tunnel. But there was an escape route. As the endless re-enactments of *Billy Goats Gruff* gave way to what I regarded as 'proper lessons', I knew we were inching gradually towards a way out.

Braille is a very simple system to learn, but a very difficult one to read. There's nothing complicated about a configuration of six dots in two vertical lines of three. Every letter and many contractions for common combinations and even whole words can be extracted from them. I had already acquired the rudiments, taught to me by Colin using six marbles fitted into holes cut into a piece of wood. The fiddly business of reading and distinguishing those dots with your fingers causes the trouble. Very few people who come to Braille after the ages of seven or eight read it fluently, and not many can who come to it before that. Colin is typical in that he can read Braille, but not lose himself in it. But by some amazing stroke of good fortune, Braille and I fitted like a hand and a glove. It felt as if the system had been designed with me in mind. Much of what has happened to me since springs from this happy marriage.

Not that the union was instant. We started timidly enough with something called a Braillette board, in which the shapes of the Braille letters are picked out with metal pegs (I thought Colin's marbles were far more sophisticated). But we finally moved on to real Braille on real cards. I remember you had to go and fetch a card out of a box and you couldn't go back for another one until you had deciphered the first. As I progressed, faster and faster, I had the first joyous inkling that this Braille lark wasn't going to be too difficult. And finally, a book, a real live book! It was called *First Steps For Tiny Folk*, as I recall. Shakespeare and Tolstoy could never have given such pleasure as Nig and Nog going up a hill did to me, even if I can't remember what manner of creature Nig and Nog were. Not that the battle was over yet by any means. I remember grappling, all one long summer holiday, with *First Steps For Tiny Folk*. Things kept cropping up which shouldn't have been there. Frequently I was reduced to tears by bumps which just didn't make sense. It looked like the three dots that make up an H, but it was too low down, and in any case it preceded M and Y, which I already knew was MY. But there was no such word as HMY, surely? It turned out that a lower H was something called 'open quotation' marks, but Dad had a hell of a job explaining why they should come along and spoil things just when I'd got the hang of MY. If Nig and Nog were speaking to each other, it would surely become obvious soon enough.

During the following term something odd happened. I was still struggling along, by now with *Second Steps For Tiny Folk*. Some godforsaken rabbit was hop, hop, hopping somewhere or other, and I was reading one word, guessing the next, reading another, guessing the next. I urgently needed to press on, to find out what was going to happen, but the English language kept getting in the way. I knew all the letters, but some of the words they added up to seemed to have no rhyme or reason to them. I knew that OO after Z said zoo, and that OO between F and D said food. So how was I supposed to know the OO between G and D sounded like the U in pudding, which shouldn't have sounded like that anyway because it should have sounded like the U between M and D, which said mud? And how could I possibly know that when O turned up in front of R in the next word, it sounded more like OO when found between D and R, and that ING said what it did say. In short, how was I supposed to know all the bloody rabbit was trying to say was 'Good morning'? I did not, and was told off for it and ordered not to guess.

The following Tuesday I could read. And not just stumble through. I'd suddenly become fluent. Miraculously, things like 'Good morning' gave me no further trouble. I was skimming along like a bird. I still became stuck on the odd unfamiliar word, but somehow I could get over it now. I had discovered context. Even if one brick was missing, at least the whole building didn't fall down. Instead of finding a clutch of mutually confusing sounds, now, when I read, I was at one with the English language. Somebody told me the other day that researchers were very excited by the discovery that the process of learning Braille was the same as learning to read by print. It wasn't an exclusively eye–brain operation. I could have saved them the bother. Twenty years after my victory over 'Good morning', I watched my son learn to read with a similar blaze of discovery. I could have danced for joy.

My reading became more and more voracious. The doings of Dick and Dora, Nip the dog and Fluff the cat were skimmed through, briefly noted and cast aside. Scarcely bothering to register the existence of Ted and Janet and their good friends Mark and Pat, I was off on the trail of real books. Long books. Books about animals like *Bambi*, *Bambi's children*, *Doctor Dolittle*, *The Wind in The Willows*, *Black Beauty*, and *Beautiful Joe*, a dog who'd had his ears and his tail docked. I discovered the joys of Enid Blyton and the Famous

Five, and thrilled to the deeds of the men who'd made Britain great, like Biggles and Bulldog Drummond. 'Relevance' might be seen as important in contemporary children's literature, but I don't remember being overly concerned that my real world was not peopled with dogs and deer that talked, or that my father had been not an air ace but a lance corporal, or that the school stories I read were about the public schoolboys of Greyfriars and St Jims. These were stories I loved and they were about as far away from Bristol as it would be possible to get. Indeed for real lack of relevance, my favourite school stories, Enid Blyton's Mallory Towers series, were for girls. Did I want a role model I could identify with – a knock-kneed, gap-toothed blind kid who was sick when he had to go to school? I don't think so. There were some books about a blind child detective, Bob Morris, but most of us thought him a bit of a wimp. At this stage, though, provided it came between covers, I'd read it. Bob picked up secret conversations over phenomenal distances, due to his uncanny hearing, counting steps so that he knew exactly where he was, stopping just short of the edges of roofs when chased by desperadoes. And, of course, he had a phenomenal memory. He was a role model all right, reinforcing every myth about blindness. We hated him.

My Braille-reading prowess was rather freakish, enhanced by a rather unusual Braille-reading technique which I developed quite by accident. Many people find they can only comfortably read Braille with one hand. Better readers use two, but usually in rotation, one picking up from the other. But a few of us read with both hands simultaneously. In my case as soon as my left hand begins a line, the right hand finds its place further along it, ready to take over, at which the left hand moves down a line while the right hand is still occupied. For some of the time both hands are reading different bits of text and the brain is somehow sorting it all out, making some kind of sense. It doesn't appear to be a method you can teach, and it turned me into something of a child prodigy. At the age of six, I became the youngest person to join the NLLB (National Lending Library for Braille), which boasted the largest collection of Braille books in the world. I filled in my initial list of forty books with huge pride. Many of them proved to be way beyond my age group and for years afterwards I received a weird and wonderful selection of books through which I waded religiously, simply because they were there. Visitors to the school used to be dragged along to watch me perform, and at home guests made an ideal captive audience to hear the little genius do his stuff. Being an appalling show-off I was happy to oblige.

When I was seven Bristol decided to enter me into the National Braille-Reading Competition. Bristol very rarely had anything as academic as this to crow about, but I walked away with the prize for my age group that year, and the subsequent three years that I entered. This regularly caused great jubilation among the teaching staff. When I returned home from London triumphant, late on Saturday nights, I was regularly marched along to the private quarters of the usually rather remote principal, Mr Getliffe, to be patted on the head. A somewhat different fate awaited me when I rejoined my peers in the dormitory. 'Bin mixing wiv all them posh kids, Whitey?' David Cope enquired. Paul Lock was more succinct: 'Stuck-up little git!' he grunted. In many ways these were more satisfying responses than those of Mr Getliffe. The Braille-reading competition was quite a big deal then. The prizes were presented by the Queen Mother the second year I went, and I almost dropped all my trophies trying to curtsey to her; the following year T.S. Eliot handed over the prize and said I showed a great sense of humour. My already wide reading told me that this was a great compliment from the man who'd written that very funny novel *The Mill on the Floss*. When such celebrities attended, radio and television came along too.

I'd already been interviewed on BBC radio newsreel, had my reading broadcast on the *Today* programme, and been on the telly with the thinking man's crumpet of the fifties, Jean Metcalfe. Paul Lock and David Cope might sneer, but they knew that this Braille-reading lark helped you reach places basket-weaving never would.

Compared with the ability to read, the rest of the sum of human knowledge rated pretty low with me. Reading Braille might look complex, but writing it is even harder. In those days all the little dots had to be punched out by hand using something elegantly called a 'dotter', which was basically a pin on a stick. As the holes you made with your dotter came out as bumps on the other side of the paper, everything had to be written upside down and back to front, with all those letters whose shapes you'd agonisingly learnt being embossed in reverse. The business of mastering writing had no great charm. In any case, at this time I had no great desire to express myself. I simply wanted to gobble up the wisdom of others.

I was reasonably competent with numbers. If it took three men two hours to dig a hole eight feet deep by four feet wide, I was quite happy to let them get on with it. For me the main appeal of arithmetic was another piece of strange special gadgetry. The implements we used to express numbers were short, squat pieces of lead placed in a board with holes. On the top of these were two small bars, one marginally raised above the other. As you slowly revolved the bars with turns of forty-five degrees, the relative positions of the bars to each other would represent different numbers. Keen mathematicians among you will nevertheless have spotted that the possible combinations can only give you digits from one to eight. To get nine, zero, and mathematical signs such as minus or plus, you had to turn the little beggars over, where the configuration of bars had a slightly different feel. Ingenious: undoubtedly. Inviting: undoubtedly not. But if they weren't a turn-on to the world of mathematics, they made particularly good stinging missiles when fired from catapults, and later on served as currency in card games.

I treated other branches of learning with varying degrees of indifference, with two notable exceptions: music and hand-icrafts. For these I reserved a particular hatred.

This loathing of music may shock those of you who cher-ish a picture of all blind babies emerging from the womb humming Mozart-like sonatas, and beating out Duke Ellington jazz improvisations on their cots. George Shearing, Ray Charles and Stevie Wonder have a lot to answer for, including my own six years of purgatory. In fact, blind people run the gamut of musical ability, from genius to tone-deaf corncrake; if you show just the slightest hint of childhood promise, your ticket's booked for Carnegie Hall.

My mistake, aged three-and-a-half, was to pick up a mouth organ and produce a tune on it. My dad, a bit of a pub pianist himself, had a cherished belief that if you could knock out a tune you'd never go short of a pint. As far as I can recall, this was the only piece of careers advice he ever gave me. I clearly recall standing outside his local pub on summer evenings at the age of four, serenading the rather bemused punters (they were obviously more tolerant in those days). Unfortunately the news that I was a musical prodigy must have filtered through to Bristol, and at the age of seven I was turned over to Mr Hayden, the senior piano teacher. He was a gentle, kindly man and, after a couple of lessons, I felt things were going pretty well. Then, abruptly, I was told that from now on my lessons would be with Miss Lanham, who was the usual teacher for the juniors. On asking why, I was told curtly, 'Oh, we thought you were something special, but you're not.' As I'd always firmly been of the opinion that I was most definitely something special, piano lessons lost their allure forever.

My running battle with handicraft lessons is perhaps

more understandable. I found anything demanding manual co-ordination virtually impossible, with the exception of reading Braille. Yet Bristol saw it as one of its major tasks to lead you on to the undoubted joys of basket-, brush- or mat-making, not surprisingly, since this was its stock-in-trade. But, with me, they were on to a loser. Manfully they tried to lure me with their blandishments of what could be achieved with raffia, the endless satisfaction that could be gained from inter-weaving pieces of cane, or, failing all that, the exciting possibilities of French knitting. It was all to no avail. After mangling tons of the world's doubtlessly scarce supplies of raffia, tangling miles and miles of perfectly good weaving cane and half strangling myself with my own French knitting, they finally gave up, and left me to read during handicraft classes.

Drama was a different matter. Despite my early strictures about time wasted on *Billy Goats Gruff*, I grew to love play acting. The first thing I liked was not thinking myself into the part, or trying to divine the intentions of the author, but the cloak-and-dagger business of securing the best part. I soon learnt that there was a subtle art to this, which involved pushing yourself forward to the extent that you weren't over-looked, but never so much that you annoyed the teacher in the process.

After being cast as a tree chopped down by the woodman in *Little Red Riding Hood*, I aimed for a starring role next time. Mrs Miller had decreed that the Tinies would perform *Rumpelstiltskin* on what was to be my first Parents' Day. There was only one male part worth playing, particularly as Rumpelstiltskin did a fair amount of hobnobbing with the Queen played by Julie Hardyman, and had the very satisfying finale of stamping his foot into the stage in a flaming temper. I went for it for all I was worth. By a judicious combination of teacher-creeping and impeccable timing I won the part. And when Mr Getliffe told the assembled audience of parents,

'And by the way, Rumpelstiltskin is six years old today,' my cup was overflowing – top billing and a solo curtain call. The technique now perfected, I secured the role of Prince Charming at Christmas (guess who was Cinderella; I think Roger was a pumpkin). From then on, barring accident or illness, I could usually rely on snaffling the best male parts in any play.

The mechanics of putting on a play in which the whole cast is blind are complex. Firstly you have to ensure that the actors and actresses don't spend most of the time falling off the stage, so very early on during productions we would transfer from the classroom to the stage in the gym where it would eventually be performed. An enormous amount of planning went into knowing exactly who would be where and when, how many steps you had to take to get to a door without fumbling, and always, crucially, how far you were from the footlights at all times. The aim was for us to look as 'natural' as possible. It's a tribute to the skill with which this was done that I can't think of one single funny incident which happened on stage because of our blindness.

My second great discovery at Bristol, which almost although not quite eclipsed reading, occurred outside the classroom. The Tinies was a very female environment. Nurses such as Patricia Mapson and the beloved Nurse Palmer bullied us, cared for us, cleaned us up, and sometimes read to us. The Tinies shared their playground with the bigger girls. Nothing so unruly as an older boy ever strayed into our lives. Instead we were by turns scolded and mothered by emerging women aged ten and eleven. And then there was Julie Hardyman. I discovered girls.

From the age of six I thought a great deal about girls. Despite my early age, there was a lot of good old-fashioned sexual fantasy in how I saw them. The sex might have been sketchy and ill informed, but all the elements of the fantasy were there. Girls were special, girls were unattainable, but in the perfect world they were there to be simultaneously possessed and protected. It may not have been very politically correct. At six I don't suppose anything ever is.

My fantasies fastened on to some pretty unlikely subjects, and respected neither age nor reality. Older girls in the playground featured heavily, especially if they had nice names, although tastes must have changed. I can't imagine Dilys, Rose, and Gloria featuring on my hit list these days. Sometimes they were girls I didn't know but had heard quite a lot about, which meant I could create them to be just the way I wanted. David Cope had a sister called Marion who fell into this category. I was so keen on Marion that I named one of Grandad White's rabbits after her. I rarely strayed into the rather forbidding territory of nurses and teachers, although I did at one stage conceive a rather bizarre passion for one of our music teachers, who was well into her forties and herself blind. Did I feel she was more vulnerable, more needful of my masterful protection?

Other unlikely concubines of this time were various women and girls from *The Archers* and *Mrs Dale's Diary*, and favourite characters from books I read. Some of the things I used to do with the girls of Mallory Towers would have made Enid Blyton sorry she'd ever invented them. The subjects of my fantasies didn't even have to be human. At one time I was quite keen on Ginger, the bad-tempered horse in *Black Beauty*!

In my fantasies I would get inside their lives, books, radio serials, and join in. Rescue them from things. Generally sort things out for them. See off people who upset them, that kind of thing. Was I blind in these fantasies? I'm not sure – it never cropped up somehow. The really awkward thing about sexual fantasies when you're six is that you never quite know how to end them. At sixteen of course, she shows her gratitude in the usual way, but at six you haven't a clue what the usual way is, so they just peter out.

The other odd thing about these fantasies is that they never included people I really cared about, such as Julie Hardyman. Julie was an angel – the kind of angel that knows it. Everybody loved her: teachers, care staff, boys, girls. Except in those plays, where I could use my intelligence as leverage, I couldn't get anywhere near her. Rugged types such as Roger won out every time. Instead I did the next best thing: I befriended her best friend Rosamund. Rosamund, as Julie's best friend, was plain, a nervy child who suffered from asthma and eczema, which made the skin on her hands dry and kind of warty. But I nobly forgave that, just as she forgave me my buck teeth, squeaky voice and scrawny body. Deep down I think we both knew we were made for better things, but once I'd clasped her warty hand in mine, and almost bitten her nose off with our first kiss, something clicked. Until our brains betrayed us at eleven and we went off to different schools, we shared a quite beautiful and sensitive relationship. I do hope those warts have cleared up!

For real sex, though, I had to wait for graduation from the almost exclusively female world of the Tinies, to the equally exclusively male world of the juniors. The change, at about seven, was abrupt and absolute. Everything of significance now happened either in the yard, the boy's playground, or the dormitories, where the staff did not rule. In the yard the dictatorship of older boys was, on the whole, benevolent. They decided which games were played and by whom, who was in and who was out of favour. Fights broke out, of course. People were always threatening to 'bash you up'. Scraps erupted and subsided with equal suddenness, but usually among equals. Bullying was remarkably rare. Smaller boys were simply tolerated, provided they skulked in their own little corners, and didn't get in the way of bigger boys.

The dormitories, however, were a very different kettle of stinking fish. I don't know whether the male staff at Bristol in the fifties were merely innocent of the attraction small boys held for slightly bigger boys, or whether they just didn't care. The accepted idea of dormitory discipline was to take one of the older boys and place him among the little ones to keep order. They came in three categories: the gauleiters, the grumblers, and the gropers. Pete, the first dormitory prefect under whom I suffered, was a gauleiter. He chivvied us from pillar to post, revelling in his new-found authority. I suppose he could only have been about fifteen or sixteen, but he seemed much older and bigger. One morning, because I had allegedly turned over in bed too noisily and woken poor old Pete up, he made me write out 'I must not wake up before the bell goes' 100 times. Invariably awake by 5.30 a.m. and knowing this was a natural phenomenon I could not control, this convinced me once and for all of the sheer lunacy of adult authority. I remember hearing a little later that Pete had fallen downstairs and broken his arm. Perhaps this should have convinced me there was a god after all.

The majority of dormitory prefects fell into the grumbling class. They did it because they had to, moaned about it quite a lot, but on the whole gave us very little trouble. Some of them were even quite nice to us, in an off-hand sort of way.

But occasionally, by the law of averages, you were lumbered with a groper. On the first occasion Harold invited me to go and sit on his bed and feel his private parts, my main reservation was that I was trying to get to sleep at the time, and that this excursion from a warm bed would wake me up. But you didn't argue with dormitory prefects, so I obliged. I felt no strong aversion to it. I frequently felt mine, so I had no particular problem with feeling his, if it kept him happy, but it was a bit of a bore, particularly when you were trying to drop off, and all he wanted was for you to tell him over and over again how big it was. Provided it stopped there, I wasn't unduly perturbed. It was when he started to use me as a runner for more questionable pursuits that my flesh began to crawl. Harold, it appeared, liked to smack arses. Not mine, oddly enough; I think my brains were already earning me a little protection. But on one occasion he made me wake up my friend Michael, the other object of his attentions, from a deep sleep. Still only half awake, Michael was thrashed on his bare arse half a dozen times for some trifling, even, we suspected, invented offence. This outraged every bone in my body. Sex was one thing, injustice quite another. We talked about reporting Harold, having a pretty shrewd idea what he'd been up to would get him into trouble, but somehow we never did. It didn't seem important enough at the time.

Better the devil you knew, I reasoned. He wasn't such a bad bloke really. I never needed much sleep even then. When the others had dropped off he would talk to me about books and sport and girls, three of my favourite subjects, as if I were an equal. Sometimes he'd get a book out of the library, and I'd read it to him after lights out. They were often too old for me, but my fast improving reading speed enabled me to cope, and it made me feel important. That reading speed was already proving to be a prodigious asset.

Despite the regular beginning-of-term trauma of leaving home, things at Bristol moved along pleasantly enough once I'd established myself. People find it difficult to understand how blind children can amuse or enjoy themselves, burdened as they are with the pathetic images of blindness used by charities to raise money. 'But what do you do with them in the holidays?' people used to ask my mother, as if we were inanimate objects to be picked up from one place and deposited down in another. We did the same as any children: we fought, we frolicked, we flirted. Every game known to man has its *blind* equivalent.

We played cricket or football with a bell ball – a rubber ball with several holes cut in it and a small bell inserted so that you could hear it coming. These balls received extremely rough treatment, and were endlessly patched up, bound with Sellotape – anything to keep them going. Endless improvisation took place if a real ball wasn't available. Boys with some sight used to play with paper balls – strips cut out of Braille magazines, soaked in water, rolled together and tied with string. Magazines could be put to further good use without even being opened. Rolled up, they made very handy weapons. Cricket had its own rules allowing people with varying degrees of sight to play. Apart from the standard ball games, strange crazes would sweep the yard. There was a season for 'bangers', strips of Braille paper folded together in such a way that whizzing them through the air at just the right speed created a satisfying report like that of a gun. Then there was a season of stilts . . .

When you grew tired of the delights offered by the yard, you could go to the field at the front of the school, which stretched practically the whole length of the front drive. It had swings, a roundabout, a jungle gym and plenty of trees to climb. One of its chief delights for me was that it also contained a donkey and a goat. The donkey, called with not a little irony Happy, could sometimes be bribed to take the smaller children for rides, while the poor goat, called Polly, frequently allowed herself to be led around on a rope by over-affectionate kids like me, miles from home and missing their normal pets. The field was a place where you could lie and chew grass, blow dandelion clocks (which allegedly made you wet the bed), and just 'muck about'. Its size and odd nooks and crannies made it a favourite spot for those who had discovered that affection does not only spring up between boy and goat, though I didn't remain at Bristol for long enough to take full advantage of these possibilities.

The dormitories, too, were not so much places to sleep as playgrounds with beds. As we progressed through the juniors, the menace of gropers seemed to diminish. Indeed, I don't recall us older juniors having prefects to supervise us, which was odd, since twenty-nine ten-year-olds in twenty-nine beds possessed an almost unlimited capacity for mayhem. Boys were always skirmishing and fighting, leaping from bed to bed, plotting, playing hide and seek and Torched Touch, a peculiarly inappropriate game for a blind kid where the next person to be caught in the beam of a torch was 'it'. It's not hard to imagine the scope this provided for cheating by those who had a little bit of sight, but it's a measure of how unimportant we regarded our blindness that no one really thought this worth remarking upon. We totally blind kids played Torched Touch with the rest, oblivious of the fact that our success depended on the honesty of the others.

I can't stress enough how unconcerned we were about our lack of sight. Visitors, even the parents of pupils, even – God forbid – my own mother and father, probably regarded our antics as terribly sad and pathetic. Of course we held our hands out when we ran, of course we collided, of course we swung our feet or our bats and missed the ball. But we didn't care. We were all in the same boat. We may have been sad from time to time, but this wasn't because we were blind, but because we were miles from home. Proponents of integrated education overlook the fact that to us blindness was the norm, and as such we felt no great need to apologise for it. Our self-respect may have been based on myth, and of course competition in life wouldn't simply be with other blind people. Once established, self-respect takes a great deal of dislodging. I just wonder how much self-respect blind children at mainstream schools have when they have to sit out games because there's no provision for them, or when they're constantly described as having 'special needs'.

The very hectic nature of Bristol's dormitories paradoxically meant they fulfilled another of my needs: privacy. When
twenty-nine people are available to play sardines or hide and
seek, one absentee more or less is rarely noticed. If I felt like
it I could read to my heart's content. One distinct advantage of
Braille is that you can continue to read however cold and however dark it is. Books under the bedclothes are one of the most
comforting images of my youth, and if I were immersed in a
book I would carry on with it long after Torched Touch had
become exhausted, waking up again at five and starting all
over again. If no book absorbed me, I lived a rich inner life as
the dorm slept on. I might be fully occupied rescuing David
Cope's sister from a desperate gang of kidnappers, or ventur-
ing into darkest Ambridge to get one of the Archer girls out of
yet another scrape with the squire.

Sex was not the only trigger for my imagination.
Numbers, dates and lists were all grist to my nerdy mill.
Sunday mornings were toughest for me, for though we were
allowed an extra hour in bed, my internal clock made no
allowance for this and still woke me up at five. Having worked
out that there were 900 seconds in a quarter of an hour, I
attempted to fill the time between 7.15 and 7.30 one Sunday
counting to 900 precisely, then checking the clock. Satisfyingly
I was only about ten seconds out. I'd also become obsessed by
dates (mainly, I suspect, because I was always either counting
the number of days to the beginning or the end of a term).
Having been told one Friday by my grandmother that it was
3 April, I always knew from that day on precisely what date it
was. For some reason, I took a mental photograph of the time,
and it stuck. My childhood memory is littered with banal
events neatly filed under precise dates. I also discovered a
series of quick quasi-mathematical tricks which enabled me to
calculate rapidly on what day an event would fall, such as
someone's birthday, and even, more ambitiously, the day of the

week on which they were born. They were simple techniques, when you knew them, but it became a party trick which served to enhance my fast-growing reputation as some kind of freakish prodigy. If this failed to amuse, I had one more goody left in my kit bag of diverting mental gymnastics: I would go through all ninety-two football league teams in alphabetical order, from Accrington Stanley right through to York City. By the time I had retraced my steps a couple of times to pick up an errant Grimsby Town or Port Vale, someone else was usually awake.

I had one other refuge in the dormitory. This period marked the beginning of my long-running love affair with radio. I'd been fascinated from an early age by the strange variety of sounds which issued forth from Mum and Dad's old, bassy wireless set at home. At that stage I was mainly captivated by the music, but soon I began to listen more carefully. It was from an *Any Questions* programme, for instance, that aged six, I discovered that Father Christmas did not exist and was, as I had always suspected, another example of adult untrustworthiness. By seven I was listening avidly to everything, any kind of music, plays, sport, comedy, even political discussions. Anything that came out of the radio was automatically greeted with a kind of reverence. For obvious reasons, in an information-obsessed society like ours, radio has made great steps in evening up the score for blind people, and is probably more significant than anything actually invented with us in mind.

The first wireless I ever owned only remained intact with the aid of copious amounts of string. It worked both off mains and battery and normally I relied on the batteries, but on the last day of one term David Cope and I decided, for some reason, to attempt to plug it into the lights. A couple of amateur electricians, sublimely confident in their nine-year-old abilities, set to work to effect this simple piece of engineering.

The result was a sharp crack and the stark realisation that we had fused the lights throughout half the school. Retribution was quick and to the point. As the owner of the instrument of destruction, I was told that, if I brought the offending radio back next term, it would be confiscated forthwith. The spectre of Bristol without a radio haunted me throughout the holidays, but somehow I hoped against hope that even they wouldn't have the vindictiveness to carry over a punishment from one term to the next. On the last morning of the holiday my sobbings and vomitings were even more violent than usual, and I finally succeeded in telling Mum what had happened. She promised to telephone the school to try to have the sentence removed. We should have known better. She made the call, but the moment I set foot in the school they pounced. The radio was seized, and I didn't see it again that term.

Times at Bristol were by no means all bad. The best days of all were the 'special days' when your parents came down to see you.

It wasn't easy for my mother and father. Money was tight, and when I first went to school they had no regular means of transport. Winchester to Bristol was a pig of a journey by bus, and too expensive by train. Finally, urged on by my near hysteria at being away at school for such long periods, Dad bought a motorbike.

I awaited these visits with agonised impatience. As the time drew nearer my anxiety grew to fever pitch. Something would go wrong; they wouldn't be able to make it. On a couple of occasions my worst fears were realised, and after working myself up into a crescendo of nervous excitement, the telephone call I dreaded would come through, pleading bad weather or illness. Still, they usually made it; they knew how much it meant to me. When they arrived we never did anything very exciting. There wasn't much to do in Bristol on a Sunday. It was difficult even to get a cup of tea. I think we made eight visits in all to Bristol Zoo, getting to know all the animals intimately and by name. Once we were even reduced to making a visit to a museum. But I didn't much care where we went. As long as they were there I was happy.

Sports days were a success. Bristol organised this event with great care and almost military precision, and everything ran like clockwork, including the kids. Preparations took place for weeks in advance: heats were run, some events were actually decided, and points were added up. There was bitter rivalry between the three houses: Beaufort, who wore blue, Colston, who wore red and Conrad, who wore green. I belonged to Conrad, and was intensely proud of the fact. When I first arrived at Bristol, Beaufort was very much in the ascendancy, but as time went by the pendulum swung, and Conrad became the best house. I was delighted to be in Conrad because people in Beaufort were all a bit supercilious, and people in Colston were just wet! Without exception.

On sports day itself the organisation was phenomenal. Once the next event had been announced, team captains would come round and start to chivvy their contestants to the starting line. There were kids with more or less sight hurtling everywhere; large kids, tiny kids, thin boys, fat girls. They raced an enormous number of races. As well as the more orthodox sprints, throws and jumps, there were a plethora of novelty contests: three-legged, egg and spoon, sack, wheelbarrow, potato, obstacle races. The whole carnival came to a crunching finale with a series of tugs-of-war.

One of the main elements was parent participation. On his first visit to a sports day Dad was asked civilly enough if he would consent to being a 'buffer'. Not knowing quite what the duties of a buffer would entail, he gladly agreed. He was duly stationed at one end of the track. Compared to the 5 feet 3 inches and 9 stone of my father, Bernard was very large, even by Bristol standards, about 6 foot and weighing in at 14 stone, and took his athletics seriously. Imagine then, my father's dismay, when he saw in the distance Bernard, head down, legs pumping, bearing down upon him. Suddenly he realised that the buffer's job was to turn Bernard round when he reached the end of the track, preventing him from powering his way relentlessly towards the Welsh border. At that moment, Dad was faced with a supreme test of character, and he met it as only a small man can. He moved smartly out of the way. For all we know Bernard is running still.

I was no super-athlete, but I was wiry and strong, and somewhere in the clutter at home are a couple of bronze medals which say Peter acquitted himself nobly enough as a junior. My other delightful memory of sports days is that on one of them I said goodbye to Bristol forever.

Almost from the day I went to Bristol I'd realised that the real route to freedom was not the fire escape, but Worcester College. Worcester was the equivalent of a grammar school, where just a few of the brainy kids went. When I was seven Colin passed his 11-plus exam, and as far as I was concerned that made Worcester a must for me too, partly because I desperately wanted to get away from Bristol, partly because I wanted to join Colin, and partly because I knew that if the less precocious Colin could pass then everybody would expect me to do the same.

Worcester was treated with a strange mixture of respect and contempt by people at Bristol, particularly by those who knew they hadn't a snowball in hell's chance of ever going there. Worcester boys were soft. Worcester boys acquired posh accents. Worcester boys thought they were better than everybody else. Unfortunately, they also had a habit of proving that they were. They always seemed to beat us at football, handball and swimming, and nobody could question their brains. Once I'd passed the exam for Worcester, I became something of an outcast, and when people weren't ignoring me altogether they were trying to persuade me that I wouldn't really be happy there. I think I had more serious fights in those last couple of months than I had in the previous six years. Even some of the staff seemed to share this jealousy of Worcester College, implying that I'd turned traitor by leaving. My attitude to other people certainly didn't change when I'd passed the exam, but afterwards I was constantly being told: 'I suppose you think you're too good for Bristol now, but won't you feel the draught when you get to Worcester?' I was intimidated into believing that, though I'd passed, I would ultimately prove unworthy. All my faults – my untidiness, my anti-social table manners, my cheek, my lack of a sense of direction – were marshalled as evidence of my inevitable downfall when Worcester really discovered what they had admitted. Even mother joined in. One night I had been lying in bed cheerfully picking my nose and sticking the results on the wall behind me. Mum came in and pointed out with some asperity that that sort of thing wouldn't be tolerated when I was at Worcester. I rather enjoyed her implication, born of an inside knowledge, that it would have been perfectly acceptable behaviour at Bristol, assuming anybody had noticed.

Some of Bristol's teachers did understand the value of getting out of the school into Worcester, and they moved heaven and earth to pilot those of us with a sporting chance through entrance exams. Four of us took them that year, Michael and I for Worcester, Rosamund and a Polish girl called Danuta for Chorley Wood. We had special coaching during the evenings. And then the day of the preliminary exam arrived.

I've always had the impression that this was one examination which by rights I should have failed. I remember deciding that there was an awful lot on the paper that I didn't know. There was a question about European seas which found me placing the Baltic in the Irish Sea and the Irish Sea in the region of the Aegean. There was also a question about figures of speech in which I assured the examiner that 'burying the hatchet' meant that you were hiding something, and 'blowing your own trumpet' was another way of saying blowing your nose (I had a rather literal mind when I was ten). Despite these mutilations of the English language I passed. The next step was a three-day residential exam at Worcester itself.

I went up on the train with Dad. I was a little worried, but strangely not as nervous as I had been about the preliminaries. Even from an early age I've always had confidence that I could achieve far more when face to face with people than when depending on a dry exam paper.

My first impressions of Worcester College are of light and space; I remember walking up to the school across the wide close-cropped front lawn, and being immediately aware inside the school that the place had an airy spacious feel. Looking back, Worcester College was no palace but in comparison with Bristol it was like walking into a luxury hotel.

The exam wasn't difficult. We read, did comprehension tests, wrote essays. All my English subjects were strong, and I must have done well on them. We also did maths, and I discovered too late that we were expected to understand decimals, which we hadn't studied at Bristol. We spent a lot of time in the gym, which I enjoyed. We'd also been tipped the wink that throughout the three days we would 'be watched', to see how well we did on our own, how well we managed practical tasks like looking after our own clothes and coping with our food, and how sociable we were. I probably made an appalling impression on the first two counts, but in deference to the third Michael and I separated on reaching the school, and hardly spoke to each other for the duration. I doubt if it made the slightest difference. A week later we both heard that we passed. All I remember was feeling numb with joy and relief.

Bristol Fashion

At the end of the final sports day I prepared to take my leave of Bristol. I suppose I should have been deliriously happy, but I wasn't. I've always been rather on the conservative side. Somehow I'd got used to Bristol: it was a situation, however horrific, I could deal with. I had made good friends there: the two Roberts, John and some of the girls, as well as a number of the teachers. I looked about for somebody to say goodbye to, but nobody seemed to be around.

So I climbed into the car and left.

3

Train Stopped Play

Throughout the ages torturers have known that pain is far more effective as a weapon when interspersed with short periods of pleasure. Make torture the staple diet, and your victim becomes accustomed to it, even enjoying it in a perverse kind of way, but interrupt it with shorts bursts of relief, and the prospect of starting all over again becomes unbearable. This was how I viewed the relationship between term-time and holidays, which were oases, cool places of relief and rest in which to recharge my batteries and brace myself for the next spasm of agony.

Holiday euphoria began in those last few days of term, heralded by the winding-up of school projects, the clearing of desks and lockers, and, on the penultimate morning, the mysterious reappearance beside your bed of 'private clothes'. Hateful symbols of domestic bliss, they were presumably stored away in some dark cupboard during term-time to be returned to you under cover of darkness at the last conceivable moment. Just the smell of them on waking – a mixture of mustiness and mothballs – was enough to send my mind racing homeward way ahead of my body. All that then remained was to get through some half-hearted end-of-term junketing, a near sleepless night of anticipation, and then at last I would be on the train:

> Bristol Temple Mead – I wonder how Sally the
> dog is.
> Bath – Will my library books be there waiting for
> me when I get home? Please don't let it be Sir
> Walter Scott again!
> Bradford-on-Avon – Who should take part in the
> first garden cricket match of the holidays: England
> and Australia, or Hampshire and Somerset?
> Salisbury – What gramophone record will Mum
> and Dad have bought me for my birthday? Bloody
> Ruby Murray I expect.
> Romsey – Only fifteen more minutes only fifteen
> more minutes.
> Southampton Central – and there was Mum
> slightly breathless but never late. And after all that
> we don't really know quite what to say to each
> other but it didn't matter as we trundled up to
> Winchester on the Hants and Dorset number 47
> bus. I'd made it. I was home.

'Home', the object of all this fevered adulation was still, and remained throughout my childhood, that house with the well-remembered bare floors, loud ticking clock and cracked lavatory pan. By now, however, Mum and Dad had turned it into a modestly furnished but very comfortable house with a well-tended garden.

When I finally arrived, there were several time-honoured rituals to go through. The first was to be flattened by Sally the

Alsatian. Sally took my frequent prolonged absences rather hard, and seemed to hoard all her considerable ebullient affection for my return. As soon as I set foot in the house she would launch herself upon my person as if fired from a cannon. She invariably floored me but this was one of the joys of homecoming. After a quick spot check to ascertain all furniture and possessions were where I had left them thirteen weeks before, the next step was to find out if any library books had arrived. The postmen of Winchester were always the first people to be apprised of my impending return when one of them was required to stagger up our path with an outsized pile of Braille books. Then, before tea if Colin were at home, there was the inevitable first game of cricket.

The full realisation that I was finally back home never really came until the next morning: that exquisite sensation of waking in my own bed, hearing the familiar sounds of Mum preparing breakfast in the kitchen, the laboured gurgling of the lavatory cistern directly beneath my bedroom, the resonance of our extremely bassy radiogram downstairs booming out the news from the West of England Home Service, the sound of the Bournemouth Belle, the fast train from Waterloo to Bournemouth shooting through and almost seeming to bisect the bedroom as it passed, and Mum's entreaties to Dad, delivered in a hoarse whisper intended to take account of my supposed slumber but echoing through the house like a piercing scream to 'get up or you'll be late for work'. Finally he would go galloping down the stairs, with me trailing close behind. I could never bear to luxuriate in bed on that first morning. Pent-up excitement and the need to vomit invariably brought me leaping from my bed. As a child the great passions of my life tended to be mirrored not in my face but my stomach. It treated 'joy and sorrow all alike'.

Home meant comfort. You couldn't avoid the constant comparison with the austerities of school: the delicious simple food, the smell of cleanliness, the stiff, smooth feel of clean sheets, the kind words and most importantly the feeling that here you mattered; that you weren't one of a huge horde for whom someone had to take responsibility but about whom nobody really cared.

I became a miser with days. I would count up the days of the holiday lovingly and then try to eke them out as slowly and carefully as possible, determined not to waste, by any inattention of mine, a single moment. This had the ironic effect which accompanies all miserliness: I ended up afraid to spend them at all. I avoided outings which I knew I would enjoy because they would take me away from home and, therefore, according to my convoluted logic, rob me of another precious day. The danger with enjoyable things was that they made time pass quickly, the precise opposite of what I wanted to achieve. So I read, idled and fretted my holidays away. The rich promise of their beginning gave way to steady routine, the steady routine to dissatisfying boredom and suddenly there I was at the end of the holidays filled with inexplicable regret.

This sterility was more a feature of later holidays and had as much to do with adolescent angst as anything else. Earlier holidays were packed with fun and games that suffered strange adaptations to allow for Colin's and my blindness.

The two chief venues for these games were the Square and our tiny back garden. The few square yards of dead-end at the top of the cul-de-sac of the Square were not a particularly prepossessing playground. It could hardly be said to provide unrivalled opportunities, particularly as it was bounded by the gardens of a group of people who seemed to regard children with about as much favour as slugs and ants. The slightest incursion on to their sacred plots were greeted by howls of rage and the time-honoured cry, 'Why don't you kids go and play over the rec?' But the recreational ground in question, only a few hundred yards away and stocked with real goal-posts, climbing frames and proper grass, somehow never had the same appeal. This was just as well for me, since it was outside my permitted area.

It's difficult to assess from this distance how 'well integrated' Colin and I were, to use the current jargon. We were certainly accepted, we made sure of that. Me with my tongue and Colin, quite often, with his fists. Colin's rather surprising propensity to settle arguments with his knuckles was discovered early by the residents of the Square. The first to underestimate his capacity for self-defence was a boy with a stammer called Derek, who fancied himself as something of a sniper. He would occasionally take it into his head to throw stones at Colin and I, thinking that he couldn't be identified. Unfortunately for him, like most of his elders, he thought that 'blind' meant 'stone blind'. He hadn't bargained for Colin's small degree of vision and Colin's right hook eventually caught up with him. That evening the fallen sniper's mother was on the doorstep complaining bitterly about the bullying of her little man. I think Mum and Dad derived a good deal of suppressed enjoyment from this encounter. They hadn't really expected that they would have the pleasure of defending their children from accusations of bullying. Another unsuspecting child one day tried to block the progress of Colin's bike by poking a stick in his front wheel. He received the same summary justice. After that attempts to take advantage of us virtually ceased. No doubt we were exploited in other ways from time to time, but it's my impression we held our own pretty well.

The real problem with friendships at home was that they were constantly interrupted by term-time. You would have begun to establish a good relationship with someone then you'd be off again for three months. By the time you returned the whole scene had changed. There was a new pecking order. Your best friend was someone else's best friend and you had to start all over again. Colin, with his more accepting, more adaptable nature, seemed to be able to cope with that. I could not. The uncertainty, the impermanence of it worried me. I retreated into my house, into my books, into my daydreams.

The one spur which could draw me out of this self-imposed retreat was having Colin all to myself. Although he had more friends outside than I did, Colin would sometimes simply decide to stay at home and then we would play games of huge complexity for hours on end. These days were sheer bliss. Although I was supposed to be the more dominant, the one who always knew and got what he wanted, there is no doubt that I hero-worshipped my older brother. In my eyes he could do no wrong. He had all the things I didn't have. He was practical, able to set up a complicated network of model railway lines in a trice, even build his own train given time. He was endlessly patient. He could sit down for hours, carefully working out the rules of some elaborate game which we wanted to adapt. He had that small degree of sight which is invaluable currency in the country of the blind where the one-eyed boy is truly king. Yet central to it all was that despite our differences we genuinely liked each other and complemented each other's deficiencies. If I used his patience, practicality and eyesight then he certainly fed off my boundless enthusiasm, my combative nature and my admiration for him.

Of all the games we adapted, the most memorable were our marathon games of cricket. Our version evolved over the years. When we first started to play I had a tiny bat made by Dad, a bell ball and a wicket improvised from one of Mum's old bread tins. My bat was so tiny and my technique so poor that in those early days every time I prodded forward I would scrape the back of my knuckles on our concrete pitch. By the end of an innings my hands were usually red raw and finally mother had to construct for me a special set of pads to prevent me filing them down to the bone. We played in the passageway leading down to our back gate, but as it was only some 9 feet wide and the bread tins were placed right up against the gate, this restricted our potential stroke play to the straight drive and the forward defensive push. As our cricketing ambitions outgrew this restraint we moved to the wide open spaces of the back lawn, which must have been all of 8 yards by 10. This opened up a whole new world of leg glances, cover drives and wild swings. The only restriction now was that we were bounded on two sides by other people's gardens, while straight ahead lay the council allotments and behind us mother's kitchen windows. This daunting array of obstacles demanded far more ingenious stroke play than would be needed for the tightest Australian field setting. The 'over the hedge and out' rule wasn't really necessary on the leg side, since a natural desire not to lose your wicket was far outweighed by the terror of having to approach No. 4 for your ball back. Certain shots developed distinctive names of their own. For example the 'bike shed push' got its name from the lean-to Dad had built for his motorbike, in a suicidal silly mid-off position, while a 'loppy drive' would send the ball spinning into some unfortunate's runner beans in the allotments (I was under the impression at the time, not having seen the word written, that allotment was spelt with a P, hence 'loppy'). Dad had rather inconsiderately planted two small trees on the pitch, one at mid-on, one at cover point. Having failed to persuade him to uproot them we made the best of a bad job and commandeered them as fielders who, on occasions, would make the most spectacular catches and then quite unaccountably muff the simplest chance.

The game itself was just about recognisable as cricket but we made a number of concessions to each other. First of all the ball had to bounce at least twice before reaching the batsman to give him time to get a 'sighting' of it. As fielders we were also allowed to take a catch off one bounce. The bowler was required to allow the batsman the courtesy of a clear and audible 'ready' followed by 'play' before hurling the ball at him.

We spent hour upon hour playing cricket, fighting out endless test matches and county games. When these games became really tense we were reluctant to stop, even for meals. Not for us the irksome stoppages for rain, or hail, or snow. It was not unusual for Mum to have to plead with us to come in since we were obviously deciding the fate of the Ashes in pitch darkness. Only one natural phenomenon was ever known to interrupt our play. At fairly frequent intervals the very busy London to Weymouth trains would come thundering through a few yards from our garden. For the duration of their approach, deafening arrival and gradual departure, cricket was quite impossible. Even worse, disaster of disasters, a train would be brought to a total standstill at the signals near our house. This was the age of steam, and a stationary train was by no means silent. In extreme cases this had been known to put an end to cricket for half an hour. These occasions were referred to as 'bad light' or 'train stopped play'.

At one time or another we bent the principles of various games and sports to fit our rather individual needs and the cramped nature of our stadium, but none transplanted so successfully or enduringly as cricket. Football tended to degenerate into long and sterile bouts of aimless hacking (whenever we hadn't lost the ball altogether), and other games tended simply to be crazes catching on suddenly and obsessively but running dry within a week or so. Golf and tennis both fell into this category. For a short time the whole object of our existence was to pot a ball in one of Mum's washing-up bowls, placed in the centre of the garden and masquerading as a golf hole. Repeated eighteen times this became, quite believably, a round of golf, just as it was quite reasonable to believe, divided by an imaginary net, bouncing the ball off the back wall for the other one to catch on the first bounce, that we were Hoad or Rosewall, Laver or Emerson, fighting for our lives at Wimbledon.

This sportsmania meant that the first evidence of our holidays was often the sound of breaking glass. Keen gardener though he was, Dad had long given up the idea of ever owning a greenhouse. The toll on our windows was enough to persuade him of that. The fastest recorded case of a broken window occurred one year just half an hour after stepping off the number 47. A short rising delivery landed with precision on the join between the lawn and the concrete popping crease – always a bowler's target in our games – then bounded wickedly, caught the shoulder of Colin's bat, and thudded into the kitchen window behind him with a sickening crash. We had a point of honour that, however unplayable the ball, any resulting damage was still the batsman's responsibility, but another unwritten rule dictated that, wherever possible, I would take the blame for anything likely to cause Dad to lose his rag. I could get away with it. Colin couldn't.

This one was easy. Dad's routine on coming home from work even on the first day of our holiday was unchanging: he walked into the kitchen, put down his carpenter's bag and went to the sink to wash his hands. On this occasion I climbed up on the box which covered the drain outside the window, poked my head through the gaping hole and said ' 'Ello Dad.' He laughed. 'I see you buggers are home then.'

Dad's attitude to children was complex. His abrupt and sometimes sharp manner with them led some people to assume that he didn't like kids. Maybe, as an amorphous group, he didn't. But when a Child, a Game, a Project caught his attention, no one could be more involved, more inventive, more unpatronising. When you were playing a game with him, you never felt that he was doing it to amuse you. He played to win; he hated rules to be broken, and he hated half-heartedness. I don't think he would have claimed to like children but I've always thought that in some way our blindness brought the best out of him as a parent. It may have upset him deeply but it also posed a challenge. Every game we played needed its amendments. Every explanation had to make sense without using visual vocabulary. I think the solutions of these problems suited the temperament of a man who was never satisfied with other people's explanations or ways of doing things and always liked to find his own. Beneath that abrupt exterior he was enormously soft-hearted. At Christmas, when mawkish visits to children's hospitals came on radio or television he would switch them off or leave the room. Apprentices whom he took under his wing when they first left school were still visiting him thirty years later. So, after a hard day's work he may have taken a little prising from his armchair but once embarked on a game he played with a will.

It's a measure of the extent to which anyone at home took our blindness into account that among the most popular games we played was hide and seek. Although on second thoughts, since the main object of the game is to hide yourself from view perhaps it's not so illogical after all. At any rate if our methods of detection were unorthodox, our strike rate of discovery was pretty effective. On one famous occasion, when the hunt was at its height I pushed open the bathroom door, paused, sniffed and said with utter confidence, 'He's in here Colin, I can smell him.' A lightning search revealed Dad crouched in the empty bathtub, hovering between amusement and indignation. It took a while to convince him that the odour in question was the sawdust which always clung to his clothes after a day working with wood.

Our teamwork was not always so effective. Sometimes Dad would remain hidden for what seemed like hours. It must have felt like hours for him as well, and it was not unusual for his patience to run out. Lying on top of the wardrobe in their bedroom one evening, watching Colin pass beneath him for the fifth time, temptation overcame him. He reached down and flicked his ear. Colin reacted as he always did to sudden shock: with an ear-splitting yell. Play was suspended for the day.

In order to relieve his boredom we then developed the rule that you were allowed to move about after a decent, though unspecified, interval. This rather changed the nature of the game, turning it from a methodical and painstaking search into a feverish hunt. At such times Colin became the scheming strategist, I the obedient foot soldier. As we passed each other in the hallway for the umpteenth time, Colin issued his terse instructions.

'Right. I will comb the house from top to bottom. You, stay here and guard the junction between the stairs and the front room. On no account let him through.'

'Sah.'

I braced myself, prepared to withstand the charge of the Light Brigade if it meant winning the approval of Captain Colin. Time passed. Nothing happened. Then I heard it. A faint footfall behind me. I never hesitated. Launching myself on our adversary I brought him down swiftly, sat on his head and waited for Colin's return. Then I heard the master's voice. Sadly though, it was not behind but beneath me. 'It's me, you daft bugger. Get off.'

As we grew older games became more sophisticated, but no less competitive. Crazes would grip the household taking it over for weeks at a time. One holiday it was racing cars. Colin and I had been collecting a series of cars numbered from one to ten. They must all have been based on popular current sports car models, such as the Triumph TR4. When pushed along they all made very different and distinctive sounds. No. 4 for example was a rather squat unattractive car but it ran with a pleasant bell-like note. No. 7 on the other hand, though long and sleek and went like shit off a shovel, had a rather flat, bland sound and could excite no enthusiasm in me. The sounds meant that we could race these cars from one end of the room to the other confident that by sound alone we could identify the winner. Of course, it was never a simple race but a complex edifice of points for drivers, points for constructors, building to a thrilling world championship climax on the last days of the holidays.

On another occasion the whole focus of our world rested on a bagatelle board. This simply consisted of a wooden board 1 foot wide and 2 feet long, dotted about with a series of numbered slots or configurations of pegs and a pull-back spring handle. The object of the game, as far as the manufacturers were concerned, was to place a marble in the little alleyway on the right hand side of the board and fire it off with the spring to see which numbered hole it ended up in. You were given ten marbles and you simply added up your score.

Needless to say this was much too simple for us. Far from being a game of mindless chance, bagatelle was one of the supreme tests of skill yet devised by man. A moron might simply pull back the handle and loose off his marble at random, flukily landing it in the 150 hole (the highest score achievable on our board). It was far more satisfying to execute a delicate push, calculating with precision the angle at which your marble left the starting alley, hearing it ricochet agonisingly between high scoring pins and holes eventually to plummet back to its starting point, having scored nothing. We often bought games from shops only to be bitterly disappointed when we got home to discover they contained some vital visual element which made them useless to us. The beauty of the bagatelle board was that its designer, almost certainly by accident, had produced a game that signalled all its highs and lows with distinctive sounds. In truth there really was an element of skill to it especially when the spring handle wore out with repeated use and we were left in control of the power of our shot. We devised strategies to land the marble in one of the high-scoring numbers. The score crept relentlessly upward. Meals had to be postponed as the dinner table was required for bagatelle practice. Bedtimes were temporarily put on hold because potential world champions don't allow their mothers to tell them when it's time to stop playing. Dad had professed to find this game beneath him but he had his competitive instincts titillated and demanded a turn. Finally, late one night, I posted a score of 860. It was beginning to look as if bagatelle's equivalent of the maximum break had been achieved.

We slept late, waking next morning to sounds below of rolling bagatelle balls. Hurrying downstairs we found a strange and suspicious scene. Dad, who never came home during the day, had just happened to 'pop home' for elevenses. While drinking his tea he had, apparently absent-mindedly, posted a score of 915, the last 130 having been sunk as we burst through the door. We cried foul but mother, loyal as ever, swore she'd seen the whole performance, including three strikes in 'all dead balls back'. Despite the steward's enquiry, the record was never beaten or even approached. The following holiday the bagatelle board never emerged from the toy cupboard.

Monopoly also, appropriately enough, monopolised our attention for a brief span. It was not so much playing the game as making it playable that so entranced us. Dad had bought the game for thirty bob, but when he brought it home he realised that Colin and I wouldn't be able to play in its current form. The solution was that the whole house was immediately turned into a Braille printing press while we embossed everything in sight: title deeds, community chest and chance cards, even the money. The only thing we didn't

Braille were the squares on the board themselves. We simply learnt those off by heart. I can still conduct you from Old Kent Road to Mayfair without missing a square. As you might imagine, once converted, we played the game in our usual cut-throat fashion, although the playing never quite matched the making of it.

At Christmas time the process just went into overdrive. The Whites lost touch with the fifties and sixties and plunged headlong into a traditional Victorian Christmas. The television set disappeared upstairs, not even coming out of exile for the Queen's speech, and we entered on a games marathon which seemed to stretch from Christmas Eve to the New Year. Not content with all the old favourites – charades, twenty questions, quizzes – various other traditions developed, most of them inspired by Dad. He rather fancied himself as a poet and our cupboards were stuffed with examples of his work to mark special family occasions. On the birthday of a cousin who with a mate had three motorbike accidents that year: 'Up the road go Rob and Mitch, they're off, they're on, they're in the ditch.' In celebration of my youngest son who turned out to be a bit of a thug: 'Kids are sighing, kids are sobbin', I know why, they've just met Robin.' The nation lost a potential Laureate when it turned its back on our Dad. Christmas had its own poem marking key events of the past year, with special verses dedicated to everyone present. As we always spent Christmas with Mum's parents and her sister and husband, this turned the Christmas poem into an enterprise which in length, at least, matched the *Odyssey*. As I grew older it became clear that I'd inherited, along with so much else, my father's penchant for doggerel. I was roped in to help, being allowed to stay up late to search for new ways to insult the family. Every foible was latched on to and ruthlessly exposed: Colin's timidity, Mum's obsessive tidiness, Nan's idleness, Grandad's state of hen-peckery, Aunt Ruth's stupidity and

Uncle Tom's tightness with money. Dad and I collaborated with glee, only retiring to devise insults for each other.

Later still the poems turned into plays, beginning as impromptu sketches devised giggling in the kitchen on the night, and like everything we turned our hand to they expanded. Props were introduced, costumes made, tape recordings gathered to provide special effects. Work had to start the minute the holidays began and the drama tail was definitely wagging the Christmas dog. Suddenly the bubble burst one particular Christmas when we created a positive leviathan, not just a play but a series of plays resembling a West End review rather than a family entertainment. By Christmas afternoon everything was ready, at which point, with her customary exquisite sense of knowing how to spoil everybody's fun, Nan Durham had a massive stroke. In the event the liveliest thing to happen that year was a very restrained game of Scrabble. Nan died a couple of weeks later. Although she contributed very little to their merriment, it seemed to be a signal that childhood Christmases had come to an end.

Though much of my childhood at home throbbed with ceaseless life and activity, there were fairly large swathes of time during these holidays when I was a rather solitary little boy but I was never really 'lonely'. As we grew older Colin developed more outside friendships that I. Then, betrayal of betrayals, at the age of sixteen he acquired a girlfriend, so, when Dad was out at work and Mum was busy with endless household chores, I was thrown back on my own resources. I spent vast tracts of the holidays reading and rereading my relatively small stock of books; twiddling endlessly through the radio dial, listening to everything from Radio Luxembourg to the Third Programme with a few foreign stations thrown in when the domestic ones failed me; tinkering interminably on the piano, devising tunes which had no beginning and definitely no end. Most bizarrely of all, I constructed an imaginary world with a six-sided piece of wood.

I now view this sad episode of my life with a mixture of embarrassment and awe. I can't remember exactly when I discovered that Braille dice could be agents of mass manipulation, but it has to tie in with the realisation that, just as you can score up to six runs from one shot in cricket, so you can throw up to six with the dice. It wasn't much of a mental leap to work out that from there you could simulate whole matches if you had the mind and the time. You had to solve the problem of how players could ever be out, but once again the basic symbiosis of cricket and the dice came to my rescue. One score hardly ever recorded from a single shot is five, ergo if you shook five the player was out. You could refine the process still further. Having established that a wicket had fallen you could, by throwing the dice again, determine exactly how the batsman was dismissed. The number one signified that he was bowled, two caught, three leg before wicket, four run out and five stumped. In a rare mood of altruism shaking a six deemed that the appeal had been turned down and the player was allowed to stay. I decided arbitrarily that 'hit wicket' and 'obstruction' were such rare forms of dismissal that they could safely be ignored.

It was simple and satisfying and I realise now quite subtle for a seven-year-old, using the logic that you make a choice, and from that choice emerges another series of choices. Meanwhile, it meant I could sit on my sitting-room floor in Winchester and decide the fate of not just one match, but of whole seasons, armed only with a Braille copy of that year's cricket fixtures. I would play out a whole summer of cricket, working out the points for a win and bonus points for first innings lead, until I had recreated a whole county championship league table. It sounds incredible now, but it whiled away acres of lonely hours for me. My main puzzlement now is how my mother stayed sane. In order to ensure total authenticity the dice had to be shaken in a cup before being decanted on to the floor. Mum says she still occasionally hears in her head the sound of a dice being shaken over and over again.

Having cracked the complexities of cricket almost any other dice version of a game was child's play. The plodding simplicity of soccer posed no problems. It took a mere half hour to plot the destination of that year's FA Cup, even if it did produce the unlikely Wembley final of Hartlepool United versus Exeter City. Randolph Turpin could once again quell the mighty Sugar Ray Robinson without spilling a drop of his precious blood. By combining the dice with the board on which we performed maths, I managed to restage every event in the 1956 Melbourne Olympic Games. Had I persisted with this obsession until more adult interests came along I could have found ways of staging general elections, plotting the rise and fall of unemployment, even tracing the ups and downs of love affairs, rendering the whole messy business of living unnecessary at a stroke.

The truth of it is, I suspect, that repressed energy has to come out somehow. I had bags of mental and physical energy but at home in particular there was a very restricted canvas on which to exercise it. Although in my head I just wanted to get up and go, my lack of confidence in getting around was holding me back.

Nowadays I commute seventy miles to London without a second thought; go off to cover a story in a city unknown to me without bothering to do any geographical research; visit Paris, New York or Cape Town as casually as I might stroll to the pub. In those days a foot set anywhere outside the known and familiar confines of the Square resulted in panic. I only had to think that I was lost to be lost. But it was a problem I was doing my damnedest to solve.

The first stage of my attempt to conquer the known world was an unaccompanied visit to the shops. For most kids the gentle but insistent mother-summons to 'just pop over the shops for me, dear' is one to be avoided, not feared. But for me the shops – all of 400 yards and one right-angled turn away – were a challenge as tough as any I faced as a child.

Needless to say this was a milestone Colin had reached with ease when he was six. I was bitterly conscious of the fact and longed to emulate him. At about the age of eight I began seriously to nag Mum to let me go, terrified that sooner or later she would say yes. The inevitable morning came when she finally gave in. From that point my treacherous stomach was a seething cauldron. Despite all the verbal descriptions, the maps drawn on my hands, the fact that I had walked it endless times with Mum, I just knew with total certainty that the moment I was out on my own I would get lost. Unable to eat any breakfast, I finally set out, with my list and my shopping basket, on the road to inevitable humiliation.

The configuration of the shops was a nightmare that might have been drawn up by a sadistic social worker for the blind attempting to construct the stiffest mobility exam imaginable. I was always reading about rows of shops! Why the hell couldn't *we* have a row of shops? Instead ours were dotted about higgledly-piggledy in something between a semi-circle and a dog's leg. No two shop entrances were alike. Dowlings the butcher's was approached by three steep steps, the greengrocer's was landmined with a phalanx of boxes with vegetables on display and the hardware shop hid cowardly behind a low hedge at an absurd angle to the road. A stretch of open grass – as far as I was concerned a landmarkless waste – a pillar box and a telephone kiosk were positioned in such a way that any course set to avoid one brought you into smart contact with the other; and a short but steep bank lurked strategically outside the grocer's. However good my form I was bound, sooner or later, to fall foul of one of these obstacles. I became convinced that the world had nothing better to do than watch my incompetence and a small blip turned swiftly into a series of disasters.

On the day of my first voyage things started off surprisingly well. I crossed the only road with care and without incident, went to the first shop in the group, the general store, which had a sensible wide entrance at a proper right-angle to the road. I handed over my list, got my loaf, placed it at the bottom of the bag as instructed . . . then the problems began. To get to my next port of call, the post office, I had to cross this open stretch of green. I wandered along for a while confident enough and then I began to fret. Something 'felt' wrong. Had I gone too far? Had I somehow missed the door? It was practically in a straight line, impossible to miss, but once your mind starts to play such tricks you're lost. All logic and memory of distance goes out of the window. You become convinced you have never experienced this place before.

I backtracked. No good. After a while I returned with embarrassment to the general store. Up across the grass again, but confidence shattered. I might as well have been on the Russian steppes for all the clue I had about where I was. My one hope – and one dread – was that someone would spot me and help out. It would be humiliating, but the only way to make progress. Suddenly I had a stroke of luck and walked slap bang into the telephone kiosk. A bump on the head was a small price to pay for the information it gave me about the location of the post office.

That transaction went smoothly enough, but then I had to complete the most difficult part of the journey. Charlie Hobbs, the grocer, was tucked away at the far end of the semicircle. I struggled along towards it. Fortunately someone came out of the shop as I approached giving me a line on the way in. I handed the friendly but tactless Mrs Hobbs my bag and my list. 'Going shopping for your mummy then?' she yelled at the top of her voice totally shattering my impression of a trip made nonchalantly and out of pure filial duty. 'Yep,' I muttered, rubbing the bump on my head. 'I'll put your eggs on the top, then,' she bawled, 'so they won't get broken.' 'Thanks,' I muttered, making for the door aware that my ordeal was almost over – and promptly fell down the bank.

Mrs Hobbs repacked the bag, replaced the eggs, even bathed my knee. Then, confident in the knowledge that the worst thing in the world had already happened, I trotted off home without further mishap. Mother greeted me like a conquering hero, congratulating me on having forgotten nothing. I wondered about owning up about the eggs and then decided it was the least of my worries, so I didn't bother. I might as well have saved myself the anguish. Only relatively recently I discovered that Mum, having watched me go, had followed me, always keeping about twenty yards behind. She had watched every calamity, every trauma and had somehow managed not to intervene. All the shopkeepers had known about the proposed trip and had instructions only to help in the direst of emergencies. When I finally made it safely to the home straight, she took a short cut through the allotments so she could be indoors when I arrived. Social workers had little to teach my mother about fostering independence.

Not that the neighbours appreciated this sterling quality. As we grew older, they became increasingly horrified at our antics and Mother's refusal to stop us. Colin was already using his little bit of sight to ride a bike around our fairly quiet housing estate. A pair of roller-skates followed, and because I had not yet progressed beyond the three-wheeler I achieved my thrills with Colin's aid attaching my roller-skates to the back of his bike, and whizzing around the roads after him. The neighbours looked on in outraged amazement.

The day arrived when I decided to master a proper bike.

The machine I chose for this exploit had seen better days – just as well as it was about to experience the worst four in its history, emerging a battered wreck and scarcely recognisable as a bicycle. More or less the same could be said for its rider. While I still had one foot on the ground – a phase lasting about a day – things weren't too bad. I could usually save myself from the worst injuries but when I did eventually work up some momentum I was rarely on the thing for longer than about fifteen seconds. I subsided gracefully on to grass verges, or crashed on to the gravel, flopped into flower beds or found myself strung out like washing left to dry across a neighbour's hedge. The flora and fauna of Milner Place was left looking like parts of seventies Vietnam. I fell off that bike from almost every angle: off either side, sliding like a sack of potatoes off the back, or simply flying straight over the handlebars. I constantly cracked my knees on the handlebars, barked my shins on the crossbar and skinned my ankles on the pedals. Every time I stopped suddenly – which was every time I rode it – I was jerked forward to slam my groin on some unnecessary appendage of the infernal machine. Shares in Dettol must have rocketed that weekend as I constantly went into the pits for running repairs on most parts of my anatomy. Attempts to persuade me to stop 'just for a little while' were ignored. The penance continued. On the very last day of the holidays I cracked it. The intervals at which I fell off had gradually become longer, then suddenly I realised I'd been riding along uninterrupted for about ten minutes. This milestone achieved, there was no looking back. Colin, who over the four days had progressed from scorn through impatience to a certain grudging wonder at my persistence, said he would set me a test. We would ride a marathon, round and round the Square, keeping going until one of us fell off. Round and round we went, for over two hours until, on the 826th circuit I fell off – again – but this time out of sheer exhaustion. When I went back to school the following day an accompanying letter explained that the various cuts and bruises, contusions and abrasions had not been acquired in an orgy of child-beating. The miracle had been achieved. I could ride a two-wheel bike.

4

The Blind Sons of Gentlemen

I spent my first few hours at Worcester believing that everyone was called Christopher and that nobody could sound their Rs. As I found my way to the wash room for a pee it happened again.

'Chwis?' came a muffled interrogation from the sit-down bogs.

'No, it's Peter,' I explained. There was a puzzled silence. He pulled the chain and emerged.

'Chwis,' he said again.

This was getting boring. Still, I'd only been there a few hours. Better play along.

'No, I'm Peter.'

For him, light suddenly dawned. 'You're a new sprog, aren't you?'

Funny! He should have said 'Spwog' but he hadn't.

I admitted that I was.

'Ah,' he said, 'then allow me to explain.'

There were two types of boy at Worcester College for the

Blind Sons of Gentlemen: those who were arrogant bullies, and those who were just arrogant. I'd had the luck to come across one from the second category.

'Here at Worcester,' he intoned, 'when we meet someone we say "*Quis*" – that's Latin for "who". You'll learn that by and by. Then you reply "Ego" – that's Latin for "I". Get it?'

I got it. At Bristol we'd had a similar system. You said 'Oozzat?' They said 'Me' and then you hit them. Still, this was clearly a different world.

It was certainly that. You would be hard put to find the equivalent of Worcester College on any educational map of Britain, either then or now. It was like a residential grammar school with public school pretensions yet a class base more varied than any comprehensive. Blindness, like intelligence, is not the prerogative of any class or income group. As its incidence is very small, we were all slung into the same melting pot. When founded in the 1860s, the school had been fee-paying, but by now no parent was required to cough up their own cash and the fees were almost invariably paid by local authorities or voluntary organisations. The only criteria for getting there was passing their equivalent of the 11-plus, and surviving the rather more arbitrary scrutiny throughout the residential examination. It's a system which ought to have been fair, although in my generation it did manage to screen out David Blunkett (whether for intellectual or political reasons, history does not relate) and I wonder if that would account for his oft-repeated aversion to selective education.

The upshot was that it brought together a group of boys – and it was all boys – who under almost any other circumstances, in 1958 at any rate, would not have been seen dead in each other's company. The parents were a bigger giveaway than the boys, who were already being homogenised by the Worcester gloss. Sit quietly and listen at any Speech Day gathering, and you could be forgiven for thinking you were inhabiting parallel worlds, where Ascot merged with Walthamstow dog track, the Dog and Duck with the Ritz. The braying tones of the upper classes alternated with cockney twangs. Dad's broad 'Ampshire and Mum's 'Saaf' London placed me firmly in the camp of the Dog and Duck.

It made for some strange and rather touching bedfellows. Michael and Reg were in my year and came to Worcester from a London school already firm friends. Michael's father was a dentist in Bournemouth, his mother had the distinct manner of a dentist's wife, and his sister, much fancied by all of us, went to a private girls' school. Reg's parents, Bill and Dawn, came from the Essex borders of the East End, with accents to match. Despite the fact that Dawn would have been unlikely to fetch up at any of Iris's coffee mornings, both sets of parents were inseparable at parents' weekends, linked not by class but by the fact that they had blind sons who befriended each other aged four. Mick and Reg and Dawn and Iris are all still in touch.

If the staff at Worcester were aware of their position in the vanguard of a social revolution they gave precious little sign of it. They would probably have argued that it was not part of their job to destroy the achievement of centuries of British class consciousness. As far as they were concerned, boys didn't happen to Worcester; Worcester happened to the boys. There was one role which Worcester had to perform, one which, ironically, the excluded David Blunkett would have wholeheartedly approved. Education, education, education.

The philosophy went something like this; blindness is perceived by the rest of the world as a disadvantage, but send out your boys stuffed to the gills with O and A levels and degrees, and they will at least have a chance of competing. So that's what happened at Worcester, and with a considerable measure of success. The atmosphere, in total contrast to Bristol, was fiercely academic. Of my year of nine – only nine, another crucial factor in scholastic success – seven of us got our full complement of Os and As and went on to university. The eighth left after his O levels to become possibly the most overqualified physiotherapist in Britain, while only the ninth settled for the University of Life by getting one of the kitchen maids pregnant. And our form was by no means exceptional. This is what was expected of us. With the advantages of reasonably well-qualified teachers, an adequately stocked Braille library, tiny classes and nothing better to do with our time, much of our competitive spirit was channelled into academic achievement.

The argument about the education of blind children is still a very live issue: special schools like Worcester, now co-educational but still churning out production-line university students, versus the local comprehensive or sixth form college, perhaps not equipped with as much blind-specific gadgetry such as Braille machines, or teachers trained in the needs of children who can't see but, so the story goes, sending out well-integrated young adults who don't poke their eyes and who can eat without covering their neighbour in crumbs and gravy, therefore mixing more comfortably in the 'real world'.

If you catch a note of scepticism in my tone you're right. Although the issue of special versus integrated is still alive, the special school has become a deeply unfashionable concept to defend. Members of the disability lobby who attended them have railed against the Spartan conditions – as I have done – and are deeply enraged by the segregation they underwent which implied some innate inferiority. They've even given themselves a name: 'special school survivors'. It's very hard to maintain a defence for the special school particularly for those who aren't disabled, against the vitriol engendered by such powerful and clearly painful experiences. The special school survivors have gained the moral high ground and arguments in favour of some degree of specialisation are dismissed as deeply revisionist; to maintain them is to show yourself clearly as 'not one of us'.

So why do I try? I think it's a mixture of pragmatism and nostalgia. On the practical side mainstream schools have yet to prove they can educate blind children – in the old-fashioned academic sense of imparting knowledge – as effectively as special schools. There are a number of reasons for this: Braille books and equipment are expensive; if blind children are educated singly or in small numbers (inevitable if they go to their local schools because blind children are a tiny proportion of the population) it's going to cost more. Moreover, each school has to go through its own process of learning how to accommodate blind children. They may only take one or two in each generation which would mean they would have to start that learning process all over again each time. Trainee teachers are still not required to learn anything at all about the needs of blind or partially sighted children and in some schools this even seems to be regarded as a virtue. I remember a headmaster telling me that as they didn't regard blind children as special in any way, it wasn't thought appropriate for his teachers to undergo any specific training in their needs. With such attitudes and with the well-established pressure on education authorities to eke out their resources, it's hardly surprising that for every horror story from a special school survivor, I hear another from youngsters whose sight loss wasn't recognised in their mainstream school, and who had to put up with embarrassment and bullying until transferred to a special school where teachers and pupils understood their problems; or of parents and pupils who wanted to go to their neighbourhood school, but who found themselves waging a constant battle for Braillers, books and teacher's scarce time.

Special schools like Worcester and about a dozen others throughout Britain have been at this business for a long time.

They have qualified teachers, long-established Braille libraries and a wealth of experience. They have also long given up their Spartan regimes and would now be horrified at what I was subjected to at the age of five: thirteen weeks away from home without a break. Nowadays, even children who have to board because of distance make very regular visits home. Worcester itself expects its students to acquire social skills, to cook, to look after clothes. Older pupils live in small houses rather than the main body of the school where they must learn to fend for themselves.

Don't misunderstand. If I were faced with a choice between the ideal special boarding school and the ideal neighbourhood integrated school, I would go for integration every time. But that is not the choice most parents and blind children are confronted with. Often it's the choice between a well-equipped special school and a local school with no experience and not much inclination to take on a blind child. Do you sacrifice an individual child for a theory? Committed integrationist friends with whom I regularly have this debate tell me – regretfully I hope – that sometimes you do, and until you get rid of the segregated special school system you cannot force mainstream schools to make the necessary adaptations. They argue with what they seem to regard as a *coup de grâce*: what about the long-term advantages of sighted children regularly coming into contact with blind children of their own age? Think of that.

For me that argument still won't do. An unrepentant gradualist, I worry about a generation of blind children deprived of decent, basic education while we sweep away the expertise in once place, hoping it springs up somewhere else. The joy of being responsible for educating our sighted peers about blindness fails to thrill. I would have thought we were at enough of a disadvantage to begin with, without having to take on the added task of enlightening our own generation.

One of the great bonuses of growing up with other blind children was that, far from regarding myself as special, blindness could be regarded as just another characteristic. It's interesting that in the United States, where the integration of blind children was introduced earlier and more completely than here, they had to revive the practice of blind youngsters getting together at summer schools so that they could offer each other mutual support and reinforcement.

I sometimes wonder what would have happened to me if I had gone to Peter Symonds' Grammar School in Winchester, a bus ride away from home as opposed to Worcester over one hundred miles away. I desperately wanted to, and it's a seductive thought, but even if it had been a realistic option at the time would the ultimate outcome have been as good for me? I have a vivid picture of an awkward undersized teenager desperate to be regarded as 'normal' by his mates. I suspect I would have been prepared to have done almost anything to gain street cred. Almost certainly that would not have included sticking at my books. I could see myself cheerfully straying down the path of slothful slobbery to be one of the lads. I could well have emerged a very well-integrated drop-out.

No such dilemma applied at Worcester College. Certainly the usual school tension existed between 'lads' and 'swots', but the camp you chose depended purely on your natural inclination. Proving that your lack of sight didn't prevent you from being hard was not an issue; as far as that was concerned we were all in the same boat. The reality was that at Worcester there were deserts of free time and a well-stocked Braille library. Sooner or later a combination of boredom and my natural inclinations compelled me to learn. I hold my current job with the BBC, which I love, as a result of that opportunity. As the BBC's Disability Affairs Correspondent, I often find myself enthusiastically explaining the integrationist line but I do it in the uncomfortable knowledge that I am talking down the system which enabled me to achieve the job in the first place.

But this is all with the benefit of hindsight. At the time the flaw in the special schools system was a huge one. True, we might all emerge with our differential calculus and a firm grasp of the importance of sand in the Industrial Revolution; but some of us were also going to our first job interviews, fists firmly planted in eyes, heads waggling about all over the place, wearing odd socks and addressing our well-honed and well-modulated observations on life somewhere over the left shoulder of our prospective employer. Worcester, in short was not strong at instilling social skills. The staff appeared to believe that they hadn't acquired their firsts at Kings and Balliol just so that they could socially readjust a bunch of blind kids. I suspect that, if asked, they would have said that was the job of the 'jolly old trickcyclist'. In any event, such a dangerously modern breed was never allowed anywhere near the place, and we carried on with our eccentric ways unmolested.

Worcester came up with a solution to the problem peculiarly its own. Rather than eradicate these odd quirks, it filled us all with so much braying self-confidence that most of us emerged finding it difficult to believe that anything we did could be regarded as less than totally admirable.

Despite our polyglot class origins Worcester boys developed a corporate and wholly recognisable voice distinctive not so much for any tell-tale accent – it's hard to know what kind of accent an amalgam of leafy Surrey and inner city Leeds might produce – but because of the clipped certainty of its delivery. Almost all of us acquired 'the voice', whether the confidence it suggested was real or imagined. Colin for instance, left Bristol sounding like a country bumpkin but was returned to us a crisp, rather bombastic teenager. None by then could have accused Colin of being the most decisive of souls, but equipped with 'the voice' he could deliver a line like 'I hadn't really thought' as if it were an irresistible call to action. Even now, for those in the know, the phrase 'Oh, he's a Worcester boy' conveys a world of meaning. They abound in the councils of the blind, conservative with a varying C, uniformly smug and never wrong. It's unattractive enough at fifty-five, so at fifteen it must have been unbearable. With this attitude we sallied forth into the city of Worcester, sometimes alone, but usually in a phalanx of arm-linked boys, booming our certainties to each other largely oblivious of any opinions an outsider was unwise enough to offer. If you'd asked, most of us would have claimed we longed to be part of the ordinary community and craved a more normal lifestyle. In truth, we had a pretty odd way of showing it, preferring to cling to each other for mutual warmth and reassurance.

In fairness we were young and were offered precious little help in forming more outward-looking relationships. A few boys lived near enough to pay visits home, occasionally taking a friend with them. Members of minority churches sometimes became adopted by co-religionist families, presumably all part of the evangelical recruiting process. The rest had to wait for puberty and the acquisition of a girlfriend with a family. If your sex appeal failed you, it was just a question of sitting up on the hill until the gates finally opened.

Well behind the door myself when sex appeal was dished out, I spent rather more time within those gates than was probably good for me. Nevertheless the outwardly civilised but intellectually brutal world of Worcester suited me well, certainly much more so than Bristol. I settled down to a world of books, balls, bullying and boredom, moderately well satisfied.

The ethos of laissez-faire certainly extended to discipline. The business of day-to-day punishment was placed firmly in the hands of seventeen- and eighteen-year-old boys trained for the previous six years in the certainty of their infallibility. As a result they went to their work with a sadistic vigour. Quantity was their watchword and it was accepted that hotly contested punishment competitions formed a lively backdrop to a prefect's life. There was certainly plenty of scope.

'Mornings' was a punishment requiring appearance at the prefect's bedside at some ungodly hour for late rising; 'nights' meant an early bedtime, sometimes for a week at a time, for talking after lights out. And every other *minor* infringement of rules – running in the corridor, whispering in prep, beating weaker brethren nigh unto death – was seized upon with a will. In the hunt for the end-of-term punishment league title, keener participants were quite prepared to go looking for trouble. The bell, sounded five minutes before mealtimes to summon you to wash your hands, was more often than not followed up by bands of roaming prefects, the totally blind ones lifting and sniffing your fingers to see if good honest urine had been replaced by good honest carbolic soap.

The ritual had a nightly equivalent. School rules said, for some incomprehensible reason, that, during Christmas and Easter terms, at 5.30 p.m. precisely 'house shoes' (light slip-ons) should replace our daytime clodhoppers. At the start of prep at 6.15 p.m. the finger-sniffing brigade would duly turn their attention to your other extremities, doing the rounds and feeling our feet. One noted blind lawyer possesses a full set of teeth only thanks to massive self-restraint on my part. Nightly I was tempted to remove them with my invariably clodhopper-shod toe.

Faced with a competitive police force we felt we had no choice but to form an equally competitive criminal fraternity. By the final week of term the race was hotting up at both ends of the school for our respective crowns. Indeed, in a few isolated cases I believe an element of collusion between aspiring winners may have crept in. For a while, I had the honour to hold the title of the most punishments acquired in a term. Standing at forty-five, it represented three punishments every four days. This was only matched by one of my class mates who, having returned to school late one term, managed to clock up sixty-three 'nights' in a term which for him held only fifty-six bedtimes. Needless to say they were held over for completion in the first week of the following term. Worcester justice was not unduly harsh, just inevitable and unbending.

Some aspects of the school's free-wheeling policy were deeply refreshing. In particular for the first time in my life I found myself in a position where I could wander about at will, without being obliged to give an account of my comings and goings to anyone. This would have been unheard of at Bristol where the gates weren't locked, but might just as well have been; or for that matter at home, where the worry level on both sides made the game not worth the gamble. But at Worcester nobody much seemed to care, regardless of your ability or inability to negotiate your way out of a paper bag. Indeed, there were forty-five minutes of 'walk time' each weekday, when you were more or less forcibly ejected from the school. Woe betide anyone found hiding in the bogs – another pleasurable search and destroy assignment for the zealous prefect.

In the opening few weeks of my first term at Worcester I used this unaccustomed freedom, albeit in a permanent state of terror, to maximum effect. It now seems incredible that a group of untried blind eleven-year-olds could be let free on an unsuspecting neighbourhood, particularly with the main Worcester to London road to cross before they could reach anywhere. But, used to captivity, most of us didn't need telling twice. In those early weeks my adventures including getting lost on almost every housing estate around the edges of Worcester, falling into several muddy ditches in the surrounding lanes, and somehow, in the belief that I had taken the turning for the village shop, finding myself enmeshed in a farmer's hen coop. The more I thrashed about seeking an escape, the more the hens flapped and clucked, the more frantic and unavailing were my efforts to escape. Finally a kindly if somewhat resigned farmer arrived to release me and place me back on the lethal Worcester to London road. His manner suggested that separating wandering blind boys from his livestock was something he had to do almost every day.

In the end I shattered this happy state of bucolic mayhem, not only for myself but also for everyone else, by getting run over by a rather large lorry carrying ball bearings. For the last twenty yards or so of its journey it was also carrying me on its front bumper.

I can't remember much about the incident. One minute I thought I was crossing the entrance to Dog Rose Lane in what was a permanent state of geographic uncertainty. The next I was haring down the centre of the road with the sound of squealing brakes pounding in my ears. I remember dimly some bouncing down the road on my head. Finally I was lying on the verge with a very concerned driver bending over me.

It could have been a lot worse. About half a minute later my friend Michael came along, kicked my shoe, which had flown off in the accident, and assumed, with the logic of a blind twelve-year-old, that it was my severed head. In the end it turned out that all I had sustained was a bump on the head, a dent in my leg where the lorry's fender presumably struck me, and uncontrollable shaking, which they told me was shock. The college maintained its usual sang-froid, writing to my parents to inform them boldly that Peter had had 'a brush with a lorry' but was okay. We had not yet entered the age of litigation-mad parents. Nevertheless, it didn't take long for the shock waves of my incompetence to register with the school of what might have happened.

The following term we returned to discover we had been

divided into four categories according to our navigational abilities. Group A, with quite a lot of vision, could still go where they liked and be responsible for others. Bs could also go where they pleased, but couldn't take anyone with them. Cs could also go out alone, but only within a restricted and specified area. Ds couldn't go anywhere without being accompanied by an A.

We were outraged. As the cause of all the trouble, I was more outraged than anyone. The headmaster was in his first year and had already acquired the nickname 'Holy Joe' for decreeing that there should be no school dance – the only chance we had of meeting female company – during lent. This latest fatwa turned him into a hate figure. 'Namby pamby ideas from Charterhouse, no understanding of blind kids' – that was the verdict of the mob.

Protests were lodged, demonstrations took place. The ethos of Worcester – that everyone had the right to be killed in his own way – had been shaken. In the end the protests and the system died the death. A test enabled you to graduate from one grade to the next. Everyone knew the scheme had become a joke when I, as spatially challenged as ever, was promoted from a D to a C.

The great 'grading' crisis accentuated a trend which is bound to occur at blind schools anyway. Although they were always called blind schools – we had no truck in those days with concepts of 'visual impairment' or 'lacking in visual acuity' – many of the children who attended them did have a certain degree of sight. I think they found themselves both, educationally and socially, in a rather odd, uncomfortable situation. Had they gone to mainstream schools they would have been known as 'Four Eyes', the kids with their noses pressed up against the blackboard in order to see it. But they came into an educational atmosphere geared mainly to totally or almost blind children where concepts such as print and pictures were considered a little suspect. Although many of these sighted children could read print quite comfortably with magnifiers – a few only needed a pair of strong glasses – they were discouraged from doing so, especially in their school work. The attitude seemed to be that as their sight could well deteriorate later on, they'd better start learning Braille now. It might have had an element of common sense, but, as with most rules at Worcester, it was taken to extremes. 'It might be better to keep up to scratch in both mediums' somehow became 'If I catch you reading print again, there'll be trouble.' We were also still in the dark ages of believing that using your eyes could somehow harm them.

If eyesight was considered 'not quite the thing' educationally, socially it was a commodity beyond price. After grading was introduced, if you wanted to go into town or just to the village shop you needed a half decent pair of eyes to get you there. Those with reasonable vision were shamelessly courted for ocular favours. Dignity demanded that you didn't simply ask someone to take you. It had to look as if you went in friendship. But the bottom line was a pair of functioning peepers. Consequently some unlikely alliances formed masquerading as David and Jonathan but if honestly scrutinised amounted to a blind guy in search of a permanent guide. This could, of course, be seen as putting naked power into the hands of those with sight, but it didn't always work that way. Many apparently inseparable friendships comprised a strong, manipulative blind boy and a weaker, more pliant sighted one. Independence was one thing, but there was no doubt life could work more smoothly if you involved eyesight. Shopping expeditions, visits to football and cricket matches and, later, illegal sorties to the pub were more enjoyable when the wheels were greased by a little vision. Inside school the same rule applied. Impromptu football and cricket matches progressed much better if you had someone to retrieve the ball from the bushes.

Schoolboy pranks required the services of a lookout, and print might be discouraged by the staff, but the sports pages, the *News of the World* and more blatant pornography had not found its way into Braille. We were quite prepared for our 'friends' to risk their eyesight to bring us these delights. It was a common sight to find a gaggle of boys clustered eagerly around one central figure, his nose planted about 3 inches away from the page, reading out the day's full cricket scores or the best bits of *Lady Chatterley's Lover*.

It's a moot point who gained most from these relationships. We, the totally blind, gained help and information. They, the partially sighted, achieved an importance and an ascendancy they might never acquire again. There was room for exploitation on both sides. We could exert moral blackmail, they could simply invoke the power granted by their sight. The real clue is that at one point there was a suggestion that in future partially sighted boys should go to a school of their own, while Worcester should concentrate on those with really poor vision. There was uproar, but I remember most of it came from those of us who couldn't see glimpsing a future in which we would be deprived of our 'sight slaves'.

If this all sounds unduly cynical perhaps I should add that our class of nine quickly moulded itself into a tight little group in which some firm and genuine friendships flourished. Even those not admitted to inner circles were treated with tolerance, something which could not be said of many others in this unforgiving climate. We were the beginning of a challenge to that conservative and insular arrogance. With a loathing of the mindless authoritarianism of the prefect system, we progressed through the school challenging it at every turn. First we employed dumb insolence. Later, when we were expected to maintain discipline ourselves, we refused to play the game. Having proudly held the record for incurring most punishments, it was with even greater pride that in my final year, I was hauled up before the headmaster so that he could berate me with my pathetic showing of imposing just one punishment. (And that was carried out under extreme provocation.) My answer was that something was wrong if you couldn't keep order in a school this small without endless punishments. This seemed to puzzle and even sadden him.

By no means untainted by the school's patrician philosophy, we nevertheless seemed to be the first year to have collectively grasped that the world was changing; that rock 'n' roll was here to stay; posh accents didn't mean big brains; some people do better if you talk to them, not bully them. By the mid-sixties, when we had reached the top of the school and the Beatles ruled the world, we were challenging an ethos which had given us egos the size of Kent but expected us to face the world unable to cook, sew on a button, hold our drink or chat up a girl.

But when I arrived in 1958 the school possessed an air of breezy combativeness, the importance of being bright, the presence of people who could hold their own and even beat me in an argument. It had almost edible food, more freedom and teachers who at least seemed to know a little more than I did. Worcester was nourishment to my starved soul. Only as the gloss wore off did I find that I needed more to keep me amused. At the end of my first year a new headmaster arrived. The old one had, by all accounts, been a bit of a martinet. Richard Fletcher, who took over was scholarly, mild-mannered and almost certainly a nice man. He once told me that the last problem he'd expected to have to deal with at a school for the blind was discipline. My next seven years at Worcester were a one-boy crusade to show him just how wrong you can be.

5

The Blind Misleading the Blind

As the blows rained down on my head I desperately tried to figure out what could be happening. One minute I had been sitting in a maths class contentedly conjuring up the partially clothed body of Carol, one of the nurses in *Emergency Ward Ten*. The next the world exploded. Had her boyfriend caught me? Had the roof collapsed? It was about the time of the Cuban crisis – perhaps the fully expected nuclear war had begun with Worcester as the first target. Then light dawned. I was being assaulted by the beefy arms of Reg Bonham, our blind maths master, goaded beyond endurance, yet again, by the baiting of his wholly unsympathetic blind class. Dismiss any thoughts that sharing his disability might have made us considerate towards his situation. We baited teachers, blind and sighted alike, of course. One of them being blind simply evened up the score and enabled us to start on a level playing field. He was still a teacher, after all.

In fact it was far from a level playing field. Reg Bonham was no match. A kindly, avuncular genius, he had swept the board in maths prizes at Oxford and also represented Great Britain at chess, but strangely for a man to whom the mysteries of geometry were 'obvious', he had absolutely no sense of direction. He even made me look like Vasco da Gama. We ruthlessly and repeatedly exploited this fatal flaw. Stories of his navigational disasters were legion. Once, on his erratic journey back to his house, only a few hundred yards from the school, he accidentally collided with and knocked over a small child. Then, so legend had it, he bent solicitously, picked her up by her ankles and boomed comfortingly, 'Are you all right little girl?'

The fun with Reg Bonham's classes began before he ever made it into the room. Firstly we had to decide where to put the teaching table – pushed over into one corner, or in one of the side aisles, or even right at the back of the class. Reg seldom found it. Occasionally he would drop all his books and teaching aids at the place where the table ought to be, scattering them all over the floor. But this was a bonus. Usually he would simply meander around aimlessly for a while in search of it, then give up and continue to teach on the walk. Strangely, for a man with no sense of direction, he liked to teach on the move, and this placed some terrible temptations in our way.

One of our favourite tricks was to take a large Braille map, about 18 inches square and made of stiff, unyielding hardboard, and place it so that it was protruding at about throat level on top of a book on one of the sets of shelves running the length of the classroom. The result was predictable and always satisfying. Happily chuntering on about arcs and hypotenuses, the stream of incomprehensible information would suddenly be abruptly cut off as the edge of the map came into smart contact with Mr Bonham's windpipe. If we tired of this – and it took a long time – we would place the map a couple of shelves lower and pile it high with anything that came to hand –

boxes, the waste-paper bin, sometimes even a chair. Many a revelation about tangents and cosigns was lost in the deafening crash as Bonham sent the whole crazy edifice crashing to the ground. And if he strayed from the edges of the room an even crueller fate awaited him. As he moved uncertainly between the desks we would wait for him to pause, hovering above some hapless dunce, and then the desks around him would be gradually and silently edged in his direction. Only when he had finished some totally obscure point and attempted to move away would he discover that he had been corralled, unable to budge in any direction. This left him with only one conceivable course of action – and thus my reverie about Carol from *Emergency Ward Ten* came to be so rudely interrupted. In this particular case I had had nothing to do with the latest entrapment, but we bore him no ill will for these random attacks. Punishments like this, while never finding the right victim on the right occasion, were deemed to even themselves out over a longer period. The province of Bonham-baiting was by no means exclusively ours. It was a sacred trust, handed down from generation to generation, though some generations performed with considerably more subtlety than we did.

If Mr Bonham could extract any satisfaction from his protracted persecution it would have to be that (a) we didn't patronise him and (b) he was by no means the first to suffer in this way. An earlier blind English teacher had had to endure similar treatment. One class had attached a banana skin to the light shade above his head by a piece of string, then, the boy sitting directly beneath proceeded to swing it gently backwards and forwards. On the first few swings it merely grazed the teacher's hair gently, evoking no more than a puzzled frown. Made bolder, the boy manoeuvred the string so that the banana skin caressed his face. Suspicion quickening, he flapped at it ineffectually, then subsided again into the Romantics, contenting himself by observing that the moths

were bigger than ever this year. But no one constructs an engineering masterpiece just to create a mild irritation. The next
time the banana skin caught him full in the face. This would
have had to have been a moth of truly gargantuan propor-
tions.Roused to a wild frenzy he reached up, grabbed the
string (which hadn't been pulled away quite quickly enough)
and with a massive tug pulled down shade, wires, light bulb
and half the ceiling too.

I wouldn't want you to run away with the idea that we
were cowardly. We never knowingly shrank from dishing out
an equally hard time to sighted teachers, though with most of
them, in order to keep the scales even, we resorted to psychological rather than outright physical warfare. The principles of
good teacher-baiting were the same for us as for any pupils:
find a weakness, then play on it until you bring them as close
to nervous collapse as you dare.

Jimmy Downes's great weakness was his voice. It was
not exactly a stammer or a stutter, but his sentences took forever to get underway. They would begin as a low growling
noise coming from deep in his throat, rather like one of those
little two-stroke motorbikes heard way in the distance, and
gradually grew until just when you thought you had the
chance of a recognisable word, he would have to pause for
breath. But the nature of his stammer was that, having
breathed he couldn't pick up from where he'd finished. The
whole motorbike routine had to start again from the beginning. This might have been all right if he'd been discussing
football or the price of fish, but Jimmy was a history teacher
so that even when the sentences did finally produce something you knew he was only going to drone on about the Great
Reform Bill or the Battle of Unkiar-Skelessi. I rather liked
history but others were less patient. One boy, exasperated
beyond endurance, one day took a Morse buzzer into class
and placed it beneath his desk. As soon as Jimmy embarked on

one of these half-groan, half-coughs a foot would descend on to the buzzer and remain there until either the sentence began or the class's mirth made the whole exercise untenable. Jimmy was so deep into the intricacies of Palmerston's attitude to the Schleswig-Holstein question that it took him a while to figure out what was happening. Eventually though, his gunboat diplomacy was every bit as summary as the great statesman's.

His real name was Robert Leslie, but everyone called him Jimmy; nobody could remember why. He lived on the premises and seemed to have no real home of his own. Rumour had it that he had been disappointed, both in love and in the level of his degree (he only got an upper second rather than the first he thought he deserved). I think, looking back, he was a rather sad, even lonely figure, but he took revenge on us for all the indignities we heaped on him by roaming the corridors at night – he was a chronic insomniac – seeking out breaches of discipline. His favourite pastime was crouching outside doors for minutes on end, trying to catch boys talking after lights out. This was a very fruitful exercise, since we invariably were.

Jimmy had his good points. If you had the fortitude to last out to the end of his sentences he wasn't a bad teacher. There's never enough literature on any subject available in Braille, so Jimmy had to read on to tape whole truckloads of books on and around the syllabus. Strangely enough, he never stammered when he read aloud, but there was another hazard to negotiate in coming to terms with the Turkish question and Pitt the Younger's sinking fund. These were the days of quarter-inch tape played on monolithic machines. Given my manual dexterity, most of my history revision nights ended with tape tangled around the recording heads, my neck, my feet and halfway across Jimmy's bedroom. He took these examples of historical macramé very well, often coming in close to midnight to extricate me from my latest pickle, comforting me with a story of one even more ham-fisted pupil than I, whom he had discovered leaning out of a window trying to disentangle the taped version of Martin Luther's ninety-five theses from the branches of a nearby tree. Every Friday night he invited anyone who cared to listen to his room where he played the classics and his vast collection of British and American comedy records. Comedy was much better attended than serious music, but it revealed a more human side to his character. I tried to repay him by securing an A in history although even here I insisted on the last laugh. For a bet, I managed to achieve this without mentioning one battle or one date.

Ramsay Baxter had not one but four weaknesses to contend with, which left him open to attack from a variety of angles, depending on your taste:

(a)   He was incapable of keeping to the point.
(b)   He was easily flustered.
(c)   He also had very poor eyesight, although not
      quite on the scale of Reg Bonham.
(d)   He taught French.

Why do French teachers inspire pupils to new heights of insubordination? Probably it's just plain English Francophobia. Baxter certainly went through the mill. Some classes seemed to be quite content to pray on weaknesses (b) and (c), being cheeky, winding him up and also on occasions playing the old desk-corralling trick. After one particularly tempestuous encounter he became so enraged that he swept from the room slamming the door behind him. Only after he'd taken a couple of steps was he brought up short by the realisation that he had slammed his gown in the door. Consequently he had to go back, open the door and confront the smirking faces of his tormentors. For some reason – and this was unlike us – we took a more merciful line with Mr Baxter although one firmly rooted in good honest self-interest. We discovered that his repertoire contained about half a dozen interminable stories, all dealing with his travels in France or his early teaching days in southern Ireland, which could be triggered by key words or phrases and we became expert at getting one or other of these hares up and running. On being kindly reassured that he had never told us the story about the actor/manager Miles Malleson and his productions of Molière, or about the eccentricities of the Irish dual-language examination system, he would be off. The perfect timing for one of these key words or phrases to be dropped casually into the conversation would be about twenty to twenty-five minutes into the lesson. Getting it exactly right would mean no more French that day, and guaranteed that he would still be going strong when the bell rang, which in turn meant that he would almost certainly forget to set us any French homework. With the combined efforts of Miles Malleson, Irish schools and a new one involving an apparently uproariously funny joke hinging on the double meaning of a French word, we managed to avoid French homework for eight weeks, a clear and undisputed record.

Ray Follett's Achilles heel was a very strange one for a PE teacher. Known more or less affectionately as 'Old Wheezer', he was a chronic asthmatic with a gammy leg. Going on a run with Mr Follett always felt a very hazardous business which would be best attended by at least two doctors. Somehow, though, he always survived, puffing and panting sometimes even fighting for breath and then at the end producing a quite amazing turn of speed.

Although I loved sport at school and took part in most athletic pursuits with boundless enthusiasm, if limited skill, for some reason Ray Follett and I never hit it off. He was an odd mixture. In some ways he was a radical: he was a Second World War conscientious objector who apparently told a military court in what must have been an almost unique example of brevity, 'My job is to make men, not break them.' But against that he was an absolute stickler for what was fitting, a conformist who thought there was a right way and a wrong way to do everything and who regarded as an irrefutable argument the phrase 'It's never been done before'. Ever the non-conformist, I fully realised the depth of our schism when he summoned me to him to explain why, yet again, I had been passed over for prefect. 'I'm afraid, White, you're just an odd one out.' I felt a surge of pride. 'You say the sweetest things,' I said.

Richard Fletcher, the new headmaster, did not teach that often. When he did it was usually religious instruction. This did not bode well for our relationship, since at this stage I was keen to flex my rampant atheism at every opportunity. Mr Fletcher was a kindly, rather gentle soul, although much firmer of purpose than we originally thought him. He would try desperately hard to engage me in discussion of the finer points of the spiritual life, but sadly the more reasonable and understanding he became of my point of view, the more exasperated I became by his. For a while our battle dominated RI classes, until I finally succeeded in breaking his spirit when I delivered the sincerely held – but I now realise not very original – opinion that St Paul was a bigoted old bastard. Mr Fletcher considered this for a while, then said he felt that possibly we had no more to say to each other on the subject of religion. In future he would prefer it if I would keep my opinions to myself and give the rest of the class a chance.

A number of teachers succeeded in stimulating my already considerable interest in books. Most notable was Doug Folley, who told us a month before our O-level paper that we all knew enough to pass, then proceeded to read to us from Laurie Lee's *Cider with Rosie* for the rest of that month. Every year Doug Folley would put on a school play. The more unsuitable a production looked for blind actors, the more determined Doug became to give it a go. Among the things we attempted were wartime plays involving sets simulating submarines and merchant ships, forcing us to scramble up and down ladders and shin up ropes, all rehearsed with meticulous precision. For six nights and six performances of a play called *One More River* everything worked like clockwork. Only when taking the curtain call on the final night did Jeff Long, who'd been playing the barrack room lawyer, step backward with a little too much enthusiasm and disappear down the hatchway, whose cover had been inadvertently left open. Fortunately Jeff's muffled cries from beneath the stage were masked by the tumultuous applause, and Doug Folley contented himself with the observation: 'Even I can't be expected to rehearse a curtain call.'

He also rather fancied whodunnits which again often involved very complicated action sequences. In a play called *Not in the Book*, a totally blind boy, on stage alone in a scene played out in total silence, has to bring off a sequence in which several drinks are swapped around so that the right person drinks the poison. It was rehearsed hundreds of times so that at no point was anyone's belief in the reality of the situation interrupted by the realisation that the actor couldn't see. It worked every night.

Perhaps his most imaginative production of all was our version of M.F. Simpson's *One Way Pendulum*, a play from the absurder edges of the theatre of the absurd. In it, if I've remembered what passes for the plot correctly, our hero has a plan to take several hundred talking weighing machines to the North Pole and, on a signal given by the playing of the Hallelujah Chorus, he persuades the people accompanying the weighing machines to jump up and down. I forget now what this was intended to achieve but no matter!

In *One Way Pendulum* I played Aunt Mildred, an old lady who had been an intrepid traveller in her youth but was now confined to a wheelchair. This meant that, for long periods of the play, seated on stage with nothing to do, I had to pull off the most difficult trick for a hyperactive fourteen-year-old: pretend to be paralysed. Sooner or later I did what many a much finer actor must have done before me, and fell asleep. Suddenly awaking I was dimly aware of a sense of unease in the audience. Up until now the good burghers of Worcester had watched the bizarre action of *One Way Pendulum* with a mixture of puzzled silence interspersed with a few isolated tuts. But I awoke to a different sound. There was a stirring in the audience. Were they all going to walk out? Suddenly and terrifyingly, I grasped the problem. Aunt Mildred's wheelchair was on the move.

Anchored on stage for hour upon hour, it was now quite definitely sliding gently down the slight incline of the stage. Very soon it would leave the gentler slopes and hit the Cresta run taking it over the footlights and hurtling into the front row. Lourdes had never seen a swifter or more complete miracle. Aunt Mildred, rapidly rediscovering the power of movement, jammed her feet on to the stage, bringing the chair to a skidding halt half an inch before the abyss, and provoking easily the best ovation of the evening. Later investigation revealed that some malcontent, determined to turn the theatre of the absurd into a Whitehall farce, had wandered behind the dozing Aunt Mildred and released her brake.

Oddly, the two masters for whom I had most respect and affection at Worcester both taught science, a subject at which I was a total liability. Indeed, as Nobby Clark said when he caught me blowing bubbles in a bottle of acid, 'I'd rather have a barrel load of monkeys in my lab than you.' (On another occasion it was a sack full of rabbits, but the implication was the same.) In my first year in his brand new laboratory, I also succeeded in singeing my hair with a Bunsen burner – several times – reducing a pair of weighing scales to a pile of unrecognisable screws and rods and leaning on two gas taps, almost sending class 4C into a toxic coma. Despite this, Nobby Clark and I got on rather well. Despite his abrupt manner – something I was well used to from my father – he was a kindly, caring man with an eccentric sense of humour which sometimes passed us by. On seeing a boy thirty or forty yards away whom he knew perfectly well to be totally blind he would yell out, 'Don't you know you've to put your cap on in the presence of a house master?' Boys quailed totally, forgetting no such rule ever existed, just Nobby's little joke.

He and his wife had the endearing habit of inviting boys up to The Lodge for, of all meals, breakfast. It was an inspired choice. Worcester's breakfasts were generally a sad affair and sitting in Gwen Clark's warm kitchen when you were far away from home, tucking into her porridge and full fried breakfast should have been a huge delight. Sadly, when my invitation came I was going through one of my 'food is my enemy' stages, and sat in huge embarrassment, pushing the delicious food around my plate, terrified that if I swallowed any of it I would be promptly sick. I don't know whether they had come across this phenomenon before but neither of them made any comment on my strange behaviour, chatting away while my companion – we were usually invited in twos – gobbled up his and probably coveted mine. What a luxury! A Worcester teacher who appeared to understand children. Eccentric and individualistic himself, he was one teacher who did not seem to believe that being 'an odd one out' was automatically a criticism and seemed to have his finger on the pulse of what was going on among the boys, most of his information gleaned, no doubt from those breakfasts.

How Walton van Clute ever made it through the deeply conservative portals of Worcester College I'll never know. He was American, for a start, from Boston. Then there was the little matter of his participation in the Spanish Civil War, his reputed brush with the Un-American Activities Committee, his confirmed membership of the American Communist Party and his avowed atheism, not flaunted but happily discussed with anyone who asked him. We first realised that we had a man of unconventional opinions among us when, the morning after the Russians withdrew their ships from Cuban waters during the 1962 missile crisis, Mr van Clute quietly commented at breakfast that in his opinion the hero of the day was not Kennedy but Khrushchev. With Kennedy mania then at its height at Worcester, as in every other part of Britain, this was an exciting, if rather frightening heresy. The word soon got around that the new guy was a Commie. When the intendedly mischievous rumour turned out to be true, the frisson was enormous.

The man we all ended up knowing simply as Van proved to have enormous charm, gentleness and generosity. Although he had very strong opinions, he never forced them on anyone. Indeed, he almost seemed to regard teaching itself as a form of bullying, which is probably why he was so bad at it. Physics was his subject so I doubt I would have understood a word even if he'd been the best teacher in the world, but even those who were fascinated by it confirmed that he was incomprehensible. Far better to get him on to the evils of Guernica, McCarthyism and organised religion. On these he was clear and concise, his meaning unmistakable.

Fortunately most of my contact with Van had nothing to do with the classroom. He helped me enormously when, as editor of the school magazine, *The Pimpernel*, I tried to transform it from a boring and predictable noticeboard into a cross between *Private Eye* and *Marxism Today*. Reviews of the school plays, sports results, lists of leavers and newcomers and the inexhaustible memoirs of ancient teachers were axed and replaced by a heady diet of politics, sex and religion.

Governors quaked; more conservative parents demanded to know what sort of institution they'd sent their sons to. But having replaced the magazine's lackadaisical sales policy with one of aggressive marketing on parents' weekends and daily forays into the housing estates of Worcester, we more than quadrupled our distribution. I had panicked and fretted as publication day approached, arguing over proposed censorship by the headmaster, haggling with the printers who I felt were exaggerating their costs, even losing a whole 2,000-word article on the evils of compulsory chapel attendance, over which two fourth formers had probably risked expulsion. Through it all Van, who had worked on a real newspaper in the United States, kept me calm. *The Pimpernel* hit the streets on time and I bizarrely won that year's prize for citizenship.

But Van's greatest contribution to my welfare were the hours that I spent at his house seeking refuge from a school and a system from which I was feeling increasingly estranged: its stifling rules, its ridiculous pretensions and the cumulative effect of thirteen years of boarding school education. When my own battle against compulsory religion eventually led to my exclusion from Sunday services, I would escape to the home of Van and his equally lovely wife Stella, drink their beer, eat their sausages and imbibe their bracing yet free and easy philosophy. Van taught me you could be clever without being cruel, acerbic without being arrogant and that you could hold strong views without ramming them down other people's throats. I haven't always practised these virtues, but, because of Van, I can never claim I don't know they exist.

I had first arrived at Worcester on a windswept September day in 1958, full of hope and good intentions. I was here to work, to be a star, to fulfil my obviously huge potential. Early impressions of Worcester had been favourable. First stop, the library, of course; it was infinitely better stocked than Bristol's with more Braille books in one

116

place than I'd seen in my life. As well as all the things you'd expect – Dickens, the Bible, unfathomable poetry – there were books a boy might actually want to read: school and adventure stories, humour, stacks of crime fiction, even a handful on cricket and football. Within days this library had become my personal fiefdom. I crawled and clambered over every inch, poking into all its corners, discovering secrets which boys who'd been there for years, and the Chief Librarian, didn't know. For the next few years, even when my hell-raising was at its height, I spent every spare second in this haven. Starting books, dipping into the middles of books, reading their last paragraphs. I would become arrested by them, reading them wherever I came upon them – crouched on the floor, perched on a table, halfway up a library ladder (no mean feat when you need to read Braille with both hands). The one place you would hardly ever find me was sitting at a table with a book neatly placed in front of me. Somehow that was far too planned.

By this method I gained a huge superficial knowledge of books unsupported by any real depth of understanding. I could have told you who wrote almost anything, but very little about what he or she was trying to say. Sometimes I found it inconvenient to leave books in the library and very soon I became the first and automatic port of call for the school librarian when anything went missing. It wasn't a difficult deduction, my bed was about six inches higher from the ground than anyone else's, raised by all the books piled beneath it.

Browsing was a luxury I never again enjoyed after I left school. I still miss it. A few years ago I returned to Worcester to report on a story. I rediscovered the library and eventually had to be prised away kicking and screaming.

Along with a sweet shop on the premises; freedom at last to roam a little; a well-equipped gym where we played endless games of football at the weekends; and friends I could finally talk to, it looked as though Worcester was going to be pretty good. In that first year the work was pretty easy too. Nelly Siddle was a Lancastrian woman who taught the eleven-year-olds. The mere fact that she was a woman was unusual enough at Worcester, but at the time the intake year was definitely regarded as separate from the rest of the school. Nelly called us 'chaps' and was slow to anger, although you could wind her up if you were prepared to work really hard at it. Lessons continued much as they had at Bristol, with an accent on English and no awkward concepts such as quadratic equations or the declension of Latin verbs to disturb me. I was comfortably in the top three at most things although at this stage there were only seven of us in the class. And 1959 was an idyllic summer. As temperatures rose through June and July, Miss Siddle allowed us to push our desks on to the veranda outside the classroom and there, at the back of the school, facing the Malvern Hills, we disturbed nobody and nobody disturbed us. Cliff Richard and the Everly Brothers were booming out of radios and tape recorders, England was winning a cricket test series 5–0, I had the aggregate top score in our summer exams and a long holiday stretched endlessly into the future. Life could not have been much better.

So how did this dream of academic delight turn into an accident waiting to happen? The answer is, I think, that on attaining the dizzy heights of 4C and the second year I suddenly realised for the first time that I was not destined to excel at everything. And at some subjects I was simply appalling. There was an even worse revelation. At some subjects I was just average. Being the best I expected; being the worst at least ensured notoriety; being average I found unbearable.

My lack of spatial awareness turned any mathematical concept beyond simple numbers into a nightmare. The science lab was a disaster zone and I was not, much to my own surprise, particularly talented at foreign languages. In short I was not the genius which the unchallenging atmosphere of Bristol had led me to believe. To keep up, let alone forge ahead, I had to work. Worcester was not short of real geniuses, boys who ate up knowledge and spat out spectacular results. I came to the conclusion that if I could not match them, even by working flat out, I would have to find another way of making my mark. On looking at Worcester a little more closely it gradually dawned on me that undermining a disciplinary system based on eccentric teachers and over-mighty prefects was not a bad alternative.

So began a more or less puerile series of escapades which kept me amused and authority enraged for the next three or four years. Some were carried out alone, most with some level of support. I was usually found somewhere near the centre of anything going awry.

One of my most regular victims was the visiting typing master, Charles Hodges, head of the typing pool at his firm and pillar of his local church – a natural target. He often told us that what we learnt from him would be the most useful knowledge we would acquire at Worcester. With the increasing importance of computers, he was almost certainly right. Our tricks were relentless and regular. The eleven alarm clocks timed to go off at five-minute intervals during his hour-long typing classes were among the more effective.

Sometimes our jests had, we thought, a serious purpose. John Earle was a white South African who had the misfortune to join us as a guest teacher for a year in the early sixties. We associated his brash self-confidence with the ruling classes in South Africa and it therefore seemed quite reasonable to us to lay at his door all the evils of the apartheid regime. Drawing on our sketchy knowledge of the subject we began by calling after him, 'What happened at Sharpville then?' John Earle countered this adroitly. Having identified Chris Davies as one of his most persistent persecutors, he demanded a 2,000-word essay on 'What actually happened at Sharpville?' As Chris would probably have had trouble constructing a full sentence on the subject, we decided it was necessary to change our tactics and resort to our normal methods. As his bed-sitting room was just along the corridor from our dormitory this proved simple enough. He was noisy as well as brash and would frequently sweep from his room with a thunderous crash, leaving his keys in the lock. It was a moment's work, too simple to resist, to nip along to his room, lock the door, remove the keys and, as a final and typical embellishment, hide them under the head boy's pillow. The results were swift and more satisfying that we had dared to hope. We'd assumed that there would be a spare key and after a few minutes of satisfactory swearing and cursing it would all be over. Instead we had the full treatment with sound effects – bunches of keys being shaken, tried and rejected; ladders placed against windows; hammers taken to locks, a full hour or more of conventional cursing and swearing with Afrikaans additions. When somebody finally went looking for the key, we were the first port of call. The searchers were faced with the standard dumb insolence; but we were more co-operative when the head boy suggested that perhaps we should all sleep on it. We were able to say, with some conviction, that we thought this was a good idea.

By the morning authority had recovered its cool, as well as its assurance with the dirty tricks. The last resort of the school master – 'If no one comes forward I will have to punish the whole school' – deposited the key back in Mr Earle's possession and four fresh stripes on my backside.

Occasionally pupils buried any differences and turned as a body on an external enemy. Such was the fate of the parish church of the little village of Whittington. Its downfall lay in its hospitality. The college's new chapel was part of a wing being built when I arrived, so the parishioners invited us to share in their worship. Their kindness was not appreciated. We had a long walk in both directions and an hour in an extremely draughty church permeated with the smell of paraffin lamps. The vicar appeared to have spent most of his adult life in Nigeria and for some reason thought we would like to know about it – every week. The phrase 'When I was back in Nigeria' unleashed a sound like a volley of grape-shot. Its source was almost certainly unknown to the villagers or the vicar, but we knew it as the sound of the hinged lids of fifty Braille watches being opened, checked, then snapped shut again. Betting on the length of his sermon, with side bets on the precise duration of Nigerian diversions, was the only enlivening feature of the visits to Whittington Church.

Initially our discontent only took the usual form of mutters and moans. Then someone let off a stink bomb; thinking that over-reaction would only make matters worse no action was taken. Then the Stop Whittington Church campaign began in earnest. At this time I was not yet into my full hell-raising stride, but I was used as a letterbox in what developed as a shadowy web of communications. I still don't know to this day where my instructions were coming from.

The first time we were not consulted. While the first hymn of the morning was belted out with the college's usual lusty fervour, the next one sounded distinctly weedy. The third one was back to speed again, then the fourth one was as pathetic as the second. By the end of the service it was perfectly clear that something was happening.

The following Saturday night, I found a Braille note in the lid of my desk: 'This week: alternate verses.' I passed the message on. The effect, this time, was embarrassingly stupendous. Sixty youthful voices belted out the first verse of 'He Who Would Valiant Be' for all they were worth – then nothing, just the thin reedy voices of a few little old ladies, the post-colonial quaverings of the vicar and the painfully off-key bass of the village shopkeeper. Then with the third verse a tidal wave of sound again engulfed the church. Because of the dramatic effects we created, we performed with even more gusto than usual. We returned to college well pleased. Still nobody said anything . . .

Next Saturday evening . . . Short note: 'Alternate lines.'

Alternate lines turned out to be devastating. I can't have been the only one half hoping that someone would do something, say something, to stop us and avoid the embarrassment of what we were about to do.

They didn't.

It was like some awful pub sing-song routine where the blokes are on one side of the bar and the women on the other but only the women really want to sing. The sound swelled and died. The parishioners kept on going. Goodness only knows why they allowed us to ruin their services for them. I suppose they were proving a point too. Finally it was over. We trailed back to college, no longer triumphant but stunned and apprehensive. What would they try next week? Alternate words?

There was no next week. The following day after assembly, Nobby Clark strode to the front of the gym. He said he had been worshipping at the church of St Philip and St James for the past seventeen years, 'and that in that time I have never been so embarrassed and humiliated as I have by your behaviour over the past few weeks'. He said he had never encountered such a display of bad manners as the one for which we had been responsible and that he would find it difficult to hold up his head in the village for some time. He said a great deal more. There were no threats, no 'If the person responsible does not come forward . . .' nonsense. He concluded by saying that such guttersnipe behaviour must cease forthwith. It did. We continued to troop down to Whittington Church for a while, although it must be said that when the heat had died down, we resumed Sunday services in the gym before the completion of the new chapel. There was no triumph. We all knew that at best we had boxed a very dishonourable draw.

We finally began to grow up, putting our energies into more adult irresponsibilities: hanging around in pubs, desperately trying to look fourteen let alone eighteen and staying clear of the ones we knew were used by the staff; hanging around in smoky coffee bars, hoping against hope some girl would talk to us and running a mile when one did; sliding into betting shops to put our scarcely adequate shirts on horses of which we knew nothing; creeping into the little shop at the back of the station to buy dirty books for our one pair of dodgy eyes to read to us. Some boys seemed to have the knowledge and the poise for this kind of thing. Most of us were gauche and out of our depth.

Work played very little part in my scheme of things. I did sufficient to achieve the exam results expected of me, but not enough to fly high. Nothing really caught fire. No piece of poetry made my spirit soar, no great idea helped me identify my purpose in life. I was becoming interested in politics, but not interested enough to wade through the manipulation required to persuade somebody to read the great columnists of the day to me. Altruism extending to reading out the cricket scores for others did not encompass turgid political leaders.

I still had one last battle before I left Worcester. Our year had great plans for our final twelve months at college. We were going to liberalise this prefect system; fight for the removal of petty restrictions; turn Worcester from a place aping public school traditions into one capable of turning out adults ready and able to face the sixties. But we hadn't bargained for the subtlety of Richard Fletcher, the headmaster. Peaceable and mild-mannered he might be, but he had confounded my prediction as a cocky twelve-year-old that he wouldn't last five minutes. Now, obviously aware that we were hell-bent on trouble, he outflanked us with the simplest of expedience. In our first prefects' meeting he coolly announced that he was going to relax the school rule about drinking in pubs so that it coincided with the law of the land.

It was a tactical master stroke. The would-be reformers were all just over eighteen. We had been handed on a plate a concession for which we thought we would have to fight tooth and nail. We tried not to feel grateful. We tried to tell each other it was just a strategem to get us off his back, but we were grateful. We could drink and be normal in our final year. The rest of the school could go hang. Most of our reforming ideas were left on ice as we enjoyed our new found freedom.

But one battle would not be given up, even for a fear-free pint at the Swan. For as long as I could remember – maybe even from that first day at Bristol when I argued about the number of hymns we had sung – I had chaffed at compulsory church attendance. Religious instruction was one thing. As I grew older I was quite happy to accept the argument that Christianity was a central part of our culture and that we should understand it and, crucially, in an RI class you had the freedom to argue. Attending Christian service, though, was an act of worship, with its essential language of gratitude and obeisance entailing belief. I bitterly resented the hypocrisy of appearing to accept the existence of a god I did not believe in. Throughout the week I was being urged in class to think for myself, challenge ideas, form my own views. Suddenly on Sunday I was expected to swallow what seemed to me a load of mumbo-jumbo without a murmur. It stuck in my gullet. I did not intend to leave school without having made a stand against it.

Initially plans were elaborate and ambitious. Everyone stood with me. Even the believers claimed to accept the unfairness of it. Worship should be freely given. If not we were going to organise a mass boycott of chapel. We would threaten with the weapon we knew they feared most – publicity. We would tell the *Daily Mirror* and the *News of the World*. That would show them.

It never happened. We confronted Mr Fletcher with our plans and, with all the liberal understanding at his command, he agreed to have a meeting with us. He used every tactical trick in the book, flattering tough nuts like me with his respect for our intellectual honesty, playing skilfully on the spiritual doubts of the waverers, invoking the good order of the school and wondering aloud, at crucial points in our negotiations, how certain people's parents would feel about all this. By the end of the meeting he had successfully isolated two of us sticking to our guns, Michael Beck the head boy, and me. No boycott; no *News of the World*.

He hadn't finished yet: he offered individuals exemption from attending chapel if our parents were fully in accord. That worked in Michael's case, and, almost to my great surprise and indignation, in mine too.

The last person from whom I'd expected opposition on this matter was Dad, the prime source of my atheism in the first place. At the last hurdle it appeared he was going to stand in my way. His argument astonished me.

'It has nothing to do with religion,' he said. 'It is a school rule from which you are seeking to be released.'

I was hearing the 'good order' argument again. I fretted and fumed. He stood firm. Only in my penultimate term, when I walked through the door at home with an offer of two Cs from Southampton University, an academic target I didn't expect to miss, did he relent. He gave me the signed letter I needed to rid me of those turbulent priests. Four months later I would have been free to do as I liked anyway, but what the hell. It was the principle which counted.

The story had a sequel. I'd heard so much about good order that I'd assumed that daily assembly, which I had understood was compulsory by law, was still required and that I had been released from Sunday services only. But after attending on the first day of the summer term, I felt a sharp tap on my shoulder as I filed out of the chapel.

It was Fletcher.

'What are you doing in my chapel?' For him it was almost a bark.

'I though morning assembly was compulsory, sir.'

'Not for you, it isn't. I don't want to see you in my chapel again.'

A demon stirred.

'What if I experience a sudden conversion, sir?'

He paused. It appeared to me he trembled a little.

'Then you see me first!'

That was definitely a bark. It occurred to me with some satisfaction that should such an unlikely event as my conversion ever occur he would almost certainly do his best to talk me out of it. I took this as the victory I had been searching for.

6

Long, Tall Janet

It began as a titter, felt its oats and developed into more of a snigger but always stopped short of the full-throated guffaw. Nevertheless it sounded as if fists and handkerchiefs were being firmly stuffed into mouths to prevent it.

As I was the person walking down the centre of the gymnasium at the time I must have caused this suppressed merriment. What could be the reason? Was my zip open? Were the contents of a toilet roll lodged in my turn-ups, unravelling in my wake? Was I enveloped by a cloud of dandruff? I reached my quarry in an agony of apprehension. 'And Peter's partner for the evening,' intoned Mrs Folley, the dancing mistress, 'is Janet.' At this point I could practically hear teeth biting into knuckles.

The protocol for this evening had been clearly set out. When we were introduced to our partners, we were to reach out and shake hands. When I attempted to do this I realised what all the mirth had been about. I missed, clutching at some nameless part of her anatomy, at which point a hand clamped on to my wrist from what seemed like a great height. Somewhere way above me a voice boomed, 'Hello.'

Janet was vast. You didn't have to be very big to dwarf my gawky four-foot, six-inch frame, but Janet must have been a good twelve inches taller than me. To start with I only had an impression of height. A few minutes later I grasped her around the waist for a ridiculously ambitious attempt at a tango and realised she was big in all ways. The daughter of a policeman, she had inherited not only his giant's genes but also a policeman's stolid devotion to duty. As we swayed in a mutually bewildered fashion around the floor, my nose now resting conveniently on her burgeoning bosom, she uttered not a word of complaint. In fact she uttered not a single word. Janet and I were ill matched in every conceivable way.

I don't know which joker inserted equal numbers of blind twelve-year-old boys and sighted twelve-year-old girls into a room and then paired them off in this excruciatingly public way. I'd still like to get my hands on them, even after forty years. We had been wildly excited at this idea of a 'social' in which we were to meet real girls. The alternative of us milling into the centre of the gym and grabbing at the first female who passed might have been equally disastrous, but at least Janet would have had the sense to avoid me and pick someone her own size. As it was, if marriage had to be arranged, someone might have taken the trouble to see if we were even remotely compatible, let alone whether we could actually reach each other.

Not everybody had a wasted evening. A charming story emerged of one of the more successful partnerships, in which the host chivalrously escorted his lady down the drive to the car of her waiting father. Sensing his chance, he tried to kiss her but she fended him off.

'There's a car with bright headlights coming.'

Thinking he'd been given the brush-off, he was just

about to leave her when she said, presumably not sure if his hearing as well as his sight was defective, 'It's gone now.'

There were no such entanglements for Janet and me, although on further acquaintance she emerged as a good-hearted girl. Desperate that no opportunity of female contact should escape us, however unpromising, most of us phoned our consorts after the social and tried to make dates. Amazingly Janet accepted my invitation, probably, I now realise, under pressure from her mother who may have seen it as the nursery slopes of a training in social work. On three successive Sunday afternoons Janet and I ambled up and down the Spetchley Road, exchanging banalities about friends, schools, parents and musical tastes. The nearest it ever came to sex was when she told me she'd seen a picture of Brigitte Bardot with no clothes on. Had I had the smallest shred of self-confidence I might have seen this as a come-on but the idea of stretching up to kiss Janet was so ludicrous as not to merit consideration. The relationship soon petered out.

There was no question of not liking girls. Julie Hardyman, Rosamund and all those girls from *The Archers* should have made that clear. I may have been no lady-killer but I was at ease with girls. But like many a segregated public schoolboy before and since, separation lends enchantment, ignorance and fear in equal measure. The added problem for a blind boy or girl is that the anatomical ignorance which gives piquancy to our quest for each other is deeper, darker and more impenetrable. With no clandestine photographs of a naked Brigitte Bardot to help me, all that I really knew about the organs after which I lusted were their names and then almost exclusively the vulgar ones. In my dreams I visualised what was really convex as concave, and vice versa. What was wet was dry, what was hairy was bare. I had not the vaguest notion of a breast or a vagina. I realise now that my fantasies about girls and women were about beings so unwomanly they might just as well have been Martians. Even the clothes in the fantasies bore little relationship to what women wear. One of the bonuses of playing Aunt Mildred in the *One Way Pendulum* was that I got to put on and therefore take off a bra. I still had no clue of what went inside it.

I open myself up to the accusation of thinking about women as objects, but objects – and not very accurate ones at that – were all I had to go on. When you can't meet them in the flesh, and whenever you do you're not sure what that flesh consists of, you are left with few options. During the sixties a rumour swept through Worcester that in Sweden, the home of all notions liberal, blind children were encouraged to examine real live naked models to fill this gap in their knowledge. We pleaded for an exchange arrangement between Worcester and Stockholm. It never materialised.

It wasn't just girls. My ignorance extended into every area that might be of the slightest interest to the late fifties–early sixties teenager. I could certainly describe what had been restored during the Restoration, the influences working on John Keats in his *annus mirabilis* and industrial wool production in the Calder Valley – fascinating stuff, no doubt, to a poetry-reading, sheep-shagger with an historical bent. None of it proved much of a chat-up line for the girls I was trying to impress, or much of a contest for the blokes against whom I competed. Take clothes, for example. What were young people wearing? Certainly not the school blazer and trousers I thrust myself unthinkingly into every morning. I knew about Teddy Boys of course. I'd heard all the hysterical outrage about their threat to society, which made them sound quite attractive, but I hadn't got a clue what they looked like. I was aware of drainpipe trousers, and winkle-picker shoes, but only in the same way that I was aware of breasts and vaginas – as words with no substance. I am now happily better informed about the latter but winkle-picker shoes, one of the icons of twentieth-century fashion, are still a total mystery to me.

Girls' clothes were an even deeper mystery. I was having enough trouble conjuring up accurately a pair of knickers, without getting involved with such nebulous issues as length of skirt, cut of coat, style of hair.

It's an ignorance which has remained with me throughout life. Despite being the right age to take sides, I hadn't the vaguest idea what Mods or Rockers regarded as their uniform. I was well into the music of Flower Power but the outward expression of self-absorbed hedonism completely passed me by. By the time Punks came along I was an old married man and probably wouldn't have wanted to join in anyway, but I was denied the pleasure of grouchy disapproval. Glam, Glitter and Grunge have similarly rocked the world and left me untouched.

When I first went to university good friends tried to disentangle me from the school blazer and the cavalry twill trousers Mum thought were 'smart'. They carted me around Southampton, kitting me out with shoes, shirts and polo necks which would stop making me look as if I'd just escaped from Greyfriars. I trailed obediently in their wake, grateful and desperately trying to drum up some interest. I was still attempting to get my sex life started, and this was apparently the way to do it. But if truth were told one pair of trousers, one shirt and one jumper still felt much like any other to me. When I discovered that having the right gear didn't automatically bring the girls rolling in either if you didn't know how to wear them, I relaxed back into my previous passive indifference.

A high-minded view might say that aping fashions I have never seen would merely be playing at being able to see with no real reference to my own sense of reality, and that I'm well out of all that cultural conformity crap. Now that I'm practically in my dotage I have a lot of sympathy with this view, but when you're sixteen and more at home conversing about the Stuart settlement than blue suede shoes you're regarded as a nerd. What do I suggest? Replacing double history at blind schools with the fondling of winkle-pickers (or something more nineties perhaps?) and the groping of Swedish models?

I had other equally blind spots. It was the era of the dance craze for instance, and every week, so it seemed, a new one hit the streets. But how to keep up? When I was ten my cousin Christine and her friend Sheila taught me how to jive. It was probably the greatest leap in being culturally hip I was ever likely to make. Even then, swinging my arms around like a demented dervish to the strains of 'Claudette' and 'Johnny Be Good', I could see its limitations. Dancing is a communal activity, its apparent lunacy tempered by the fact that other people are being equally lunatic alongside you, but learning and repeating a series of actions which you never see anyone else perform renders them meaningless. The pressure to conform is there though. As jiving was closely followed by the Twist, the Hully Gully and the Mashed Potato, the garbled instructions of Chubby Checker and Little Eva were never enough to keep me up to speed.

Strangely, even in the arena of music, where you would think we blind and sighted people were on completely equal terms, the huge visual factor of the enjoyment of rock music was an element that prevented me from ever feeling completely involved. I loved the sounds, but always felt I was missing something. What did Elvis do on stage which reduced girls to jelly and parents to impotent rage? Why did it matter what image Billy Fury projected, or what he stuck down his trousers (allegedly)?

Three of us formed a band, the W Brothers. Musically, we weren't bad at all. I was the weak link, but the other two still work in the profession. But, all totally blind, we had no idea what to do on stage other than sing. For some peculiar reason that didn't seem enough.

The school made some effort to fill these gaps, particularly on the girl front. The junior social at which I had encountered Long, Tall Janet was a one-off but further up the school a real attempt was made to foster relations with local girls' schools. It would be nice to think such unaccustomed liberality was inspired only by the joyous realisation that boys need girls and vice versa. Unfortunately I suspect a rather more sinister motive. A whiff of eugenics was in the air.

The staff at Worcester and our sister school for blind girls, Chorley Wood, were obsessed by the fear that we might, as they so delightfully put it, 'marry blind'. There was plenty of evidence that this was prone to happen. At that time blind youngsters tended to be steered into jobs such as physiotherapy and office work which had separate segregated training centres. The consequence was that many blind people in their late teens, after seven or eight years cooped up in single-sex boarding schools, suddenly found themselves thrown together at residential training colleges. It doesn't take a genius to work out what happened. Suffice it to say that rabbits stumbling across such scenes might have felt themselves to be shy and inadequate by comparison.

But marrying blind was not considered a good thing. Attempting to justify the attitude scientifically, I'm sure people would point to the increase in the genetic risk of producing blind children when blind couples get together. Though this may be factually correct, it's nobody's damn business but that of the couples themselves, who will be quite capable of ascertaining the facts and weighing up the risks. But I also suspect a rather more subversive thought at work: blindness is a problem and by doubling it you simply create twice as much trouble. At its very kindest this attitude can be seen as a way of our solving our domestic problems by finding some nice sighted girl to tidy our clothes and spread butter on our toast. Perhaps it's not surprising that many of us grew up with the fixed belief that the only way we could prove we had become truly integrated was to catch, bed and marry a sighted girl.

I first became aware of the regular dancing classes long before I was old enough to join them. The juniors' dormitory overlooked the front drive and every Monday evening at 9.15 on the dot delicious sounds and smells wafted up to us. Clacking heels, girlish giggles and just the merest hint of feminine perfume sent my ill-informed fantasies into overdrive as the girls of the local grammar school or the nearby convent departed after another session grappling with the square tango, large undirected feet and gallons of pent-up male testosterone. They sounded happy enough when I heard them, but perhaps that's because they were leaving. I often wondered in later years how on earth they ever persuaded so many to come to the school week after week. Was it some specially created badge for Worcester girls in the Duke of Edinburgh's Award scheme? A punishment for particularly wicked girlish behaviour? 'Do that again, Monica, and you'll be sent to dance with the blind boys.'

But they came, God bless them. And joining the dancing class was a high point in your school career.

Unfortunately these classes were fuelled with such unlikely expectations that you were doomed to certain disappointment. Dreaming of exotic sexual adventures on the first evening, what actually happened was the worst kind of boy/girl cattle market. Like many school events, they took place in the gymnasium. They began with the boys at one end champing uncertainly at the bit, the girls at the other backed up against the wall bars like the Sabine women about to be snatched by the marauding Romans. On the command 'Take your partners' we surged forward full of purpose, only to find ourselves flailing around in the centre of the floor, uncertain what to do next. In the ensuing confusion all the best-looking girls were snapped up by the experienced Lotharios from the previous year, while we rookies got what was left if we were lucky. Sometimes there were not enough girls to go round – some emboldened Monicas had made a break for it presumably – and you were likely to be taken in hand by the dancing mistress, Mrs Folley.

This could have its compensations. For one thing, you might actually learn to dance. For another, Mrs Folley was quite an attractive woman whose main dancing instruction was to utter the words 'Hold me tighter' in a husky voice which we chose to interpret as a fever of desire. In our imaginations we turned Mrs Folley into some rampant predatory Mrs Robinson who presumably started the classes so that she could be squeezed half to death by a pack of spotty fourteen-year-olds.

I managed to talk to some girls though: nice girls, friendly girls, chatty girls. A gawky, buck-toothed diminutive teenager, as stiff as a ramrod when it came to dancing, I was hardly likely to be top of any girl's hit list, but I had one saving grace. I could make them laugh. Often I had what I thought were quite promising encounters as I spouted wit and wisdom about the causes of the Counter-Reformation and unusual glacial formations in mediaeval France, and they chortled away fit to burst. All the following week I would dream of my dawning relationship with Julie or Penny or even Dawn, starting of course with violent sex but ending with marriage, children and a happy, fulfilled life. Somehow though, Julie, Penny and Dawn seemed to have seen it differently. They were rarely there next week. If they were I couldn't find them.

If dancing classes were a big event, term dances sent the upper school into a frenzy of anticipation. Dancing classes

were transitory affairs with no time to develop beautiful relationships, but the dance gave you all night to try to find your
wicked way. These dances were no more or no less than crude
girl hunts where the time-honoured system of stars – one star
for a kiss on the lips, two for a feel outside upstairs, right
through to six, going all the way – measured your success.
Most of us would be lucky to hold hands, but it never stopped
you hoping. The girls' grammar school and the convent were
supplemented on these occasions by the Dame Alice Otley
school, where girls were locked up as boarders like us. Rumour
said they were as sexually desperate too, although I never saw
any great evidence of it.

Hope never triumphed over experience. The day of each
dance was spent in a flurry of pointless preparation. Parts we
barely knew we had were washed and clothes that would have
done little for Casanova were donned with exaggerated care.
Scruffy school ties were tightened and straightened one hundred times and patent leather already shiny dancing pumps
were rubbed dull. Worcester dances were rather like football
matches. The first few minutes were crucial. Score early, and
you might be on a spree all night; miss those opening chances
and the game could settle into a sterile, self-fulfilling agony.

If you found a girl you liked in the mêlée accompanying
the first couple of dances, you had to hang on to her for dear
life. The sole object of dance nights was to have a girl in tow
when you reached the interval. You would then gulp your
supper as fast as possible, wash it down with a couple of
glasses of fizzy cider for Dutch courage, and then conduct the
hapless creature on a tour of the school's most captivating
points of interest: the music room, the woodwork room, under
the school stage – anywhere you might have a chance of being
on your own and begin totting up your stars. The following
day wild stories circulated concerning the most unlikely
venues for acts of passion. The more artistic ones liked to take

their girls to the library to show off our wonderful collection of Braille books, although the inspection usually ended up in the darker recesses of the reference section. The door from the library led into the chapel, where it was not unknown for sacred exploration to be followed by its more profane counterpart. Others made no pretence at high-mindedness and were quite prepared to press cloakrooms, boiler rooms and Mr Gwilym the Gardener's potting shed into service. Most stories were highly decorated versions of the truth.

Trying to find somewhere suitable was rather like looking for a seat on a busy commuter train: doors were eased open, prior occupation was established, disappointed clucking followed, and then on to the next carriage. You would have thought that older boys with studies would have been in a better position, but even these were shared by three or more people so that during the interval hurried and complex negotiations had to take place between those with and those without female company.

I, of course, usually found myself in the latter group. Luscious lovelies, somehow acquired in the anarchic lottery of the first skirmishes, mysteriously melted away after the opening foxtrot, leaving me with a series of unsatisfactory one-dance stands. As the evening progressed the girls you danced with became increasingly less enticing as all the peaches were gobbled up (the girls must have noticed the same phenomenon). Even when I had somehow contrived to acquire a partner for that all important pre-nosh last waltz, some call of nature or need to rearrange her perfectly arranged hair gave her the means of escape before we filed into supper.

I'm not sure if Rene Barker was too slow, too stupid or too nice. Whatever the reason, one Saturday night at around the age of sixteen we found ourselves embarked on the great ritual railway carriage search. She was from the reputedly rapacious Dame Alice Otley School, so I concluded it a certainty that my virgin state would soon be at an end. I hadn't a clue what this entailed, but I hoped it would come instinctively to us when the moment arrived.

The start was not auspicious. This was a real rush-hour train of a night. Woodwork room – occupied. Nobby Clark's laboratory – locked of course, but I had a master plan.

'How would you like to see our school shop?' I enquired.

After all, what girl could resist a whistle-stop tour of the Crunchie bars, cheese and onion crisps and bottles of Tango?

I knew that the shop – in reality a converted scout room – was sometimes used for late-night larks with the bolder kitchen maids, so that afternoon I had made a point of acquiring the key. Gauche I might be, but I had been the lower school's foremost trouble-maker for years and forward planning was something I understood.

Sadly, on this occasion, I was up against other boys rather than the staff. As I turned the key in the lock I heard a scuffling noise and some muffled squeaks. Another set of keys was evidently in circulation.

Things were now desperate. We had reached the equivalent of the guards and luggage vans. We finally came romantically to rest on a radiator at the far end of the corridor more suited to engineering piles than passion. I had reached that point of paralysed misery where speech, let alone action, requires a massive effort. She seemed equally passive although I suppose I could hardly expect a firecracker in view of the evening I was giving her. In the end, with time running out, and in the absence of anything else to do, I tentatively put my arm round her and then to my own utter amazement kissed her. Nothing disastrous happened. We didn't clash teeth or bump noses. My nose didn't run, and the kiss wasn't a slobber. Quite the reverse, it was the most arid, soulless, pointless event of my short life. Far from whistles and bells, it just felt like two pieces of sandpaper brushing against each other.

We didn't attempt to repeat the exercise.

We trudged in silence back to the gym and, after the first dance of the second half, she, of course, had to answer a call of nature. I found someone else to dance with – anyone – just so that she could complete her escape.

On another even worse occasion I filed girlless into supper but as we sat at the table I thought my luck might have changed. From my right rose a subtle but alluring perfume, and I thought I heard a low, attractive girlish giggle. By her silence I deduced that, like me, she had been abandoned at the last moment. Plans to rescue her, cherish her, raced through my head. We passed salt, pepper and cider jug courteously back and forth while I searched desperately for an ice-breaker.

'Not bad cheese and tomato sandwiches,' I finally hazarded.

He agreed that they weren't. A bit heavy on the old aftershave, I suppose.

What far more frequently happened was that I found myself alone in my study – assuming I was allowed to stay there – playing sad songs. On one particular dire occasion I even found myself comforted by Jimmy Downes, who assured me with unwanted camaraderie that 'they weren't worth the trouble'.

They were, of course, but I seemed to have a fatal talent for investing my effort in the wrong places. I had an unerring weakness for other people's girls. It seemed that, relieved from the pressure of actually having to make a move, I relaxed and blossomed.

The parents of one of Colin's friends had a little seaside bungalow practically on the beach at Bracklesham Bay in Sussex. Our family stayed in the bungalow for nothing if we took care of their son Bill during the holidays. We spent two of the best summers of my childhood there, enhanced for me by the fact that I interpreted the deal as including taking care of two of Bill's successive girlfriends. I fell temporarily in love with both Margaret and Ann, who responded to my infatuation with generous older-sisterly tolerance. I think both of them thought I was even younger than I really was – I certainly looked it – and they therefore allowed me the kind of licence a genuine rival for their affections would not have been permitted. As a result, frolicking around in the sea with Ann one day, I almost discovered what was found in those damned bras. We played cricket on the beach, went to the fun fair at Southsea and, because it was a wonderful rabbit warren of a house with weird entrances and exits all over the place, we acted out endless sessions of Murder in the Dark. Whenever I drew the jack, which designates the murderer, I stalked Ann with gentle purpose. Her distinctive perfume made this easy, although I was frequently hindered by Bill who, with the lights out, was stalking her for another purpose. Judging by how long it took her to scream as my fingers circled her throat, she wasn't totally oblivious of, or averse to, what was going on.

The same phenomenon occurred later at university. Still incapable of getting my own girls, I stole, albeit temporarily, not one but two from my best friend. He is still my best friend thirty years later giving some indication of my fearsomeness as a rival in love.

In fact I was too uptight, too scared, too self-conscious to forge a relationship and not arresting or sympathetic enough to tempt any girl to try to rescue me. When I did make contact I suspect the combination of my brains and my nerves made me appear prickly and arrogant. The famine continued.

Not for everyone at Worcester though. Despite the dreadful cattle market of dancing classes and the competitive orgy of speed-groping during the dance intervals, love somehow bloomed. Several long-standing relationships developed, even a few marriages. One was Colin's. When it came to girls, he had it over me every time. Better co-ordinated, better dressed, better looking. His customary caution and fastidiousness added to his charm. Colin also had – still has – a dry wit which is sometimes rather more acceptable than my barbed tongue. Jean came from the local girls' grammar school. They met at the dreaded dancing classes, love blossomed, surviving separations when they left school, and they eventually married in 1965. Initially I was rather jealous. I got on well with Jean but, increasingly isolated and friendless at home, I had lost my playmate and hero, particularly when Jean starting coming to stay during the holidays.

However there was one huge bonus. Unable to get a girl of my own I inherited by proxy Jean's family, and the all important bolt-hole, a real house in Worcester.

Jean's mum was a warm motherly woman who thought it was totally natural not only to be acquiring a blind son-in-law but also his younger brother as a frequent house guest as part of the deal. Even after Jean went off to teacher-training college she would sometimes come and rescue me from school on her weekends and take me home to 12 East Street for lavish teas and a reminder that normal people lived in normal houses. During my period of tortured and extended adolescence Colin and Jean often provided a haven, both before and after they were married. When times were rough, and being at home meant offering explanations about what was or wasn't going on, their flats and houses provided a sanctuary for my introspection.

My class was rather less successful at the mating game, with one very notable exception. Dave was a Jack the Lad from Streatham, more uncomfortable than most with Worcester's delusions of grandeur. Only an average scholar, he was well above average when it came to pulling girls. Many nice chatty girls who seemed to like my sense of humour nevertheless ended up in the arms of Dave Thomas, who obviously possessed a certain attraction. Strangely we didn't resent Dave's successes. He was upholding the honour of the class in an area where most of us were conspicuously failing. It seemed a fair division of labour that we would do the studying and the trouble-making and leave Dave to get on with the shagging.

Sadly, though, it led to a predictable enough conclusion. One Friday toward the end of our first term in the sixth form we suddenly heard that Dave, due to see out the year and go on to physiotherapy school, was instead going to leave. Further enquiry yielded the information that one of the maids was pregnant, and that Dave was responsible. In keeping with the mores of 1965 he was going to marry her. Convinced he'd been kicked out, one of those passionate, ill-informed Worcester campaigns gathered pace. 'Save our Dave' was its message. Dave himself had to quash it, explaining patiently that it was, in fact, his own choice. We contented ourselves, still to his embarrassment I suspect, with a very public collection of cash to which the staff were very publicly asked to contribute. A few months later he brought the baby back to see us. His hero status was complete. What he'd done seemed so much more real than A-level history and festering in a single-sex hothouse. Sadly, I believe it all ended unhappily, but at the time in our eyes Dave had joined the real world.

I was now good and ready to do the same. I was likely to get reasonable A levels, ensuring my place at Southampton University reading law. What could stop me joining what I perceived to be real life – a job, a home, a family? I was shortly to learn the answer was that I needed to do rather a lot of rapid growing up.

7

All Dressed Up and Nowhere to Go

I earned the A levels (including the dateless A for history) and won the university place, but I found the world an oyster which stubbornly would not yield up its pearls. For the next four or five years I couldn't even make up my mind if I liked oysters. I oscillated crazily from one contradictory ambition to another, one minute seriously considering a career in politics, the next thinking I could quite happily settle for an easy life proofreading Braille books for the Royal National Institute for the Blind, then quite seriously contemplating dropping out altogether and living off the state, unable to see the point of any human activity. Classic adolescent guff certainly, but it is difficult to subdue or deflect when the option of working on a building site or hitchhiking around the world is not readily available.

My pendulum had in fact been swinging wildly for some time. At the end of my O levels I declared that I'd had enough of school. I was going to leave and take articles with a solicitor, and if A levels were really necessary I would take them externally. Schools and universities were an irrelevant vanity; the only game in town was a job and an income.

By the next term I had swung completely the other way. We were only here once and we should aim as high as our talents would take us. I put my name down for Oxford. Perhaps in an attempt to reconcile these U-turns, I spent most of the essays for my Oxford entrance exam panning the Oxbridge system of privilege for an elite and making a plea for a modern education system. I was turned down with the suggestion I try again the following year when I might have 'matured a little'. Then it was all red bricks again, the only hope for a meritocratic society in which brains not breeding determined your fate. I tried to demonstrate my dedication to this principle by applying to Southampton. If the going got tough I knew I could be home for supper in half an hour.

Consequently I went to Southampton for the wrong reasons, to read the wrong subject and with the wrong attitude. Fed up with fourteen years of boarding school I thought I could combine the biggest educational adjustment of my life with nipping home for sausage and chips, running repairs on my clothes and a pint with my dad. Uncommitted to my new life I was programmed to fail. And fail I did.

My first weekend should have told the tale. First evening: Go for a drink at the union bar, or get an early night? Opted for early night. Day two: Accused of being a poof for walking arm in arm with a student who was showing me into a lecture hall. Visited student union for a drink. Discovered chatting up girls was going to be no easier at university than it had been at Worcester, although at least, there were some there to chat up. Day three: Went to watch Southampton play football with my brother. Saturday night, stayed in.

On day four, though, I thought I might be getting the hang of things. I went along to the freshers' bun fight, where all the university clubs and societies had stalls and bid for your interest. I had found myself well able to resist the Bridge club, the A.A. Milne society and even an organisation dedicating itself to the cleansing of the nearby river Itchen. I flirted briefly with the humanists, before making my only commitment of the morning, a promise to consider writing something for the university newspaper on 'first impressions of a blind student'. About to leave, through the swaying throng I suddenly felt a hand on my arm and heard that familiar question: 'Do you need any help?'

It was a girl! Ergo I needed some help. Deciding that simply asking her to show me the door would involve losing her forever I developed a sudden, if passing, fascination with Thomas Hardy and Staffordshire pottery, both of which had clubs dedicated to them. She accompanied me patiently through the interrogation of their chairman about membership fees, trips and the chance of high office. When I turned back she was still there. Patient, biddable; after ten minutes' acquaintance I was convinced I had found my pearl.

It improved. As we left the students' union she said casually, 'Have you eaten?' I hadn't. 'Fancy a spot of lunch? My house is just down the road.' It's no longer necessary to describe the avalanche of erotic speculation this innocent invitation provoked. As it's tricky to ravish and chat simultaneously, this meant I had to leave the conversation to her. She wittered on about brothers and sisters, her geography degree and the terrible price of university scarves, while I was busy increasing the size of our family to three, became a barrister and bought a large house in Surrey.

The first crack in my dreams appeared when she opened the front door. To my ears came the clatter of knives and forks and the buzz of conversation. Geared to a long uninterrupted afternoon of love, I had never imagined multiple occupation in a student residence. I thought desperately of ways of persuading them all to go out for a bracing afternoon walk. How many of them were there? Her next words turned my nagging doubt in to a clanging bell.

'I'd like to introduce you to Peter, he's come to share our modest repast with us.'

Something was terribly wrong about all this. What had happened to my bucking paramour? What was it with the twee archaic language? And how come our romantic encounter was for her the acquisition of a waif picked up on the way home? What happened next confirmed all my worst fears. They all rose, each one gripped my hand and said, 'Welcome, friend.' I knew only two categories of people who assumed friendship on so short an acquaintance: Americans and religious sects. Far from having been snapped up for my sexual prowess, I had been 'fished' as a potentially vulnerable recruit. After only three days at university assorted Bible-bashers had already come tapping on my door but this attack had been much more subtle. My self-esteem in tatters, I was at least now firmly back on home territory. I hadn't extricated myself from an institution's compulsory worship only to be sucked in to some loony cell. So I ate their roast pork – which was very nice – while explaining at interminable length why I was an atheist. Expert at repelling doorstepping Mormons and Jehovah's Witnesses, I found discomforting these novices child's play. Aware that the perceived blind victim, ripe for spiritual solace and the laying on of hands had unaccountably developed into a threat, I was ushered out as soon as was decently possible. Being Christians though, I was offered a lift home, not by my original captor, but by one of the boys. I never saw them again.

This day ended with a befitting disaster. I went to the pub for a little of the balm my own soul preferred. On the way home – by no means drunk – I tripped, cut my hand and ruined one of the 'smart' pairs of trousers Mum had bought me. Consequently day five was taken up with rushing home for running repairs. Thus began a cycle of minor disasters followed by major retreat. I never succeeded in extracting myself from it.

Matters were made worse by the early realisation that I'd chosen the wrong subject. For years it had been assumed that mouthy Peter White, who would argue about anything with anyone, would make a good lawyer – surely that was what the law is about, taking a case, mastering it and arguing it, whether you believe in it or not. It seemed a fair summary of my behaviour to most people who knew me. Sadly the freedom allowed you by a verbal punch-up at the pub and the constrictions placed upon you by a precise, pernickety and already tightly argued body of law are hardly comparable. After the first two lectures, dwelling in minute detail on, respectively, the discovery of a snail in a ginger beer bottle and the sale of a totally spurious nineteenth-century remedy for flu, I began to ask myself whether I had really arrived at the apex of academic debate. Donahue versus Stephenson may indeed, as everyone assured me, be the cornerstone of English common law but my grasshopper mind rebelled against the archaic language, the smallness of vision, the sense of dry decay.

To make matters worse I had no one to blame but myself for this situation. I hadn't been forced or browbeaten. My latest world position was that vague arty subjects like the history I loved could be read at any time and at my leisure. University, on the other hand, was the time to grapple with a complex substantive body of knowledge which could build into a profession and, in so doing, reduce your brains to jelly. In the next five years full of nihilism, doubt and downright depression I may not have done myself much ultimate harm but I do have one lasting regret that I passed up the chance to have fun reading the subject I loved. It was a singularly stupid thing to do and I should have learnt my lesson from it. It's a testimony to our self-destructiveness as humans that despite paying a high price I'm still an occasional prey to the sin of self-denial.

In the end, though, the choice of subject could not be blamed for my failure to come to terms with university. I was just ill prepared. I had never before had to take responsibility for organising my own life. At Worcester, I threw my dirty clothes on the floor and they somehow got washed. I turned up in the dining room and there was a meal on the table. I galloped down the stairs at five minutes to nine, straight into my classroom. No briefcase to pack, no roads to negotiate. All my work could be presented in my beloved medium, Braille. All the staff could read it, if not by touch, then by sight.

At Southampton, everything was different and required so much more effort. Suddenly, for the first time I had to think about how long I'd been wearing my shirts and my underwear and whether they needed washing. It was a great chore this, particularly bundling it up into polythene bags and lugging it home on the number 47 for Mum to wash. There, of course, could be no question of my cooking for myself. I didn't know one end of a frying pan from another. I could avoid starvation by eating in my hall of residence or at the students' union refectory, but introducing any variety into my diet meant searching for a cafe – which I couldn't afford. Otherwise it was back on the 47 again for a bit of home cooking.

My biggest surprise was how exhausting I found travelling. When I consider now how heedlessly I career around the world, it seems absurd, but in those early months of university that mile-long journey from my hall of residence to morning lectures felt like ascending Everest. Even before I set out there was the business of sorting out the books and relevant notes I needed to take. And having to do the walk itself day after day wore me to a frazzle: crossing busy intersections, picking the right turnings, dodging shop signs and lamp-posts. When you reached the campus itself matters were ten times worse. Southampton, like most university campuses, is open and for a blind person pretty featureless, without the regular pattern of pavement and road providing something tangible to follow. Buildings are set at weird angles to each other and paths go off in bewildering directions unmarked by any tactile signal. I'm sure it all looks very pretty but it's a nightmare if you have to navigate by touch and sound. One Friday morning, about three weeks after the start of term, I'd made it on to the campus but suddenly realised that during my search for the entrance to the law faculty – which involved a half turn at precisely the right moment to arrow you towards its door – I had become completely disorientated. I was crossing a landscape as featureless as the Gobi Desert. I turned. I retraced my steps. I took another half turn.

I fell into the ornamental fountain.

The shock of one minute being on solid ground and the next floundering around in freezing cold water is profound, but not as profound as the humiliation. As I staggered about like a beached whale, shoes full of water, trousers weighing about thirty pounds, I tried simultaneously to maintain the stance of a student nonchalantly on his way to a lecture. Presumably I was hoping to pass as a marine biologist. It failed, of course. On to the scene came the inevitable helper, at once welcome and embarrassing. The rescuing student had a car. I was deposited back at Connaught Hall. The sequence of events was now predictable. Shower, change of clothes, bundled the wet ones into a polythene bag, back on the good old 47.

Even when I hadn't decided to go deep-fountain diving I was still returning to Connaught Hall halfway through the afternoon exhausted. Many memories of those early weeks at university consist of lying on my bed half asleep, dimly aware of the *Woman's Hour* serial or *Afternoon Theatre* on the radio.

I had never felt so tired in my life. Essays weren't being started, background reading wasn't getting done.

This was partly tiredness, partly ennui and partly an unwillingness to adapt to unfamiliar methods. I'd been used to writing my essays in Braille and having them read and marked without fuss. For the first time I had to type them. Bitterly the words of typing master Charles Hodges drifted back to me. 'This is the most useful thing that you'll ever learn at this school.' I still found the process frustrating: not being able to check my work; not being able to go back and titivate; not being able to draw a line through your last turgid paragraph. A knock on the door and a brief break to lend someone a spoon or answer a phone call would cause you to completely lose your train of thought with no way of retrieving it.

I was equally out of sorts with reading. I was by no means the first blind lawyer and there were quite a number of books available in Braille. But law books date quickly with changing case law and legislation, so the vast bulk of my material was recorded for me on tape, either semi-professionally from the RNIB's tape library or by a willing troupe of more or less literate, more or less nubile students. I had hoped that my requests for readers, dotted about the noticeboards of the law faculty, would bring a string of girls running so that I could more easily select my future partner. They came but rarely stayed long, driven away by a combination of the appalling dreariness of what they had to read, the awfulness of my coffee and the endless stream of my male neighbours who dropped by on various pretexts to ogle them. I would put the tape recorder on, sit on my most uncomfortable chair and prepare to look interested in the delights of conveyancing. An hour later they would wake me politely, thank me for coffee and leave, never to return. I found it no easier to take in when it was safely on tape. Their reading efforts went largely unregarded.

Problems mounted up. Late essays became more difficult to start as I ducked another battle with the typewriter. Boring voices and tangled tapes closed off my usual methods of reading my way out of trouble. The prospect of dicing with Wessex Lane, the fountain and the half turn to the law faculty to attend a tutorial, where I would have to plead for another extension on 'The role of the bona fides purchaser for value', simply kept me in bed. After the first few weeks, and particularly in the second term, this became a regular habit. Lying there for hours mulling over my problems, listening to pirate radio – then at its height – or *Mrs Dale's Diary*. And trying not to masturbate, the *only* form of self-denial I was practising at the time. It was a welter of self-indulgence. My record was to rise at 5.40 p.m. for a brief dinner, then go back to bed at 8.00 p.m.

I was in despair, but could not show it. I'm sure people would have helped, but I became a master of evasion. I had by now made some good friends – that element of integration was not a problem – but they didn't know what to do. I was skipping lectures – but who wasn't? When friends turned up for a coffee or to go for a drink or chew the fat, I was bright and bubbly, the life and soul of the party, the blind kid who turned out to have a black, self-deprecating sense of humour. They assumed I knew what I was doing. In truth, although I needed the company, I came to dread their footfall outside my room. When I heard them I would leap up, sit at my desk, look busy. No one was going to know that Peter White couldn't cope.

It was no easier for lecturers and tutors to help. They nagged about late essays but I was by no means the only lazy, reasonably bright student they had to deal with, doing as little as they could to scrape along. When I finally handed in a couple of essays they were good, satisfactorily hovering around the upper second level. When I showed up at tutorials

I was bright, argumentative and clearly understood the subject as well as most. The iceberg inside me always unfroze with human company. The show-off awoke and all seemed well. But what could they have done? They were mainly Oxbridge academics with no knowledge of the working methods I was trying to use, and no training in the psychological problems I might be experiencing. Besides I wouldn't confide in anyone. In any case we were approaching the summer of love: 1967. To have a student at work in the run-up to the summer of '67 was a bonus, not the norm.

I knew I was on a collision course with failure but I couldn't find the brakes, the accelerator or even the steering wheel. In June, the inevitable happened. I flunked my first-year exams.

That's an understatement. I turned up, sat in front of my detested typewriter and wrote not a word. It wasn't that I knew nothing, but nothing I knew seemed worth writing down. My quandary was that I wanted events to force me to leave because I hadn't the bottle to say I'd had enough. On the other hand, failing the exams meant looking stupid and incompetent. I froze and allowed passivity to do the rest.

It focused attention on my situation. Having spent two sets of three hours staring into space, I couldn't face a third. I finally rang my tutor at home, telling him I was in trouble and that I couldn't sit the next exam. I didn't want to go on with the course. He came down to the exam room, deployed all the sensible arguments, then gave me a lift back to Connaught Hall.

My friends were as sympathetic as the limited amount of information I gave them allowed them to be. I glossed over the full extent of the disaster, implying that I just hadn't done very well. I had to tell Mum and Dad the full story. They were glum. Fed on a diet of my largely uninterrupted academic success, they were unprepared for this. They couldn't understand what was going wrong. Hardly surprising, neither could I.

I sat at home for a couple of weeks trapped in circular thought processes. Then, after all this pondering, I made a stupid mistake. I could have changed courses or taken a year out, but faced with tutorial common sense, the puzzlement of friends and parental glumness, I opted for resitting the exams. I had not yet come to terms with the obvious fact that the law and I were never going to be ideal partners. Throughout that summer, while others were going to San Francisco, I tortured myself with the law of contract, the English system of courts and the concept of *mens rea*. In September I scraped through my resits.

And then, in the second year, I did it all over again. Initial enthusiasm, growing apathy, denial, evasion, then paralysis at exam time. The only difference was that this time everybody got the message and I left. Nobody tried with any conviction to stop me.

I have never experienced before or since such despair. I had closed off the most obvious option for providing a decent life, without giving adequate explanations to anyone. The usual bolt-hole of home had become a trap where I seemed always to see the disappointment and bewilderment of Mum and Dad. With few friends at home and the links with university broken, I had no one with whom I could be heedlessly forgetful. And the world in general seemed intent on deepening my gloom. The year 1968 was lousy. The swinging sixties were going seriously sour. Martin Luther King and Robert Kennedy were shot, Czechoslovakia was invaded by the Russians, and nobody lifted a finger. And never a fervent radical in world events, the student riots in Paris, far from filling me with revolutionary zeal, convinced me more and more that the lunatics were taking over the asylum. To top it all, I was deep into Alan Bullock's biography of Adolf Hitler. I wasn't exactly doing much to lighten my mood.

For the first and last time I endured the misery of being unemployed and without status. I grew to dread that most innocuous of questions, 'So, what are you doing now?'

Until a month before, I had been able to say, with absolute truthfulness, 'Oh, I'm at Southampton University,' even though I was doing very little there. Suddenly I was reduced to those defensive ground strokes: 'Oh, this and that,' 'Looking around,' 'Not a lot,' forward defensive pushes designed to ward off further enquiry. When my parent's friends came round I would skulk off upstairs, desperate to avoid their unanswerable questions. It was rather like being four again and hiding behind the sofa pretending to be 'out'. I could almost feel myself shrinking, cowering away from the light, wanting to be invisible. For someone who had always been insufferably bold and comfortable with myself, even when others were not, this was a new and deeply humiliating experience.

It never occurred to me that I had an excuse. Many people expected blind people to be unemployed and would not be unduly shocked or even surprised at my situation. *I* was deeply shocked. That was the problem.

In this welter of self-pity I sought a solution. If I was destined to be one of life's watchers, perhaps I had better start thinking about how I could make a living at it. I rang round all the journalism courses. They all said the same. 'Postgraduate I'm afraid. You'll need a degree.'

OK, sod 'em. A degree was something I had resolved I was not going to get. What about all those foreign correspondents whose autobiographies had them starting off at the *Knaresborough Advertiser*, making the tea and covering the flower shows? My tea was undrinkable and I didn't know a wallflower from a buttercup, but there must be something I could do. I went half-heartedly along to see the news editor of the *Southampton Evening Echo*. He said they didn't do it that way any more. Had I tried the journalism courses? They'd need a degree, of course. Of course.

It was well established that blind people could do certain jobs without degrees, but I didn't want to do any of them. Colin for instance, although certainly bright enough to do A levels and go on to university, had opted for one of them. Physiotherapy conforms happily to one of the most cherished stereotypes of blindness: long sensitive fingers deftly using our heightened sense of touch to heal the sick, a kind of Bartemaus in reverse. Our approach to careers neatly sums up the difference between us: me reaching for the sky, not weighing up the consequences, not listening to anyone's advice; Colin coolly assessing the options and settling for the least worst, and, I have to say, doing it very well. For the past thirty years he's been a very successful physiotherapist. With his genuine manual skills, his reassuring professional manner and the blind card, he's built up an enviable reputation in and around southern England as a cross between Doctor Finlay and a minor deity. Had he cared to go private I reckon he could have made a small fortune, but his genuine socialist support for the NHS persuaded him not to take this course. Among blind people he's a classic example of someone who's taken the limited opportunities offered and made the absolute most of them. For someone like me though, even had I had the temperament, the long sensitive finger jobs were out of the question.

I had one trump card up my sleeve. I could always proof-read Braille books. It wasn't the height of ambition, true, but I'd read Braille books all day and most of the night since I was six. Why not do it for a living? I wrote to the National Library for the Blind and the RNIB, conscious that I was selling myself short.

I received the Institute's reply first. They said that these days they liked their proofreaders to be fluent in at least two languages and to be expert in Braille mathematics notation. If I could fulfil these criteria they would consider me for a post. The National Library was more succinct. It said it had its full quota of proofreaders and was not planning any recruitment. Even the dead-end jobs were turning me down.

If I couldn't sell my services, perhaps I could give them away? What about VSO? I'd heard all the romantic stories about youngsters setting off as boys and returning as men after a year's teaching in a fly-ridden mud hut. I thought a year in the back end of Africa would just suit my mood. I contacted VSO but they replied coolly that VSO was no longer offered as therapy. They wanted people who could offer something, rather than those who were looking for something. I retreated, chastened again.

I eventually found help in the most unexpected place, the Royal National Institute for the Blind's careers service. My previous experience of this august body had not been particularly encouraging. Its usual approach was as old-fashioned as its name suggests. When they had come to Worcester to advise us, the approach seemed to be simple. Good with your brain: lawyer. Good with your hands: physiotherapist. Don't want to do either of those: clearly you were a bit of a misfit who would have to sink or swim on your own. So I went to London without any high hopes of success, primarily to fill another day with the appearance of activity.

Tony Aston was a total surprise. He was under fifty, and listened rather than lectured. I had only intended to present the bare bones of my dilemma, smile politely, and then go away again. Instead I found myself telling him more about the awfulness of the past two years than I had yet told anyone. Amidst all the self-pity I think I probably burbled on a little about journalism as an ultimate goal. What I said I mostly needed at the moment was a break from education, and something which involved working with people. Instead of telling me I sounded like a contestant for Miss World, he picked up a phone.

He talked to community service volunteers, the domestic version of VSO. Apparently they weren't so sniffy about giving a leg up to ne'er do wells. Tony told me reassuringly when he put down the receiver that they very rarely turned down anyone, however hopeless. That did my confidence the world of good, but it led to remarkably swift action. The following morning a form arrived in the post. After filling it in I was summoned for an interview within a week. CSV supports existing projects by sending in voluntary help, youngsters who get their board and bare subsistence paid. I was asked what I wanted to do. I hadn't got a clue. I was asked if there was anything I wouldn't do. I said I didn't think I could work with people with learning disabilities, an honest answer I don't regret. At nineteen, and probably now, I would have been hopeless at it. They asked me to go and help run an organisation called Youth Action York. I understood very little about what it did, but I was a youth and I wanted some action, so I agreed to go to York.

I didn't know it then, but it was a momentous decision. For the past two years at one of Britain's foremost educational establishments, I had mentally frozen. Amongst the disaffected youth of York, many of them teetering on the edge of dropping out themselves, I was about to have the most instructive, enjoyable and – in the word's widest sense – educational year of my life so far.

8

*'Peter Goes Where
the Action Is'*

As we crouched in the tiny loft, paintbrushes temporarily forgotten, Peter Bromley's voice rose to a hysterical crescendo: 'And it's Highland Wedding . . . Highland Wedding coming up on the stand side . . . Highland Wedding with three hundred yards to go.'

It was Grand National Saturday, 1969, and a great deal was riding on this horse. Quite apart from the jockey and several hundred thousand pounds of the nation's hard-earned cash, there was my gradually emerging reputation as a guru, sage and seer. By a series of flukes and just a little pop psychology, I had managed to convince a small group of York's teenagers that their unlikely blind leader possessed a mystical sixth sense and a hot line to God. It was the worst kind of myth-making but it was the only currency I had with which to run the organisation. I used it shamelessly, and this was its latest manifestation. I was not a betting man, knew nothing about horses, and as far as I can remember until that day had never correctly picked the winner of a race, but my newly found act of total infallibility had to be sustained. When I was asked with touching faith what was going to win the National, I plucked the name of the only runner I knew and put my last tenner on Highland Wedding.

Which is how we came to be holed up with a tranny in the loft of our latest victim, who had somehow been convinced by social services that the answer to her problems was to let a horde of unskilled youngsters paint her ceiling.

'Fifty yards to go . . . twenty yards to go . . . and Highland Wedding, wearily but victoriously crosses the line.'

He'd done it! He'd done it! With one final convulsive communal leap so had we! The little old lady, cowering in her tiny bedroom below, was suddenly joined by a huge shower of plaster and dust, some long forgotten trinkets and four pairs of strong young legs. Our plans for repainting the ceiling suddenly had to be revised to include replacing it. This, of course, was well beyond our competence – as was almost everything – and Youth Action York had to organise yet another fundraising event to pay for the job. But my reputation was intact, the beer flowed freely that weekend, paid for by my winnings and the little old lady emerged with a brand new ceiling and only a minor heart attack.

I, and Youth Action York, were in far better shape now than when I'd arrived, thoroughly demoralised and rather scared, six months earlier. Then the omens had not been good. My arrival had been constantly postponed because they couldn't find digs for me. In response to my repeated and insistent phone calls, some poor woman was prevailed upon to take me in temporarily. When I arrived, lovely woman though my landlady was, I realised I had stumbled into a matrimonial minefield. By the end of my first fraught weekend husband and wife had decided to break up. White's fatal charm was working overtime again.

The premises of Youth Action York also proved to be

singularly charmless. Even before you reached our basement office you had to brave the frosty indifference of two ladies from the Citizens' Advice Bureau who worked above us. We had been foisted upon them and they regarded what went on 'down there' with the deepest suspicion. In so far as I had a plan that first Monday morning, it was to render their suspicions justified.

The interior was damp, dark and smelly and a total mess. My predecessors had been an MP's nephew and a minor member of the aristocracy. They might have been wonderful at gaining sponsorship and poncing about at charity dos but they clearly regarded housework as no part of their remit. My co-worker, Lynda, who'd already been there for about a month, proved to have many virtues but domesticity was not one of them. The office was a pigsty, without a discernible filing system. The large kitchen at the back, potentially a great asset, was simply a health hazard. Sanitation officers would have closed us down within the day. I was not the man to put any of this right single-handed, but even from the very start I was developing the beginnings of 'a big idea'.

With organisations like Youth Action York, what comes first, the chicken or the egg? If you take on loads of jobs, but don't have the volunteers to see them through, social services and voluntary organisations quickly dismiss you as a bunch of irresponsible riff-raff and cease to use your services. If you lure the volunteers but have no work for them to do, they get cheesed off and disillusioned and drift away. When I arrived I could grapple with this problem on a level playing field. We had no jobs and no volunteers, which is how I came to make the first executive decision of my life. I decided to recruit volunteers.

It wasn't a very difficult decision. If we failed to perform jobs, we ruined our reputation forever: disappointed frail and elderly people (possibly, – I often wondered how many of

the good people of York had our efforts thrust upon them.)
Most important of all it drew down upon us the wrath of Miss
Beverley, a dragon who ran the social services with a rod of
iron.

Our volunteers, on the other hand, didn't really want to
work. They needed a warm, secure, adult-free environment in
which to smoke, snog and skive off school. Provided with
these, they would be ours for life, or at least for the year which
was my responsibility. Rather like the Jesuits, we could worry
about how to get them to work later.

The events of day one could hardly have spelt out our
problems more starkly. Left alone by Lynda to mind the office
for the afternoon, the silence of my cellar was broken only
twice. First it was a phone call. I jumped eagerly to answer it.
On the other end was a breezy vicar.

'You know that fence we asked you to mend for the playgroup about a month ago?'

Was this already a complaint? I said I was afraid I didn't,
I was new.

'Nothing to worry about. We've done it ourselves.'

He rang off. Nothing exciting to tell Lynda there then.
An hour later there was a footfall on the stair. Hastily, I turned
off *Afternoon Theatre*, hid the radio under the desk and tried
to look ready for anything. The door opened slowly.
Somebody walked in, stood for a while, sucked on its teeth (I
still wasn't sure of its gender) then spoke.

'Lynda about?' It was a girl.

'I'm afraid not.' I was desperate to keep her there. 'I'm
sure she'll be back soon.'

'Don't matter,' she said. 'Tell her I called.'

Without giving her name, she left. Not bad for the first
day. Jobs lost: 1. Volunteers lost: 1. I resolved to do better.

'Doing better' involved buying a cheap dartboard, getting
in a few bottles of beer and bringing down a couple of packs of

cards. D Day was Wednesday afternoon, the time when the boys of Archbishop Holgate's grammar school faced a tricky choice. They could either be buried up to their thighs in mud while being used as a kneeler by some eighteen stone oaf, or they could opt for 'social action', which was about to involve sitting in subterranean squalor with a beer in one hand and an arrow in the other.

Not that they weren't wary. This may have been the liberal sixties but our volunteers were unencumbered with any high-falutin' ideas about political correctness. They lived strictly in a world of 'spazzos' and 'cripples'. One of them, who later became a friend, told me much later that, on asking who was now running Youth Action York, he'd been told with a weary shrug, 'Oh some blind kid. The place has really gone down the drain.' However for quite a few of them a freak show still had the nod over third fifteen rugby. By 2.30 that afternoon we'd gathered quite a crowd. It was at this point that I produced my master stroke.

'Anyone fancy a hand of poker?' I asked.

There was a murmur of interest. 'This should be worth watching,' seemed to be the feeling. I rummaged for my Braille cards. There was polite interest in the configuration of dots in the top left-hand corner of each card.

'All right, I'll play,' said Dave, who seemed to be the unofficial leader.

More joined. Soon six of us were sitting around the rickety table. I dealt.

It started sedately enough. A pair of my tens beat a pair of Dave's nines. Next hand, John was bidding pretty confidently on a jack high running flush. We reached a shilling. It turned out I had two pairs, the highest fives. I scooped up the shilling. A murmur went round the circle.

You ought to be able to bet pretty confidently on a prial (three of the same number) in a poker game. Mike did. It turned out he had three sevens; I had three tens. Serious teeth-sucking ensued. They didn't have much money.

'One more hand,' said Alan, the group's card-shark-in-chief. 'I'll deal.'

The accusation, unspoken, hung in the air.

Everyone appeared to have good cards. Bidding was brisk. Dave caved in first, telling us unprofessionally that his lowish three-of-a-kind wouldn't be good enough. It was better than at least two of the other hands. After a little more desultory bidding, John and Mike retreated too, panicked by Dave's nerves. The game was left to Alan and me.

It was the classic poker situation. Both of us were pretty sure we had enough to win, but not quite sure enough. It became a battle of wills.

'Raise you threepence!'

'Raise you sixpence.'

'A shilling.'

I was the one who broke this time. I was worried about Alan's finances. I still had a bit of social security money left from my previous summer of unemployment, but I wasn't sure how bankrupting one of my volunteers was going to go down.

'I'll see you.'

Alan paused then produced his king high full house with a flourish. It should have been enough. On any normal day it would have been enough. Almost shamefacedly I unveiled my royal flush.

There was an awed silence during which I gathered the money – almost five bob – a lot of money to a seventeen-year old still at school in 1968.

'Do you mind if I look at those cards again?' said Alan.

He took them, studied them, turned them over, held them up to the light.

'Very interesting,' was all he said.

Then he left. The others drifted away thoughtfully afterwards. They weren't used to seeing Alan nonplussed.

Later that evening there was a ring on the doorbell of my new digs.

'There's a boy to see you,' said Mrs Hutton.

It was Mike Chadwick, the quiet one. He was friendly enough. 'Someone left the light on in Youth Action York. I nipped in and switched it off.'

'Thanks.'

There was a pause.

'Fancy a drink over the Grey Mare?' he said.

'Why not!' After all I could now afford it.

They were all there. Dave, John, Alan. They gathered round not really threatening, just insistent.

'Come on. Tell us how you did it. It's to do with the dots isn't it? Just explain how it's done.'

I explained. I had just had a fantastic run of luck. I was no great card player. There was nothing special about the dots. You couldn't feel them as you dealt them. They were not marked in any other way. It was just a fluke.

Thank goodness they didn't believe me. They remained convinced that they had been successfully duped by a blind man and, although embarrassed, they were mightily impressed. After a while it seemed churlish to spoil it all by insisting on an unprecedented run of luck. And so the legend was allowed to grow.

'Anyone want a drink?' I asked tentatively.

They all did. By the end of the evening they had all their money back and more. By their own lights I had acquired a reliable group of lieutenants to see me through the year.

With the boys sorted out I could now turn my attention to the girls. For me, as usual, this was going to prove more difficult but even here reality was slowly creeping in. I knew that not many, if any, could be persuaded to fall in love with me, but there was a fair chance quite a lot of them would be more than prepared to mother me, and mothering could prove to be much more useful for what I had in mind. Motherer-in-Chief proved to be Lynda, who was large, loud and enthusiastic. She was not weighed down with academic achievements, but she could organise and motivate. There could easily have been a problem between us. She arrived in York a little before me with a confusingly similar brief to mine: the organisation of Youth Action York, with an assistant to help her. So was I. They left it to us to sort out that little minefield. Whether they were perceptive or just lucky, I never discovered, but our skills and deficiencies more or less precisely complemented each other. We hit it off, called ourselves joint organisers and got on with the job.

I now went in search of much needed publicity. The MP's nephew and the son of the minor Scottish earl had managed to keep the organisation's profile high, but since their departure there'd been a lull. I might not have any blue blood, but I did have a gimmick. I set about using it.

I'd discovered long ago that a blind person had to do little more than get out of bed to be front page news in a local newspaper. As a child I had featured in the *Hampshire Chronicle* for my Braille-reading competition victories, being able to swim and the award of a puzzling 'medal for chivalry' at the Winchester Odeon, apparently for no greater reason than having the courage to breathe in and out on a regular basis. A quick visit to the *York Evening Press*, armed with a white cane and the ebullient Lynda, ensured us a front-page spread and the headline 'Peter goes where the action is.' In the accompanying article, amid tales of my fortitude and boundless courage, I told the world I thought the older and younger generations had much to offer each other, and my aim at Youth Action York would be to bring them together. (The fact that part of the master plan was to bring the younger generation crashing through the older generation's lofts was still a closely guarded secret.) I also made an inspired appeal for a tandem, so that I could get round the area with a volunteer providing the eyes at the front while I supplied the pedal power from the rear. The response was extraordinary. Tandems in various stages of dilapidation poured in on every side. We finally selected one that looked as if it might survive more than two journeys. The sight of a furiously wobbling Lynda on the front and me perched like a sack of potatoes on the back provided yet another newspaper photo opportunity.

Although designed as a publicity stunt, the tandem proved to be a great success. True, Lynda was no Daisy, and her tandem-riding appearances were purely decorative, but some of the volunteers took to it with great gusto. After one or two dummy runs outside the office, during one of which we almost kneecapped the fiercest inhabitant of the Citizens' Advice Bureau, Dave and I set out on our first real excursion. I can still feel the sweat on the back of my neck as I recall us meandering up the Micklegate during a Friday afternoon rush hour, my feet more often on the ground than on the pedals. We soon got the hand of it, though, and the Youth Action tandem became a familiar sight cruising through the suburbs and housing estates of York, loaded up with paint pots or gardening tools, us intent upon our latest mission of mercy.

Though the notion of my actually decorating or planting anything is pretty laughable, I did discover that when it came to developing the second stage of our operation – finding something to do with all these now willing volunteers – I had an important role to play. It turned out that, rightly or wrongly, our older clients trusted me. When a job came in either Lynda or I, or both of us when it was quiet in the office and we were bored, went to see our prospective quarry. In the early days we were far more desperate to help than they were to be helped. Our visits were usually greeted with sceptical tolerance. People were unclear who had sent us and why we had come, but they were more than happy to share a cup of tea and a chat and this was where I discovered I had suddenly come into my own. Having spent most of my childhood in institutions, it was a joy to sit in someone's kitchen with a perfect excuse for being there listening to them rambling on. Most kids are fed up with this by the time they are eight, having been bombarded with wartime memories from Grandad and home-made remedies from Gran, but for me it was catch-up time. With delight I marched through the Somme, endured the rigours of the Depression and revelled in outrage at the depravity of the youth of today. By the end of the morning we were able to agree that it would be a kindness to allow the youth of today to ransack their shed, refashion their garden and attempt to build a summer house.

Lynda was equally good at this part of the job. After a while we developed a system where I took the men and she concentrated on the women. We had discovered that though old ladies mothered me and old men fancied Lynda, in the end I had a far greater tolerance for military reminiscence and Lynda had an extraordinary talent for extracting the most intimate sexual confessions, keeping the office enthralled on days when cards and darts had palled. The concept of client confidentiality was one Lynda had yet to discover.

Trust was misplaced in other ways too. White's First Law of Disability states: 'People's ability to cope comfortably with blindness is in inverse proportion to their supposed sensitivity to it.'

While apparently intelligent people are groping about for the right word to say and the correct manner in which to guide you, the down-to-earth man in the street has said, 'Get in 'ere, mush,' and shoved you bodily to the front of the queue at the bar. One of my perennial problems at university was dealing with the cloying solicitude with which my blindness was treated and the way in which the simplest practical situation would be turned into a major matter of etiquette.

Not so with my York clients. As soon as we were enduring together the heat of Mesopotamia, or unpicking the inequities of the dreadful thirties means tests, they seemed to have forgotten I was blind altogether. This was fine until it came to the more precise details of the jobs we were supposed to be doing for them, but to them it made no difference. They would earnestly seek my views on the best type of fertiliser, the most resistant wood varnish for the shed and even, on a few occasions, what would make the ideal colour scheme for their front parlour.

The most blatant example of this was Mrs Bennett. Her house was a mess and her front room hadn't been touched for about ten years. She was fond of the bottle and little else, but for some reason she took to me. Soon my word was law. When we persuaded her that the room really could do with repapering and that the girls would do it for her, she happily acquiesced. But there was one condition. She plonked the pattern book decisively in my lap.

'You must choose the paper, dearie,' she insisted.

We tried to dissuade her with logic but she was adamant. In the end, I picked one out totally at random. There was a sharp intake of breath from the girls, but they dutifully spent all one weekend hanging it for her. She was thrilled. They told me afterwards it was the most garish pattern in the book. If they'd had to look at it after a night on the gin they would have thrown up. She didn't care. The pictures in her head were probably far more bizarre than any wallpaper that I could have selected.

We were also on pretty safe ground with the job allocators. Directors of social services and the chairmen of do-gooding voluntary organisations proved meat and drink to me. My quasi-public school education always gave me a flying start with people in authority. Now that a few failures had knocked off some of my rough edges I could really be quite charming when I put my mind to it. I diligently toured the circuit of Age Concern, Arthritis Care and the WRVS, garnering all their hard luck cases and laying in a stock of goodwill for the future. Lynda and I also worked up rather a good line in presentations at general meetings and annual dinners. The combination of her earthy home truths and my plausible humour went down rather well. The blind kid and the fat girl proved to be a winning combination on York's 'good works' circuit.

Recruiting volunteers through schools proved to be a much tougher task. The message we were supposed to convey did not match the one we knew would bring in the kids. With headteachers skulking in the back row, it was difficult to tell their pupils that Youth Action York was a great place to skive off games and that it guaranteed a steady supply of clandestine booze and a reasonable chance of getting laid. Instead we faltered on about the pleasure of serving others, the fun of finding out about the lives of people born fifty years before us, the development of skills which could be so useful in later life. The boredom from the hall was tangible. After fifteen minutes or so of acute embarrassment we shuffled off stage, mission unaccomplished. Fortunately the real message spread perfectly well on its own. Dissident youth flocked in, the jobs to volunteer ratio was settling down tidily and by Christmas the organisation was humming along with an efficiency which two months earlier would have amazed everyone. Most of all me.

Our one-off jobs were soon being supplemented by the occasional big project, good for business because they used up a lot of volunteers and could also be manipulated for handy publicity. The first of these was particularly successful. We were asked to redecorate the whole of the Elizabeth Fry Home for Unmarried Mothers. Usually, with decorating jobs the girls were keener than the boys, but not on this occasion. Male testosterone was queuing up to be of service, clearly hoping that the young mums would have learnt nothing from their experience. Fortunately, as far as I know, our boys were not instrumental in perpetuating the role of the home. So pleased was the matron with our efforts that we were invited along for an 'end of decoration party', which provided some very heart-warming photos for the local press.

Our image of wholesome selflessness was reinforced by our Christmas late-night shopping exercise. Hundreds of York's frailest were caught up in an operation of almost military precision that involved them being wheeled around Woolworths and Marks & Spencer way past their bedtimes in an orgy of sock- and hanky-buying. Each client had their own dedicated volunteer on hand to fulfil their every need. It went way beyond our resources of existing volunteers, so I went on a campaign of recruitment which took in the university, art college, local factories such as Rowntree's and the telephone exchange. The shopping night went like clockwork. It earned Youth Action the York equivalent of the Nobel Peace Prize.

Behind all this virtue lurked a rather murkier world, I'm glad to say. While we posed with big smiles in front of the cameras, a subterranean life was developing in our underground premises much more along the lines I'd had in mind. Not that we got up to anything that villainous though. The all-night parties which became a regular feature of our weekends were rowdy enough, but fuelled more by cider, Watney's Red Barrel and a vivid imagination, rather than by any more powerful substances. Pop stars might have been out of their skulls on LSD in 1968, but most of us hadn't progressed much beyond uppers and downers. The sex too hadn't progressed far beyond Cliff Richard's 'Summer Holiday'. I can still recall Lynda's reaction when we were invited to a party at the university after our collaboration on the late-night shopping spree. No shrinking violet sexually, she returned after a rather protracted absence to declare with horror, 'Some student just asked me if I fancied popping into bed for a few minutes.' I'm not sure whether the invitation or its implied time limit shocked her most. As far as I know, most of what went on in our basement drop-in centre still fell firmly in the category of heavy petting.

Somehow, amid all this mayhem, somebody had to do a little work to keep the show on the road. It usually turned out to be me, although the volunteers set out to make that as difficult as possible. In particular I became the victim of a phenomenon most blind people will be only too aware of. The world divides into two sets of people: those who are embarrassed by blindness, and those who will go to almost any lengths to show how little they are embarrassed by blindness. This usually takes the form of what passes for 'humour' in which blindness is the butt. This is not offensive – not to me at any rate – but it is profoundly boring. If I had a quid for every occasion I've had to chuckle at a joke about my driving a car or eyeing up girls, or for every time I've been asked if I've heard the one about the blind man who bled to death trying to read his cheese grater, then I wouldn't be bothering to write this book. Sadly, you have to laugh. If you don't you are judged to have failed to come to terms with your blindness. It never occurs to the joke-teller that you might have failed to come to terms with repetitive jokes or people who need to cover their embarrassment by telling them.

One day I couldn't locate the office phone at Youth Action York. This was particularly galling, as it was ringing. Its muffled tones first led me to suppose there was something wrong with its bell, but when it wasn't in its accustomed place on the desk I realised we were in the presence of a joker. The impression was reinforced by the sniggers which followed my attempts to trace its wire along the desk, on to the shelves above and finally out on to the window sill. In the end I tracked it down to one of our few filing cabinets. I went to open its rarely used drawers, but it was locked. As I looked for the key the phone stopped ringing. I began to understand how old Reg Bonham the maths master must have felt. 'Find the phone' became a regular feature of slow days at Youth Action. They persevered with the filing cabinets for a while, but as I began to carry the key with me, ever more ingenious hiding places had to be found. Once someone succeeded in running it out of the window, up the outside wall and into the Citizens' Advice Bureau upstairs. The retribution this caused brought an end to that game, but plenty of others were available.

The dartboard I'd installed offered a good deal of comic potential. During the long watches of the day I was in the habit of practising my darts. I had some idea that the moment would come when I could counter one of those joker's references to my being likely to do better than the current team by proving them right. I'd memorised the board and was becoming quite adept, but the boys had several ways of subverting this simple pleasure. Sometimes they would move the board a few inches to the right or left or raise or lower it a little. When I began to adjust to this, they would remove it from the door altogether. On one famous occasion they managed to edge the door open without me noticing. The next dart winged its way through the kitchen and straight out of the open window, almost transfixing an advice seeker emerging from the Citizens' Advice Bureau.

Mike Handley was joker-in-chief when it came to darts. I've always applied intense concentration and total commitment to any sporting activity in which I am engaged. Mike's favourite trick was to wait until I had drawn back my arm, clenched my fist, gritted my teeth and was just about to throw. He would then silently thrust a piece of wood in front of me, inches from my hand and my dart, which, hurled with great force, would bury itself harmlessly in the wood. Everyone thought this a huge joke until the day when Mike thrust his arm just a little further forward than usual and my dart neatly pinned his hand to the wood. Somehow the game seemed to lose a little of its savour after that.

If Mike Handley was in charge of darts, Ian Gibson was certainly king of Braille. As I sat in the office reading for hours, the system fascinated a lot of the volunteers. One boy became so involved that he learnt how to write Braille and meticulously tapped out pornographic passages from books such as *The Virgin Soldiers* and the *Kama Sutra* for me. That's what I call public service. Ian's interest was a little less constructive. In those days Braille magazines were produced by spraying plastic dots on to paper. Unfortunately the ease with which they were put on was matched by the ease with which they could be removed. Perfectly comprehensible sentences can be wrecked by the simple application of sharp finger nails and Ian spent many happy hours reducing learned leaders from *The Times* into total gobbledygook.

If it had just stopped there it might not have mattered, but Ian Gibson had a questing mind and remembered that plastic had other interesting properties. One day I was peacefully reading an article from *Punch* when I became aware of a pleasantly warm feeling on the backs of my hands. I was puzzled. Had Lynda installed a heater I didn't know about? Was I sitting in a patch of late winter sunshine? Or had I succumbed to a very sudden fever? I pressed on with Punch, also now aware of a rather strange and unidentifiable odour. Only when the dots began literally to disintegrate under my fingers did I realise what had happened. While I had been deeply engrossed Mr Gibson had put a match to the bottom of the page. Literally, as I read, the whimsical thoughts of Mr Basil Boothroyd were dissolving into molten wax.

173

Despite the destruction by fire of the canon of Braille literature and acting as fall guy for burgeoning teenage wit, I was having a good time. I had friends, I had a social life, I had somewhere to live which wasn't an institution or family. And for the first time in my life I felt as if I was doing something useful. There was only one cloud on the horizon. It couldn't last. Community service volunteer projects only ran for a year. I was making no money and still had no qualifications. I was faced again with a dilemma. Assuming anyone would accept me, should I go back to university? I knew I hadn't really solved the problems which had driven me out of the previous one but I still hadn't a clue what I wanted to do instead. Youth Action York had been fun, but all it had achieved in terms of the big picture was to convince me that there was one more job I knew I didn't want to do. No way was I equipped or prepared to be a social worker.

In the end I compromised. I reapplied to university, and put York at the top of my list. I had fallen in love with the city and the people, and thought that maybe I could have my cake and eat it, as usual holding desperately on to what I'd got.

I may have wanted York. Unfortunately they didn't want me. The rejection letter came one bleak January Monday. I hadn't even been given the chance to shine at an interview. Simultaneously I was in despair yet relieved. Deep down I think I knew that returning to university would be a disaster. On the other hand if I was to be turned down by the college at the top of my list in a city where I'd made a bit of a splash, then it looked as if the option had gone anyway.

Within three days I was offered two interviews. The first one took me 40 miles east to Hull, which was quite attractive since it kept me within striking distance of York. Unfortunately, halfway through the interview I had the disconcerting experience of realising that somehow I'd managed to apply for the wrong course. The politics, economics and sociology degree I'd thought I was joining turned out to be social administration, a route which led straight back to social work. I went cold inside but I must not have even blinked. An unconditional offer came a week later. At about the same time I went down to Canterbury to be interviewed for the right course. I remember nothing about the interview, only the trip back to the station on the university minibus. Sitting behind me two students were having a long, convoluted argument about a bed – not about hopping into it, but about whether it could truly be said to exist! My spirits sank. The letter offering me a place the following year and the news that my local authority would once again be prepared to foot the bill did nothing to lift me.

The Youth Action idyll was drawing to a close. It had been a year of ups and downs. We meticulously organised a fundraising dance, after which one volunteer decided to waltz off with the entire takings. The sponsored pancake race coincided with a late March blizzard. Hardly anyone turned up except for our honoured guest, the lovely Jean Alexander, who played Hilda Ogden in *Coronation Street*. She struggled in the snow all the way across the Pennines on the train from Southport to bless our deserted celebrations. We rewarded her by making her have tea with the lady mayoress, a huge *Street* fan. On the personal front I endured a long, tortured love affair with Jenny, the engaging creature who had come into the office that first day, sucked on her teeth and walked out again. This relationship was so one-sided that she never even knew about it until in desperation I wrote her a long, witty, self-deprecating letter declaring my love. The sole effect of this was to make the silences between us – which until then had been quite comfortable as she didn't register them as silences – acutely embarrassing.

Our final pièce de résistance was to be a huge adventure playground project for the deprived children of York, run by our volunteers throughout the summer holiday. Lynda and I spent most of June and July garnering new recruits prepared to give up their August, scavenging at local companies for things like scaffolding, beer barrels and anything else the little buggers could play with and screwing money out of any local firms who couldn't come up with anything more useful. This project was easily the most ambitious and adult enterprise we attempted. Not only did it require major organisational skills, but we were responsible for the safety and well-being of a couple of hundred little darlings. Their parents were not overly concerned, maybe, but if anything had happened while we were looking after them, there would have been a huge storm.

It was at this moment of maximum stress that I decided that I had fallen in love with Lynda, an unlikely scenario which puzzled the volunteers and Lynda in about equal measure. For months our relationship had been a mixture of tolerance, suspicion and, in my case, mockery. I had at last found something I could do well and was reluctant to share the glory. There's no doubt I had acquired an intellectual ascendancy over many of the male volunteers, and I used it ruthlessly. Lynda, who was a bit loud, coarse and scatty, had been the butt of my gentle (probably not) humour. The boys colluded; Lynda and I collided. She was an amiable girl, and it never got nasty, but neither was it the stuff of great romance. Suddenly, after months of putting her down, I was backing her up. After consistently supporting the volunteers against her and undermining her authority, I found myself vigorously taking her side. Volunteers tutted in confusion; Lynda bowled along pleased at the change but blissfully unaware of its cause. For weeks only I knew its roots lay in pure and simple lust.

The unflattering truth is that it had taken me nine months to feel comfortable enough with a real woman to make a play for her, and then only at the moment when she was about to walk out of my life. Once the change had come about I went for it in my usual single-minded way. Nothing was too much trouble. Lynda, for instance, was desperate to become a policewoman, but mild dyslexia meant she'd have trouble with the qualifications. I rang the director of community service volunteers, who happened to know the chief constable of Warwickshire very well. Lynda was allowed to take the entrance exam anyway. I coached her, and she won a place.

A somewhat serpentine power struggle was also going on over the leadership of the adventure playground scheme. Just before the project opened we heard that the play leader we had been promised from London had to cry off. At the very last minute a third-year student from York University who'd apparently made a great success of it the year before stepped in to save the day. In the event the volunteers nick-named her Attila the Hen. Our easy-going ways did not suit her, and her final briefing to the troops on the night before we opened was an instruction to clean up our act. Youth Action, Lynda and I had never been designed as a clean act, and we left the pub muttering.

Unrest deepened as our volunteers, used to fulsome gratitude for the smallest show of enthusiasm, experienced the rough end of Attila's tongue. Lynda was most upset though. She was convinced that despite Sue's diplomas in child psychology she could do a better job from her knowledge of the real world. In the following battle of wills, Lynda lost. Sue said she'd walk out if she wasn't left in sole charge. Initially I had insufficient faith in Lynda to let her do exactly that, but I managed to be devious enough to appear supportive. I made her dry her tears, boosted her confidence, and whisked her off to watch Leeds United versus Manchester City as balm to her injured soul. I also managed to kiss her goodnight for the first time. The following day, fired by the limitless liberties this simple action had opened up, I rang Sue at home and told her not to bother coming back.

It did the trick – partially. Lynda and I became inseparable. And she did indeed make a good job of the playgroup leadership supported by me in word, if not in deed. Socially, the purification at Elland Road was followed by a Sunday in Scarborough, during which we trotted about like an old married couple. And then, untold bliss, a weekend in Blackpool.

Sadly, though, this did not live up to its dirty postcard billing. Lynda's fairly well-documented lack of virtue resisted all attempts at further tarnishment. At Blackpool we stayed with her maiden aunt Peggy. All I got for my trouble was another goodnight peck on the cheek. And that was after the big dipper and all the candy floss she could eat.

Despite these rebuffs I remained patient, hopeful and loyal. The final act of the play project was a daring experiment in social integration, as we were to take some of York's roughest kids to one of North Yorkshire's snootiest villages. Kilburn, up on the moors, was and probably still is chock-a-block with crusty colonels and disapproving dowagers. The children we took to camp at their very gates were reputed to play tag with hatchets. Only our youth and ignorance saved us from worrying about it.

We should have worried. On the first evening, as we 'adults' were preparing to decamp to the village pub, two of our charges, who'd somehow absconded without anyone noticing, were led back by their ears by one of the colonels. He said he'd caught them bombarding one of his barns with a fusillade of stones, breaking all its windows. Their version: 'It was just a deserted old 'ouse, and the windows was broken anyway.' The colonel was out for blood. A good horse whipping was the least he would settle for. Half an hour of sweet reason from me and eyelash fluttering from Lynda persuaded him that we'd 'talk about it in the morning'. We arrived the following day with fulsome apologies and, more to the point, a bottle of whisky and we were graciously forgiven. I still suspect the kids were telling the truth.

The rest of the weekend passed peacefully enough, although our visit to the local parish church, the first I had entered since leaving school, threatened to cause a riot, this time triggered by Lynda and I. The vicar's references to the tolerance owed by their peaceful community to children from the 'back streets of York' came close to getting him throttled. Our kids might be poor, but they weren't thick, and they weren't deaf.

But we buttoned our lips and that afternoon accompanied the kids on a trip to marvel at the mysteries of the White Horse, cut into the hillside just outside Kilburn by – well, who knows? The children celebrated this deepest of historical puzzles by fighting on top of it. The end result was a gaping head wound for Billy, who had to be ferried to hospital by means of Lynda flagging down a lift. I sat back at base camp anxiously awaiting the return of Lynda and potential insurance claims.

In the end Billy proved to have suffered no lasting damage. We picked him up from the hospital in our minibus on the way home. To our enquiries about his welfare nine-year-old Billy informed us he'd 'had an 'ard-on all night, what with all those nurses'.

On our final night in York we were invited to a quiet drink in the local which the office had adopted. When we walked into the Micklegate Arms just about every volunteer who'd ever done the smallest job for us was there. It was a fitting contrast to that solitary first day I'd spent in the office a year before. I was genuinely touched. I had previously left two schools and one university without the slightest twinge of regret and apparently totally unmourned. In the past year I had at last gained some self-respect and been trusted to use abilities I didn't know I possessed. I hope they had something out of it too.

179

The chapter was not quite over. I pursued Lynda halfway across England. I went first to stay at her house. Then she came to mine. I don't know what *she* was up to, but I was trying to get laid before I made another assault on university.

I think in reflection she was just trying to be helpful in a girl guides kind of way, with the sex badge. Anxious to return to a long-standing boyfriend in Bath she nevertheless offered me just enough encouragement to keep me interested. On what we both knew was the last morning before I finally hitch-hiked back home she allowed me a rather more informative cuddle than had previously been on offer. But the final mystery in the game of pass the parcel remained unwrapped. I was still sitting in the circle, hands outstretched, but when the music stopped somebody else was always holding the prize.

9

Radio Days

'I want to work for the radio.'

'Who doesn't? Have you seen the crowds outside?'

She rushed on before the idiocy of that remark in my case could strike her.

'Coming in here all morning, they have. They all think they can be the next Tony Blackburn. I ask you.'

I understood her disgust. The idea that Mr Blackburn might be replicated even once appalled me too.

'You don't understand,' I said. 'I want to do real radio. Talking, ideas, politics – that kind of thing.'

She sniffed. Clearly 'that kind of thing' was no more to her taste than Radio 1's foremost disc jockey. Inspiration struck.

'What experience do you have?'

A question calculated to dispose of most twenty-two-year-olds. I resorted to the white lie. Two to be precise.

'I've worked on campus radio and I've done a little public relations work.'

In truth I'd lent a box of records to the bloke upstairs

whose girlfriend made coffee for *The Voice of Kent*. I'd never had them back, so I thought they owed me something. As for public relations – well, anyone who says good morning in a civil manner to his fellow man is in PR, don't you think? It was enough, at any rate, to stop Wendy in her tracks for a few seconds. She'd clearly just been expecting the answer 'no'.

We were standing on either side of the reception desk at the offices of BBC Radio Solent in Southampton. I was desperate for a job, Wendy was smugly secure, three days into her appointment as the new receptionist, which she had clearly interpreted as including the duties of personnel manager. Cerberus gathered herself to repel one more Tony Blackburn pretender. 'We're not taking on any more staff at the moment,' she said. 'We shall let you know should any vacancies occur. Don't call us, we'll call you.' Honest.

I went sadly home prepared to hitch-hike back to the University of Kent, and waited for the phone not to ring. As I waited I reviewed miserably the past fifteen months . . .

Going back to university had been a mistake. I hated Kent as much as Southampton, social sciences as much as law, and university life as much as ever. With Gadarene predictability I allowed history to repeat itself precisely: missed lectures, unsubmitted essays, feckless drifting. In some ways it was less frightening. I'd been here before and recognition dulled the pain but low level panic always lurked close to the surface. If I cocked up this time I feared there might be no way back.

One thing was crucially different though. I quickly developed a network of friends with whom I seemed to have some clout. Three years previously I had just emerged from an idiosyncratic boarding school smooth-faced, buck-toothed and dressed in my church clothes. I was desperate to be liked, and apologetic about my blindness.

Now it was different. I came to Kent with the experience

of two years at university and my year in York, which had taught me that, with two pounds a week more than anyone else in your pocket, a three-year start on drinking stamina and a reasonable brain you weren't afraid to use, you could be a king, blind or not. I was beginning to rediscover my pre-adolescent ability to turn my gaucheness into intriguing eccentricity, my blindness into mystique.

New friends colluded enthusiastically with this scheme of things. I'm not sure whether I chose them or they chose me, but fresh out of school and not overendowed with simulated adult sophistication, they seemed to see something in me they needed.

If for no other reason I'm glad I went to Kent because it was there I met the closest friend of my life. We were brought together, as I have met most of my friends, over an argument. About a week into the first term a bunch of us had gone out on a drunken Saturday evening, during which I employed to the full my customary weapons for making an impression: a good head, a strong bladder and, singularly out of date in the era of The Doors and Hendrix, the gentle art of the pub pianist. Back at university we collapsed into my room where we were joined by someone simply introduced to me as 'Freak'. In the regulation drunken argument which followed Freak embarked on a scintillating and comprehensive destruction of the working-class drink ethic that said getting pissed was manly, bonhomous and healthily disinhibiting. 'Bollocks,' said Freak. It released mindlessness, cruelty, stupidity and inhumanity. 'Watch yourself when drunk,' he said, 'and you'll see a moron.' My main argument against this attack on my raison d'être was that *any* human activity watched out of context looks pretty ridiculous. Sex, I pointed out from the lofty heights of zero experience, would simply look like an absurd gymnastic routine to anybody not emotionally involved. This turned out to be a shrewd line of attack since Freak, it emerged, had lost his cherry the summer before and still thought this was a pretty big deal. As we trampled pell-mell across each other's susceptibilities and those of everyone else in the room, people gradually melted away, some in high dudgeon, some just exhausted. A little after 3.00 a.m. the room fell suddenly silent. For a moment we wondered why, then realised we were the only people left. With nobody to shock or savage we started to agree. By 5.00 a.m. a firm friendship had been forged.

Freak – really Godfrey Davis but christened Freak at school because he was regarded as . . . a freak – is generous in all the most important ways: with his time, with his care, with his insights. On a superficial level this shows itself in his always thinking about where you would enjoy to go out, what food you would like to eat, in whose company you would feel comfortable. He doesn't always get this right, but he thinks harder about it than anyone I know. Far more important to me during those fifteen months at Canterbury was his uncanny ability to cast a blinding, some would say brutal, searchlight on other people's problems. Most people you talk to about your life cluck sympathetically, mouth a few platitudes, all the while waiting impatiently for their turn to talk to you about theirs. With Freak the experience is very different. If you don't want an answer you'd better not ask. For some this can be very destructive. At the time it was exactly what I needed.

Freak went unerringly to the heart of my problem: self-pity! We disposed of that one pretty quickly. At the heart of it, he pointed out, was my continued failure to come to terms with the fact that while I said I wanted my blindness to be treated normally I still exploited it mercilessly, both as a way of blackmailing people to be useful and as an excuse for avoiding anything I didn't want to do. I think I had always known this but to have it pointed out with such searing clarity and no hint of embarrassment was a salutary experience which helped me enormously. Thirty years on I continue to do both of those things, but since meeting Freak I have never done so with my eyes closed.

Freak practised what he preached and refused to be blackmailed. On one occasion we were engaged in an argument of massive but bitter inconsequence in the middle of a large field. Eventually, exasperated beyond endurance, Freak simply walked off, leaving me without the remotest notion of how to escape from this featureless landscape. In the end I took the only course open to me and walked right the way round its perimeter until I finally found a gate. No one had ever done such a thing to me before. I was simultaneously furious and grateful. It was quite a relief to discover that somebody could do it, that there was a boundary.

Like many perceptive people, Freak could apply his talent to everybody but himself. This was his undoing. Alive to every hypocrisy, aware of every self-deception, he some-times seemed like a man perched on a very narrow ledge terrified to take a step in any direction. The knowledge that self-interest lurked at every turn gave him particular trouble in his relationships. Girls liked him and he liked them, but the knowledge that any endearment he might utter could be con-strued as having an ulterior motive, particularly by himself, appeared sometimes to encase his vocal cords in treacle. Either that, or one of his moods of splenetic destructiveness descended upon him, such as the one on the night we met. Many of the parties we unwillingly attended during those Kent days ended with both of us slinking away pursued by the sounds of male threats and female tears. It was a sure sign that yet again Freak had decided to explain to a room full of people the error of its ways. Though I deplored his methods, I was usually convinced he was right. I stuck around.

Despite Freak's friendship I was rapidly losing the plot again. The summer of 1970 saw the Labour Party lose power against all the odds. England were bounced out of the quarter finals of the World Cup by Germany. I went on a gigantic bender lasting about ten weeks. I didn't have a drink problem, I had a life problem. By now, being more or less permanently sozzled was the only way I could successfully conceal it from myself.

The crunch came in the middle of the long summer vacation. The summer term had no treacherous exams to expose me. But the knowledge the skids were under me again was becoming increasingly hard to conceal. One night, out for a drink with Mum and Dad, we met some of their old friends. The usual recipe of many memory-dulling pints was supplemented by going back to the friend's place and laying into their holiday Cointreau. Never much of a liqueur man, the Cointreau, plus much of what had preceded it, ended up in their flowerbed on the way out. Old drinking partners of my father's, our hosts thought this was a huge joke, but for me it was the ultimate humiliation. You can fail as many exams as you like, but a man who can't hold his liquor is beneath contempt. When I got home, fuelled with self-disgust, the dam suddenly broke and it all came tumbling out: I was failing again, I wasn't doing any work, I hated university, the people, the life. The only thing I really wanted to do was get into radio. I burst into tears.

Everyone was stunned. I don't think my parents were at all surprised at the revelation that I was unhappy. I'm sure that had been painfully obvious for some time. But the manner of the revelation must have been a shock. I may have been an emotional child once, but more recently I had protected my griefs and failures from my parents ferociously. I wasn't going to have them think I didn't know what I was doing. We had settled into that familiar pattern of parent/adolescent relationships where nothing is ever said but the worst is always feared. At least now it was out into the open and they reacted like all parents when at last they know what they're dealing with, saying they only wanted me to be happy. There was no point in me carrying on at university if it was making me miserable. If I really wanted a career in radio I should take a serious crack at it. Dad said, with rather more feeling that he probably intended, that there was no point in spending the rest of your life regretting not having followed your real inclinations while you had the chance. Phrases such as 'You've only got one life' and 'This is not a rehearsal' spread a little comfort over what had become a rather shocking night.

The following morning everyone was deeply embarrassed, most of all me. No reference was made to my outburst, but something had irrevocably changed. I'd said, right out loud, I wanted to work in radio. This had somehow turned it into a greater reality and imposed an obligation on me to do something about it. It could no longer be consigned to the dustbin of impossible dreams.

One other crucial life-changing event occurred that summer. I met a girl. A girl who didn't really belong to one of my friends. A girl I hadn't worked with for a year before turning to her in desperation. A girl who was as awkward, shy and as out of place as I was and, most miraculously of all, a girl who seemed to like me without wanting either to mother or nurse me.

I was supplementing my holiday social security money with a few bob from playing the piano in a pub. Despite being the era of Pink Floyd and King Crimson, my stock in trade was songs from the trenches, the music hall and the crooners of the twenties and thirties, with the odd horribly mutilated Beatles song thrown in as a sop to modernity. For some inexplicable reason people flocked in, including a gaggle of nurses from the nearby hospital. I spent the first three weeks of the holiday having the appallingly frustrating experience of girls coming up to tell me how lovely my playing was before allowing themselves to be seduced to the strains of 'My Old Man Says

Follow the Van' by one of the beery squaddies who had also adopted the pub, all the while expecting me to serenade them. One night, returning from the gents, I went to retrieve my pint from the top of the piano and found a body in the way. It turned out to be one of the nurses who'd appropriated the only chair she could see, which turned out to be the one I was using as a piano stool. After I turfed her off, she promptly asked me to play 'Liverpool Lou' or failing that 'Scarlet Ribbons'. Clearly she was an old-fashioned girl to whom the delights of Floyd Pink or Crimson King were clearly unknown.

With my usual courage I adopted a form of courtship which seemed appropriate to the era she inhabited. I did nothing. I waited on events. But, for once, in matters of the heart events were on my side.

Our pub, the County Arms, had organised a coach trip to another pub very like itself a few miles away. I went along as the pianist. As I did my stint a little voice asked if I would play 'Liverpool Lou' or failing that 'Scarlet Ribbons'.

'Don't you know anything else?' I asked.

'What about "Michael, Row The Boat Ashore",' she tried hesitantly.

At least we'd now made it into the fifties.

On the way back Dad played the piano-accordion in the aisle. Someone sat down beside me and said hello. Even to my pessimistic turn of mind over women, this was beginning to look like more than a coincidence, although in later years she claims it was merely because she was being driven from seat to seat by gropers old enough to be her father.

How to start the conversation?

'Don't ask him to play "Liverpool Lou",' I hazarded. 'He doesn't know it.'

On making my first tentative foray into the groping department, I encountered a long back and short hair. Immortal chat-up line coming up . . .

'So, how long have you been a skinhead?'

Not making much headway with that one, I tried another tack.

'So, which part of Liverpool are you from?'

There was a puzzled silence.

'I thought this sentimental attachment for "Liverpool Lou" must mean you were from Merseyside.'

'No, Portsmouth – but a family of sailors.'

Equally tortured dialogue managed to ascertain she was called Jo, she was at the end of her first year of nurse training, and that she thought Winchester was snooty. Also discovering that she seemed to have no deeply rooted objection to being kissed, we abandoned the difficult business of conversation for the rest of the journey. At the very last moment, just before I had to get off, I asked if I could see her the following night. There was a hesitation. Oh God, here we go again. Could I really have got it so wrong – again? Then she said tomorrow was awkward – but what about Sunday? I breathed again and climbed off the coach in a daze.

Our first proper date turned into a minor spectator sport. Agreeing to meet in the pub of our first encounter was not the brightest of ideas. Apart from the locals, my parents, against their usual Sunday habits, decided 'just to pop in for a quick one'. The last straw came as my final titivations had reached a point of frenzy. A friend from Southampton rang to say he and his wife were 'nipping up to Winchester this evening'. They too, it seemed, planned to 'pop in for a quick one'. I hadn't the heart to beg them not to come, as I would have liked. The only silver lining was that it would suggest to Jo how enormously popular I must be, and how she would have to fight for my attention. At that stage I didn't know that fighting for people's attention wasn't Jo's style. After I had been there about an hour, becoming more convinced by the minute that I'd been stood up, she wandered up during a lull and said, 'Hello.' It turned out she'd been there all along but wouldn't interrupt.

Finally someone exercised some tact and we found ourselves alone in a corner. To our mutual amazement the flood gates opened. I'm a talker, but not in those days and not with girls – not for about a year anyway. Jo's not a talker, full stop. But we talked our heads off, almost as if we'd never spoken to anyone in the world before. Within minutes it seemed we had gone way beyond inventories of brothers and sisters, former pets and discarded hobbies. I found myself disclosing my frustrations at university, the revelations of York and my new ambition to be the next but five Director General of the BBC. I had never unbuttoned to anyone so quickly, and Jo, whom I later discovered is normally very reticent until she knows people well, reacted in the same way. In her case the family inventory took longer as she had four brothers and three sisters to describe. Also, it soon became clear that her hang-ups, unlike mine, were rooted in a family of quite extraordinary dysfunctionality. As the gallery emerged of an admired but remote father, hopelessly over-stretched mother, feckless and irresponsible brothers, bossy sisters and dotty but domineering aunts, I felt as if I'd strayed into a madhouse. In describing all this mayhem, Jo seemed perfectly sane.

By the end of the evening it was clear that something important was happening. At the time Jo was still living in nurses' accommodation, communal, basic and with a midnight curfew. I walked her home for what turned out to be my first, and naturally delayed, cuddle behind a set of bike sheds. In a night of so much catching up it seemed somehow appropriate.

I was now faced with a ticklish and what was to become a recurring problem – how, having walked the girl home, to get back home myself? Nightingale Lodge – yes, really – was stuck in the middle of a huge and largely featureless hospital complex. To make matters worse it was undergoing redevelopment, so that the lack of well-defined roadways was compounded by bare earth, builders' rubble and other totally unforeseeable obstacles. Lured on by the prospect of a cuddle, I had pushed this problem to the back of my mind. When midnight struck, buoyed up by the confidence of new love, I decided to spurn the option of returning to the main road and take the short cut through the hospital car park.

An hour and a half later, my ardour well and truly cooled, I was still staggering around among the ladders, abandoned scaffolding poles and temporary huts of the average building site. My shins were barked and my trouser legs were caked in mud, and I still hadn't the faintest idea where I was. My questing white stick suddenly encountered thin air. I slammed on the brakes, stood still and dangled the stick over the precipice. Nothing.

My nerve broke. I turned round and retraced my steps – very carefully. Listening intently for infrequent passing cars I finally, after half an hour, managed to navigate myself back to the main road into Winchester. Here, the final embarrassment awaited me. Emerging triumphantly from the hospital entrance, I heard the sound of an idling car engine. Its window was wound down.

'Er, want a lift? Couldn't sleep. Just fancied a drive around.'

'Oh sure, Dad. At two o'clock in the morning, after four pints?'

'Your mother was worried,' he said.

I let it go. It turned out I had almost fallen into the pit dug for the foundations of the new maternity wing.

This was a recurring pattern. Jo moved house twice during the year of our courtship. On both first dates in the new places, by now fully aware of my fate in advance, I walked her home, kissed her goodnight, and became promptly lost.

On each occasion I had to be rescued, first by the police, and then by a GPO van. In each case I tried to persuade them to drop me at the bottom of our road but they were far too considerate and at three in the morning insisted on walking me right to my front door with encouraging shouts of reassurance.

Despite these traumas, and despite on our second date scaring Jo half to death by telling her I wanted children, the relationship somehow flourished. Apart from all her other attractions, Jo had one supreme asset. She was thoroughly indifferent to the issue of my blindness. As she said later, 'I didn't waste time worrying about what obviously didn't worry you.' Even when faced with my potential disembowelment on that first date, her attitude was sanguine. She adopted the view, very rare in sighted people, that I had managed perfectly well without her for my first twenty-three years, so I could presumably continue to do so for a little longer.

At the end of this love-drenched vacation I prepared to return to university with an even greater sense of its pointlessness than usual. I at last knew what I wanted to do, and whom I wanted to do it for.

One more brick fell into place. It happened on yet another afternoon at university as I sat on my bed listening aimlessly to the radio. Suddenly my attention was caught: 'The BBC has just announced its latest sights for new local radio stations. They are planned for Oxford, Teeside, Birmingham and Southampton.'

That was it! That was the shove I was looking for. I had to go for it.

. . . The phone rang. It was a man called Ken Warburton from BBC Radio Solent – for me. He had seen my white stick trailing rather dejectedly into the lift and on asking about me at reception had been told it was some nutter who wanted to be Tony Blackburn. He explained that he had been given the job of producing a 'special programme for the blind'. After my

initial euphoria, my heart sank. I needed a special programme
for the blind like I needed a hole in the head. The last thing I
wanted was to plunge back into the ghetto in an orgy of navel-
gazing. Nevertheless a small voice of calm told me to button
my lip. Ken, who had the dark brown tones of a typical late-
night presenter, suggested I meet him the following day to
'kick around a few ideas'. That sounded okay to me. I
unpacked my rucksack, rang Jo, went to the pub and told the
landlord I was going to be a famous broadcaster.

The immediate reality was a little more prosaic. Sitting
across from Ken the following morning, complete with a
hangover from premature celebration, I was sharply reminded
that I still had a long way to go. Ken's concerns were manifold.
Would I fall down manholes with 400 quids' worth of prime
tape recorder? How would I find my way to interviewees'
houses? How would I be able to set correct recording levels
using a meter? I told him that the first two were no trouble and
that it was his job to teach me the third. I then decided it was
time to go on the offensive. One rather crucial subject wasn't
getting much of a mention during this discussion.

'You've not mentioned money,' I plunged in. 'I had
intended to do this as a job rather than a hobby.'

Ken fidgeted uncomfortably. 'I'm glad you asked me
that.'

He wasn't. It was his turn to plunge in. 'The budget for
Link [the name of the blind programme] will be five pounds
per week.'

He paused for effect. 'But you won't get all that.'

Once we'd paid the travelling costs of these housebound
blind people, *Link*'s mighty budget would be decimated. He
must have seen my crestfallen expression.

'Still, if you do all the interviews, edit the tapes, write the
script and clean out the bogs, you might get fifty bob or even
three pounds per week.'

On this tenuous basis I finally packed in university for good and threw my in lot with the BBC.

I had become, more or less by accident, a freelance broadcaster. Ken had not asked me whether I knew anything about the finer points of the subject of blindness (medical conditions, social services and so on), or whether I had the faintest idea about the laws of libel or how to get the best out of an interviewee. I spoke in more or less consecutive sentences and I was blind. In his terms, that was enough for his programme. It wasn't quite what I had hoped for – salaried job with pension rights at the very least – but for the time being it would suffice. Now all I had to do was prove I could deliver.

Then Mum and Dad came up trumps yet again. The verbal joust I had just conducted with Ken was hardly a basis for crossing the road, let alone leaving university. At the time I had no visible means of support, no proven talent and no contract. Despite that, they knew that the die was cast and they bore it stoically, allowing me to clutter up their home for a little longer while I sorted myself out.

On New Year's Eve 1970, BBC Radio Solent hit the airwaves. It was the usual affair of strange squeaks and bangs, prematurely opened microphones, misqueued records, and a ponderous message of encouragement from Earl Mountbatten, who one of course knew would be a regular listener, entering all the competitions. Tacky it may have been, but I was entranced. Early on the morning of 1 January, hangover once again firmly in place, I was on their doorstep, ready to master the art of broadcasting.

At this point I have to pay another tribute. Much is said about discrimination and people's unwillingness to give disabled people a fair chance, but during those early days the attitude of BBC Radio Solent – with its skeleton staff, shoestring budget, and sharp learning curve – was impeccable. I arrived with no broadcasting experience, technical skill or aptitude, and I was totally blind. They taught me as problems arose, along with all the other vicars, sports enthusiasts and chairs of women's institutes who aspired to speak to central southern England. BBC local radio marked the start of proactive broadcasting in this country. People often wandered in off the street to air their views. The phone-in was king. 'One blind kid, more or less' easily fitted into their scheme.

After half an hour fiddling around with the controls of a standard BBC-issue Uher tape recorder, which weighed a ton and had a panel of buttons more like a piano keyboard than a piece of sophisticated recording equipment, Ken decided I was ready to embark on my first interview. Linda Smith, it appeared, was blind and yet, miraculously, she could ride a horse. So what – I could ride a horse when I was nine. This apparently was not the right attitude. 'Blind girl rides horse' was a good story and I must give it due weight, so for the first time but by no means the last I set off to express simulated amazement at the feats and courage of blind people.

Linda, who lived rather encouragingly at a hostel run by the Girls' Friendly Society, turned out to be a perfectly sensible lass who also failed to see what all the fuss was about.

'What are the main hazards for you of riding?' I asked dutifully.

'Low flying aircraft,' she answered mischievously.

I laughed.

Ken, though, was not amused. 'It diminishes the drama of the story.'

But he had a bigger gripe. My recording levels were too low. He was uncompromising.

'Go back and do it again,' he said, 'and leave out the aircraft gag.'

He thought a bit more.

'And don't do it at the Girls' Friendly Society,' he said testily. 'Let's hear her ride this bloody horse.'

I was thrilled. I was clearly not going to be patronised. The second time I got it half right. It made it on to the airwaves, and my thrall to radio was complete.

I had to adjust my attitude to radio from the idealised to the realistic. Whenever I'd fantasised about broadcasting, it was in terms of my sitting in front of a microphone – I didn't always even bother with the microphone – giving my views of this and that. Flunkies would come and go, silently and unobtrusively adjusting controls and perhaps bearing the odd glass of champagne for my guests. But this was local radio. Broadcasting meant humping twenty pounds of antiquated machinery into the streets of Southampton, seeking the Girls' Friendly Society in a darkened road of some benighted housing estate, then grappling with a bewildering array of equipment while simultaneously trying to think up intelligent questions. There was never any suggestion that because I was blind there was anyone spare to nursemaid me. Quite simply, there wasn't.

Advice, though, was a different matter. The engineers in particular positively itched to devise complex and sexy equipment to help me with my 'predicament'. The first opportunity for the would-be Professor Brainstorms was provided by the low-level recording affair. On those old Uhers the information about whether you were over- or under-modulating was given by a meter on which were numbers indicated by a light. If it was over 7 your recording was almost certainly too distorted to use. Under 4 and the most ringing declamation sounded like the squeak of a bat. How was I to read this vital information? We had not yet reached the era of synthetic speech, or the lazy man's automatic level setting.

There usually is a very simple low-tech solution to this kind of conundrum. If the control with which you set the levels had not been circular it would have been easy – you could simply have judged by touch the angle necessary for it to achieve a good recording, and set it accordingly. Unfortunately on Solent's model the controls were round. The damn things felt exactly the same wherever they were positioned.

The engineers would not be beaten. They suggested I should wear headphones when recording, so that I could monitor my sound levels as I went along. This was fine so long as I was in the studio. Working in someone's front room, however, already engaged in the tricky task of convincing them you were just having a relaxed chat while pointing ten inches of cold steel at their nose, was made even more difficult if you were sitting there like a Martian with headphones over your ears.

I timidly suggested an answer of my own.

'Why not just put on a tape, setting the level switch roughly where I think it ought to be, then do a test recording? That way I can make sure everything else on the machine is working okay, and I can adjust it if the recording levels are wrong.'

The engineers chewed on their battery gauges unhappily. This was far too rule of thumb for them.

'We'd still rather make you a proper device,' they insisted.

A few years later, sitting inconspicuously at the back of a lecture on 'Getting the Best Out of Your Recordings' given by Solent's chief engineer, I was amused to hear him say 'Don't just rely on your meter for levels. Put on a tape, do a test recording. That way you can be sure everything on the machine is working properly and you can adjust the levels if they're wrong.' Incidentally, as far as I know there is still no more reliable method of taking levels.

Other technical skills proved even more elusive. For instance, we were still very much in the days when tape was edited manually. You wound the tape through the recording heads until you heard the bit you wanted to remove, then physically cut it at a very precise angle with a razor blade, rejoining it with splicing tape. It's a fiddly business at the best of times. For someone who was kept down in the Tinies for being unable to tie their shoelaces, and who at fifty still finds buttering a piece of toast an activity requiring maximum concentration, tape editing was beyond me. In the absence of a rule of thumb which could be pressed into service, I did what I have always done when faced with something I couldn't or wouldn't learn. I employed the charm offensive to persuade someone to do it for me. Busy station assistants were begged, bribed or bullied, depending on their temperament, to do those last-minute but essential bits of polishing before items went on air, to remove the libel or rambling irrelevance, or ensure your contributor made some semblance of sense. It's a tribute to a combination of my powers of persuasion and the enormous generosity of an endless succession of hard-pressed junior staff that I can never remember missing a deadline through failing to get something cut on time.

Not that, at this stage, there were many deadlines to miss. Apart from the regular weekly *Link* programme, I had few opportunities for what I regarded as real broadcasting. 'Real' broadcasting meant anything unconnected with blindness. There still seemed to be a belief that though it was fine to have me pontificating about my disability, anything as intellectually challenging as extracting mites from your dog's ears or the Dibden Purlieu Flower and Produce Show might prove beyond my scope. However, such was the hand-to-mouth nature of BBC Radio Solent's output that, sooner or later, simply hanging about was bound to produce its own reward. One afternoon, as I sat blatantly eavesdropping in the production office, I became aware of a concerned, muttered conversation on the other side of the room.

'So – who is he then? What does he want?'

'I don't know. But he's in reception saying he was asked in to be on your programme.'

'God, well I can't do anything. I'm just going on air. There's nothing in the diary.'

'Well, neither can I. I was supposed to be in the New Forest ten minutes ago.'

I coughed. 'Er – would you like me to go and find out who he is.'

There was a pause, though there wasn't really much time for pausing.

'Thanks,' said the presenter, as he dashed into the studio five seconds after the start of his signature tune.

It turned out that Captain Snodgrass had been invited to publicise an army recruitment day taking place in the park across the road from the radio station. The station manager had met him in a pub at lunchtime and suggested he might like to 'pop over and talk about it on *Needle Chatter* this evening', but he hadn't bothered to tell anyone else about the conversation. Such was the nature of communication and research on early local radio.

I saw my chance. I went back to the cubicle and told the presenter on talk-back what had happened. I timidly offered to interview him. There were fifteen seconds left on the record he was playing.

'Bloody hell!' Two precious seconds wasted. 'Bring him in and do him live in five minutes. I've just had a gap open up. And that was Dusty Springfield, "I Only Want To Be With You". Coming up in a few minutes – how you too could be a soldier.'

I said a few bloody hells of my own. When I had offered to do the interview I'd meant prerecord it. Doing it live on air was stepping into the fire with a vengeance. Still, this is what I had wanted. I could hardly bottle out now.

I went to fetch him. Fortunately there was no time to be nervous or to think up fancy questions. Five minutes later we were on air.

'Captain Snodgrass, why are you conducting this recruiting drive in Southampton?'

'To get more soldiers to fight people with, son.'

He stopped dead. I knew gaps were there to be filled.

'So what kind of people are you looking for?'

'People who like a good fight.'

'Ah, yes. So if someone out there listening fancies being a soldier what should they do?'

'Just turn up at Hoglands Park and tell us you fancy a punch-up.'

At this point there was a crackle on my headphones and I was told I could stop now. Apparently a big story had broken. A tree had fallen down in the New Forest.

'Captain Snodgrass, thank you.'

'Thank you, son.'

And it was over. Looking back it might not have been the most riveting of exchanges, but nothing disastrous had happened, and I had got the presenter out of a hole. A few more interviews trickled my way.

Then I had two more slices of luck. Early local radio was very much 'a noticeboard of the air' and everyone from the radio vicar to the radio vet came on to deliver their message to the community. From time to time some effort was made to invest these contributions with a modicum of professionalism, which is how I, as the radio blind man, came to be on a course at Solent conducted by a couple of trainers from London. My interviewing technique still left much to be desired, but it was a little more sophisticated than that of the vicars and the vets. At the end of the training day, their noses twitching with the scent of new gadgets to devise, they asked if I'd like further tuition 'tailored to your particular needs' at the BBC in London. Naturally, I jumped at it.

The training itself was of very little value. It was supposed to tackle the vexed problem of editing, but after an hour

I had sustained two nasty cut fingers and the tape deck was beginning to look like an operating table. They decided we'd move on to the more cerebral aspects of broadcasting. This involved a journey to the bar, where I was regaled with countless stories – newsreaders being stripped naked by colleagues as they stoically pressed on with the details of fresh disasters; sports reporters describing football matches which had in fact taken place while they were comfortably ensconced in the pub across the road; salacious details of the love lives of everyone from war correspondents to the head of religious broadcasting. I left London with no more knowledge but an enormously increased appetite to become part of this raffish world.

The course had another effect. Someone a little higher up the BBC's hierarchical pecking order had taken me seriously, so Radio Solent thought they had better do the same. Many years later I discovered that shortly after I returned from the course in London a short memo was sent to producers. Cryptically it read: 'Give Peter White more work. It may have useful publicity possibilities.'

The ruse worked. Radio Solent shared its premises with BBC Television South. Doubtlessly attracted by the incentive of only having to carry their camera equipment up one flight of stairs to get a story, *South Today* asked to do a film about me. Seeing the same publicity possibilities as Solent management, I readily agreed.

The problem they faced was rather similar to the one I'd had a few months earlier over Linda and her riding. How did they make a blind man broadcasting seem really *difficult* and *wondrous*? As far as I was concerned, I sat and talked into a microphone – and that was it. I wrote scripts on a Braille machine, but that was pretty old hat. I decided to help them out.

'How do they cue you in when it's time for you to speak?' the film's producer asked.

An idea stirred. 'Well, you see, normally in radio they flash a light when it's time for the presenter to begin, the light sitting on the table beside you. But of course I can't see it, so I just rest my hand on the naked bulb. When I feel the heat through my fingers I start to speak.'

There was an awed silence.

'We've got to have that,' the producer yelled.

Alas! What my inexperience had led me to forget was that for every successful take there are at least ten unsuccessful rehearsals. Too late to draw back, though. Several burnt fingers later – the scars had only just healed after the editing course – he was finally satisfied. It was much too late to point out that what really happened was that I wore headphones and that when it was time to go the producer, if I had such a luxury, simply shouted, 'Go.' It wouldn't have made such good telly though, would it?

It did the trick. The film made a real impact and the following day the telephone rang itself off the wall with requests for more interviews from newspapers and radio programmes. The local newspaper made me its 'Profile of the Week'. Solent got its publicity and the trickle of work turned abruptly into a flood.

It was just as well. In the middle of that eventful summer Jo dropped a bombshell. She was pregnant.

At some point our non-stop dialogue had paused for long enough for us to discover proper sex. Our mutual inexperience – the depth of which we only revealed to each other gradually – made the process at first painful but ultimately joyous. However, despite my declared enthusiasm for fatherhood on that first date, a baby now was too early, if not for me then certainly for Jo. She was still a nursing student. I only had the inkling of a job. For her, it had forced a decision about our commitment to each other far earlier than she had intended.

For a fortnight our relationship hung in the balance. Getting rid of the baby was not an option for Jo, a Catholic. As a father, it was definitely not an option for me either, although there were plenty of people prepared to suggest it. But keeping the baby did not automatically mean Jo throwing her lot in with me. Finally she said yes to my marriage proposal. Typically of Jo, when she made a decision she made it full-heartedly and never looked back.

For me it was hard to absorb. Just a year before I had been girl-less, jobless, hopeless. Now I was about to marry someone I loved. I had dipped my toe into the broadcasting water and not had it bitten off. And for the first time since before adolescence, I thought I knew where I was going. I was thrilled and I was terrified.

10

Taking Off

People frequently express amazement because I now make a daily 140-mile round trip in and out of London. 'Isn't it terribly dangerous?' they breathe, and then, 'I do think you're brave.' The truth is real danger and real bravery lie in navigating blindfold the so-called idyllic villages of Hampshire and West Sussex. London on the one hand has wide, well-paved streets, is full of fairly helpful people and has a public transport system which works at a reasonably leisurely pace. Its crowning glory for blind travellers is the part everyone else professes to hate: the Underground system. Tube trains take you where they say they're going to. They do not get caught at endless traffic lights, make detours to avoid road works or drop off dear old ladies at unscheduled stops so that they are closer to their homes. You can trust the Tube to take four stops to get from Waterloo to Oxford Circus. And you can traverse its labyrinthine corridors without the fear of being mown down by a bus, cut in half by a despatch rider using the pavement for a short cut or wrapping yourself around randomly erected scaffolding.

By contrast the average Hampshire village is a narrow ribbon of road used by all the traffic in creation, travelling at break-neck speed to get somewhere else. These roads very rarely boast pavements, but have in abundance deep muddy ditches into which you frequently plunge as you attempt to avoid the traffic. You are unlikely to find anyone else foolish enough to be walking along these roads from whom you can ask any help. If you do it is likely to be either someone who has only lived there for fifteen years and therefore can't be expected to know their way around yet, or a taciturn bumpkin who appears to believe that you've disguised yourself as a blind man in order to mug him.

It was therefore probably a bad move to base my first series for BBC Radio Solent around the idea of a 'sound portrait of Hampshire villages'. It was great as a proposal on paper, but not so good on the fast-moving A27 trunk road.

However, with a new wife, an eight pound-per-week flat and a baby on the way, I had to do something. I had no great well of creativity on which to draw, so I grabbed at the only thing I knew – talking to people. Within three months of our marriage I had not one but two new series running on Radio Solent.

Talk About – the village portraits – ran for the first three years of my Solent career, three years of rising at ungodly hours to take two, sometimes three buses to places with names like Kings Somborne, Hinton Admiral and Lytchett Matravers. Having fallen into a few ditches and wandered across a couple of farmyards, I would try to extract revelations from people who believed, quite rightly, that there was absolutely nothing extra-ordinary about their village or their lives.

'Charlie,' I would say, settling myself comfortably across from the man I had been assured on the phone was 'an enormous character', 'and how old are you?'

'Eighty-two,' Charlie would say with quiet pride for having kept breathing unaided for so long.

'And have you lived here all your life?'

Pause. 'Not yet,' Charlie would inevitably say.

I was always falling for lines like that in the early days. My age was against me of course. Callow youth of twenty-three interviewing people who'd survived two wars, brought up umpteen kids and done hard physical work for fifty years. My critique of T.S. Eliot's *The Cocktail Party* and the antecedence of the popish plot must have seemed rather irrelevant to them. No wonder they took the piss, even more so when I flaunted my recently acquired school knowledge but failed to know what was common currency for anyone over forty.

During only my second recording of *Talk About* at the Isle of Wight village of Carisbrooke, I was proudly told by Bill that we were on exactly the spot where his grandfather had sounded the last post. I tried to look interested in his clearly portentous piece of information but in truth it was a term I'd never come across.

'And is the post still standing Mr Mew?'

There was a silence, then a volley of snorts and stifled guffaws. Bill finally recovered himself enough to tell me as gently as he could that the last post was a bugle lament at a military funeral. Bill's grandfather had apparently played it for one of Queen Victoria's daughters. Why hadn't he said so in the first place?

Despite such embarrassments 150 programmes featuring knarled sextons, dotty vicars, disorientated centenarians and squires two centuries out of their natural time must have taught me something. Any fool can interview a prime minister. He will give you an answer, whatever you ask. Try making a programme from interviews with people who wonder what on earth you're doing in their front room in the first place, and who believe that William the Silent was a little too garrulous for his own good.

My other bright idea for a series caused equal amounts of grief. 'Broadcast about what you know! That's the secret.' Someone told me that in my early days but my interpretation was unfortunate, to say the least. When I thought about what I knew, it always somehow, came back to pubs. Not only did I feel comfortable there, but I even managed to earn some money in them too, so I suggested that BBC Radio Solent should mount a search for 'the best pub sing-song in the south', wittily entitled *In Time Gentlemen Please*. Everyone knows that the pub is an impossible environment in which to conduct a broadcast; everyone, that is, except a twenty-three-year-old with three weeks' experience of radio. It starts off okay. The landlord welcomes your first approach with open arms, telling you of his fine bunch of customers, and what wonderful material they'll provide. Naively you believe him, completely ignoring the fact that he'll say anything to obtain that free advertising. Equally naively you do your research on a Monday evening! What a polite, decorous, charming group of people. No problem here, then – except that you've arranged to do your recording on a Friday night.

Which is how, six days after the birth of my first son, I found myself trying to present my first 'as live' radio show standing in the middle of a Southampton city centre pub, surrounded by dockers, market traders and girls on the game.

It was impossible. As the Friday night regulars flooded in, attracted by the prospect of free food and some young dickhead who was going to make a fool of himself, the situation went from bad to worse. Every Smart Alec in the place came up to clean his tonsils with the microphone, and tell the world what he thought of the show so far.

'What are we going to do?' said a terrified programme organiser, who'd come along to monitor my performance during this novel radio experiment.

'I haven't got a clue,' I admitted, equally terrified and nonplussed.

Salvation came in the very large shape of Gladys. This had been billed as a pub sing-song and Gladys had come along to the Eagle to get her very large Welsh contralto voice on to the radio. She wasn't about to allow any uppity dockers or tarts to stand in her way. She took in the situation at a glance, came up to the microphone and enveloped me in a large-bosomed embrace.

'You're a bit out of your depth here, aren't you?' she murmured. 'You just leave this lot to me.'

I was happy to comply. She took the microphone.

'Right, you ignorant buggers! Give this boy a chance. We've come here to sing, and sing we bloody well will.'

Silence fell immediately. Gladys had them eating out of her hand. From that point on she ran the show, allowing me to do the odd scripted announcement but swiftly seizing back control every time it threatened to go off the rails again.

So I got away with it. Somehow that first show was a huge success. Sadly I couldn't take Gladys with me for the rest of the series so we had to make do with learning a few lessons. No city centre pubs, no Friday nights and a few 'private party in progress' signs. Even with all those precautions, after each show I was always mightily pleased when *In Time Gentlemen Please* was finally called.

I'm not quite sure why I was trying to behave like Terry Wogan when I wanted to be Robin Day. Perhaps, at this stage, it seemed the only way in. Solent had already taken on its full quota of staff journalists, and they did all the serious news interviewing. Oiks like me hung around and waited for crumbs to fall from the table and as we were monumentally under-staffed, fall they did.

One of the great advantages of working for a local radio station in its infancy is that sooner or later you did everything.

Multi-skilling wasn't a policy, it was a survival strategy. Sooner or later, the mere fact of your being around meant you got to interview everyone: politicians, priests, pop stars, sportsmen, sailors and salesmen. Thanks to my grasshopper mind, stuffed with useless and unrelated information, it soon became known that I was a safe pair of hands when it came to the sudden or spontaneous interview. The famous case of the unannounced army-recruiting captain had not been a freak. I began to gain a reputation for versatility.

The morning magazine programme *Solent Today* was in particular a voracious consumer of items. Freelancers would hang hungrily around the newsroom when the morning editorial meeting was due to end, trying to ensure they were the first to catch that day's producer's eye, should there be any tit-bits to snap up. We would form a little cluster, like kids around Father Christmas, all busily trying to pretend we were there for some other reason. Strangely it never seemed to occur to any of us that the simplest answer would be a request to attend the morning meeting where we could make our bids fair and square.

Producers varied enormously in terms of the ease with which you could sell them an idea. Some of them would buy any old rubbish, just so long as it filled up their programme. Others, usually those on the way up, had genuinely tough news values and had to be really convinced before they would buy anything. Two commissions from one of the latter kind finally convinced me I had been fully accepted.

On the first occasion I arrived one morning to be asked if I would cover a controversial and avant-garde exhibition at the local art gallery. I hesitated. I had always used the line that I would be particularly good at radio because people would be forced to describe things to me properly, thus treating me like the archetypal radio listener, but it had only been a line.

'You hadn't forgotten I can't see it, Henry?' I said.

He paused slightly embarrassed. 'Well yes, I had for the time being. Still if they can explain it to you, they can explain it to anyone. Are you going, or shall I send Dennis?'

Dennis was my chief rival among the predators.

'Not bloody likely.'

On the second occasion a particularly nasty feud between two local gangs of Hell's Angels was gathering momentum. It culminated in an axe attack by one leader on the other in the New Forest (it's amazing how much mayhem goes on there). When his case came up, Henry approached me.

'I want you to go along to Winchester Crown Court and see if he'll give you an interview after the verdict.'

'Okay,' I said. 'But why me?'

'He's less likely to hit you,' said Henry simply.

I tried to work out whether this was a compliment, an insult or pure journalistic pragmatism. I'm still not sure. The Hell's Angel paid me the compliment of refusing me an interview along with everybody else.

I was not above using my blindness to advantage when it suited my purpose. In Southampton we were especially well placed to secure big name interviews. The great days of the luxury liners were all but finished, but the launching of the *QE2* in the late sixties gave rise to one final spasm of starlets arriving at Southampton docks.

QE2-arrival day was rather like the end of the morning editorial meeting, though on a larger scale. It wasn't just a question of competing with BBC Radio Solent freelancers, but also reporters from the two local TV stations, the local papers and, if the name was big enough, some of the news agencies and nationals too. When it came to hanging around the berths and blagging quick interviews as stars stepped down the gangplanks I was at a distinct disadvantage, but there were other methods and I was up to most of them. By assiduous cultivation of the PR men and women who surrounded these celebrities, it emerged that most of them, still addicted to the attention of the public, had something they wanted to sound off about. Find out what it was, and you had an interview. The media outlets didn't care what the stars were saying, as long as they had their voice on their show. In addition, once having secured my audience with the Great One, the Great Ones themselves often became intrigued.

They were used to receiving the standard questions shouted by the press: 'How ya doin' Mr Stewart? How long are you in England this time?' 'Miss Hepburn, are you planning any more films?' Simulated adulation masked deep cynicism and boredom.

I may have had similar feelings – I can't remember now – but I didn't look as if I had. I gave the impression of sincerity, so having once got my interview, I also tended to get my pound of flesh. Because I engaged the subjects' interest it meant I could often circumvent the wishes of their minders and turn a three-minute bash of an interview into a ten-minute stroll; this was quite a consideration. In those days we were paid for each *minute* broadcasted.

Neil Sedaka was enjoying a revival in the mid-seventies. We'd been allocated one of the state rooms for what was intended to be a reasonably in-depth interview. Neil Sedaka seemed ready to go, but he was flanked by a female minder who kept insisting that Mr Sedaka was in 'a great hurry' and had other appointments. Sedaka himself didn't seem to know much about these appointments or who they were with, so I decided to take a flier. I knew his songs, and even liked some of them, so I kept plying him about the significance of some of his lyrics. These are the kind of questions which music stations like, and which flatter song-writers. He kept on answering. I detected a bit of a chill in the air from over on my left, but by the time the minder finally cut in I had a good fifteen minutes (worth £40) on tape. Mr Sedaka and I parted firm friends. On the way out the Cunard man who'd been minding me told me that if looks could have killed I should have been dead by now. The harpy had been trying desperately to make eye contact with him, but he had been averting his gaze. Neil Sedaka was ignoring her. She was furiously aware that however hard she tried she could make no impression upon me whatsoever. Who says blindness doesn't have its advantages?

On other occasions it came up trumps too. I once interviewed the superstar couple James Taylor and Carly Simon in their cabin, which was shrouded in a curious combination of odours – perfume, dirty nappies and other more exotic-smelling substances. The interview was curious in its Jekyll and Hyde nature. Carly Simon was bubbly, outgoing and friendly, either a sucker for the blind card or, I prefer to believe, just a nice person. James Taylor, on the other hand, was mean, moody and monosyllabic. But he was bearable, because his long, thoughtful silences carried us comfortably over the eight-minute mark (£32).

The Two Ronnies were engaged to do the Christmas season at Southampton's Gaumont Theatre at a time when they were absolutely at the peak of their reputation. I had wanted to interview them for a long time, and although I got my request in very early, I was effectively told to take a running jump. The message was clear: Mr Corbett and Mr Barker's fame from their television series was such that they didn't have to bother with the likes of me.

A couple of weeks later though, just two days before Christmas, I had a phone call from their agents.

'If you would like to present yourself at Mr Barker and Mr Corbett's dressing room at the interval on their Friday night show – purely because of your persistence you understand – they will grant you a brief interview.'

The rumour was that they'd overpriced the tickets and the canny people of Southampton were fighting shy and audiences were below expectations. I didn't care about the reasons. They were the hottest property in British comedy at the time and I appeared to have been given an exclusive. I pre-sold it to other places, as well as to Solent. I was just about to leave for the theatre when a bombshell was dropped. A long-running wage dispute between the broadcasting unions and the BBC had suddenly come to a head. BBC staff were to go on strike over Christmas – as from four o'clock that afternoon.

It was quite a dilemma. As a freelancer I was not part of that particular union, but solidarity would be expected and an interview like this would stand out like a sore thumb. But this was my first big break . . . I crossed everything and slipped away without telling anyone.

Showbusiness myth is a funny thing. I had been warned about interviewing the Two Ronnies: 'The little one – Ronnie Corbett – no trouble at all, good as gold. The other one – Barker – a bit prickly. Doesn't like ad-libbing. Won't get much out of him.'

I was nervous enough as it was. In this interval I had ten minutes to do a seven-minute interview, just the kind of situation where you can get easily flustered, do the interview, then discover you haven't recorded it properly. During the first half of their show I tested the equipment about eighteen times!

When I was hustled up the back stairs during the break, all the predictions proved to have been incorrect. Ronnie Barker was waiting for me at the top of the steps, apologising because Corbett had to nip off on a call of nature. He seemed fully aware of the time constraints I was under and the nerves I must be feeling. When Ronnie Corbett came back it was Barker who bustled about, arranging chairs, making sure we got underway as quickly as possible. During the interview itself Ronnie Corbett was polite and professional enough, but Ronnie Barker was the one who seemed to be making all the effort. As we reached the point where they had to go back on stage, he made a suggestion: 'Why don't you follow me right up to the curtain, talking to us as we go on? Then you can merge your interview with the start of the performance.' It was a master stroke which turned a bog standard showbiz interview into a radio event. It always seemed to me to have been extremely generous of him.

I left the theatre in a daze and grabbed a taxi to go on to play the piano at a Christmas party in a pub. As I climbed into the cab the news came on. The BBC and its staff had reached an eleventh-hour agreement. The strike was off.

All of this was very exciting. Sometimes I still had to pinch myself to remind me it was truly happening. But it wasn't lucrative.

People tended to make the assumption that, because I was interviewing the likes of the Two Ronnies and Carly Simon, doing live programmes in pubs and beginning to do some reasonably heavyweight political interviews, I must be doing very well financially. Nothing could have been farther from the truth. We were struggling, and often losing.

For a start BBC local radio payment rates were diabolical. They were not based on a union agreement. For the village programme *Talk About* I was getting £7 a programme. For *In Time Gentlemen Please*, a fiver. Even allowing for inflation, such payments were laughable. Nobody really tried to justify them; it was accepted that the money wasn't there, and that people like me would do it for the glamour and for a leg-up in the profession. Like scores of others, I was happy enough to go along with the idea. Interview rates for local radio were much lower than national networks, but BBC local radio proved a gateway into the rest of the BBC; freelancers like Dennis and myself were paid peanuts, but it was assumed that we would sell our material on to national news programmes, magazines like *Woman's Hour* and *You and Yours* or pop shows on Radio 1. They didn't even balk at our trading with outside sources such as the British Forces Network or American, Canadian and Australian stations. Put simply, they had your material first; in return you had a desk, a phone, a contacts book, tape recorders, editing facilities, engineers and a direct line to any part of the BBC you wanted.

For people such as Dennis this accommodation worked brilliantly. He had been a salesman before he joined Solent, and his ability to see half a dozen outlets for every story was legendary. I had no such talents. I loved doing the interviews, mixing appropriate sound and music, crafting the writing so that the story was told clearly. But when it came to knocking on doors afterwards to convince producers and editors that they really ought to buy this story, I was useless. Unless I was commissioned or a sale fell right into my lap, I was missing out every time. I was depending on Solent's payments, which were never designed to be relied on, so although I was having the time of my life, Jo and I were going nowhere.

When we married in October 1972, we had moved into a flat above a doctor's surgery close to the centre of Winchester. It was a lovely airy flat, with a romantic little attic bedroom, just the place to start married life. But we could barely afford it and were frequently falling behind with the rent. In that first year I would regularly receive a minuscule – and belated – payment cheque from Solent and whip it across to the pub over the road to be cashed before it went anywhere near our overdrawn account. The only things that kept us going in those early days were handouts from parents and my pub piano-playing.

I was earning more from playing five nights a week than from my radio work, but it was also taking its toll on Jo and me. After an idyllic year when we couldn't believe our luck, the realities came crowding in. It was a familiar story. I was working all the hours God sent; getting home from Solent at about 7.30; gulping down a meal; out again at 8.00 to play until midnight; then, quite often after that, feeling starved of fun myself, staying behind to have a drink – or three – with the landlord. Jo, meanwhile, was stuck in a flat with a baby watching the bills mount up, and unable to see a way out. We both knew we were doing our best, but we both knew it wasn't good enough.

One problem had to be solved very quickly. When we'd moved into the flat we had omitted to tell the good doctors about the imminent arrival of a third tenant, and apparently the patter of tiny feet on the ceiling was thought not to sit well with the private health care they were dispensing in the surgery below. The problem created by the third tenant was then rather neatly solved by the imminent arrival of a fourth. Jo was pregnant again. Good doctors clearly could not be seen to pitch a blind man, his wife and two small children out into the street. We miraculously rose up the council's waiting list, which had been static for the previous eighteen months. With the housing market currently going through its early seventies boom there was no way we could consider buying our own house in Winchester, so towards the end of April 1973, not long before the birth of Robin, we moved into our first real family home.

This did not solve the essential problem: I was not earning enough money. Some people might argue that at this stage of my career I had come up against a form of discrimination, a subtler form than the simple 'Bugger off, we don't want you' variety, the disabled person's equivalent of the woman's 'glass ceiling'. Management is quite happy to have you around. You contribute to their own image of themselves running a liberal organisation. The problem comes when this wretched woman or blind person is no longer content to bask in the joy of being involved but wants to rise in the organisation. They even imagine, God forbid, that one day they might be able to do a senior job. I have to admit that this is a form of discrimination I buy into. Most of the knock-backs I have experienced in my career have been at the hands of people whom I have not regarded as being particularly good at their jobs. People who are confident and capable are usually keen for others to have a go, looking for answers rather than problems, a yes rather than a no. But for people who are struggling to survive, teetering on the edge of not coping, it's very different. You can almost hear them thinking, 'God, if a blind man can do my job, what does this say about my concept of myself? This is something I must stop at all costs.'

I'm not sure whether I've been the victim of this kind of discrimination – I tend to detect it more easily when it's happening to other people – but friends and colleagues felt it was happening to me at this time. As one friend said, 'If you were able to see you'd be a producer by now, without a doubt.' I had applied for a couple of jobs as producer and got nowhere, but part of me wonders whether my own lack of conviction about my ability filtered through to the BBC and stopped them taking the plunge. I still seemed happy enough to splash about in the shallows rather than striking out into the deeper waters where technical skills, which I was not convinced I could master, would be required.

Instead, after eighteen months of biding my time, I suddenly and rather typically struck out in three different directions at once. First I sent a number of stories to a producer at the British Forces Broadcasting Service, including one dealing with a fox called Robin which drank Guinness at a Hampshire pub and gave every appearance of inconsolable grief when time was called. Secondly, I applied for a job with the RNIB as its assistant public relations officer, in the belief that the birth of our second child meant it was time I had a proper job with a salary and a pension. Thirdly, I sent a number of tapes and scripts to a woman called Thena Heshel who produced *In Touch*, Radio 4's weekly programme for blind people. The interviews all occurred on the same day.

Anyone looking for a clear-cut sense of direction in this trio of applications would search in vain. The British Forces meeting was just a trawl for work. After the briefest of chats they hustled me into the bar in a very British Forces kind of way, congratulated me on having the get-up-and-go even to bother climbing out of bed in the morning and packed me off to my next appointment. Significantly, virtually the only work to be generated by this meeting was a commission to make that year's Wireless for the Blind Fund Appeal. Typecasting again.

That next meeting, with the RNIB, was considerably more significant. Even by applying for the job I was in grave danger of capitulating to the enemy. It was certainly 'safe' enough, given our temporary desire for security. To put it crudely, it was the clerical equivalent of sheltered employment. It was badly paid with poor prospects, but you would have had to mess up big time to fail.

During the interview they asked me what I would do to improve the Institute's image. With nothing to lose I went for it. 'Change your name for a start. Get rid of patronising attitudes. Stop using pity to raise your cash. And clear out your dead wood and employ lots of young blind people.'

As is often the case when you have nothing to lose I appeared to have hit many nails on heads. We parted on surprisingly cordial terms.

And so on to my third interview, and the formidable Thena Heshel. I had sent Thena, among other things, a tape of an edition of *In Time Gentlemen Please*. Consequently, as she explained much later, she was expecting a fat beery fifty-year-old to walk in. I don't know whether that threw her off her stride but to me she was mild, friendly and took it as a matter of course that there was work around and not enough blind reporters to do it. I walked out of her office without realising that I had just had an interview which would profoundly influence the next twenty-five years of my life.

A week later two letters came by the same post. One offered me the RNIB job at £1,500 a year; the other came from *In Touch*, which asked me to cover a blind golf tournament for £30. I rang the RNIB and asked them for £1,000 a year more. They gasped but made their top offer of £1,800. I turned it down. I had no more thoughts of safety for the next two decades.

From this point things took a turn for the better. *In Touch*, in particular, proved to be a blessing. It seems a shocking admission but in 1973 the big attraction of *In Touch*, the flagship programme for blind people with which my name is now so firmly associated, was the money. Still only in my mid-twenties, still desperate to be regarded as a mainstream presenter, the last thing I wanted was to be seen as a blind man broadcasting to 'his own kind'. It's a bizarre attitude if you examine it closely. You trumpet your normality, deny that your blindness makes you different in any way, yet at the same time do your damnedest to disassociate yourself from all those other blind people who feel exactly the same way. It's an embarrassingly fascist point of view. Strangely, almost everybody sympathises with it.

But I was saved from greater disloyalty by my greed. The £30 for the golf piece which Thena had commissioned (and of which I made a total mess) was followed by a succession of other reasonably well-remunerated pieces. Those little cheques, paid at national BBC rates and dropping regularly on the doorstep, really made all the difference. Suddenly everything was less of a struggle. We were not always now paid on Friday and overdrawn by Monday. And when, a few months later, Thena gave me a chance to present the programme, it really felt as if I had arrived. It might only be a minority slot, but hearing yourself booming out of the wireless as a genuine Radio 4 presenter counted for something.

It was a good moment to join the *In Touch* team. Although the programme had already been going for twelve years, it was just beginning to break out of its minority status and find its feet. For much of the sixties it had been tucked away as that most despised of animals, an educational programme on snooty old Radio 3. It wasn't even weekly, having staggered from one programme a month to the riches of once a fortnight. But by 1973 things were changing. The openings which the sixties had created in so many areas were at last making people wonder whether disabled people had a 'take' on life which ought to be heard. Certainly, many disabled people were making themselves heard more distinctly. Then, within the team itself, producer Thena Heshel was beginning to make her mark. She may have seemed mild and motherly after that first interview, but many BBC managers already had cause to know that if you picked a fight with Thena you'd better wear your cast-iron underpants. Instead of being bounced around the networks like a scheduler's shuttlecock, *In Touch* settled into a weekly Sunday slot on Radio 4. BBC bosses tinkered with it at their peril. When, for instance, we lost two of our meagre fifteen minutes to a newly introduced news summary, memos flew from Thena's pen like volleys of grape-shot. After a few months of steady unyielding Heshel-sniping, our two minutes were quietly restored. This proved the model for many a rearguard action over the years, when anyone trying to save money or follow some half-baked theory made the mistake of thinking that *In Touch* would be easy meat.

In that year another symbol of the programme's permanence appeared on the scene – the first edition of the *In Touch Handbook*, a Who's Who and What's What of blindness, which has acquired, over the past twenty-five years, a near biblical status. The book's undoubted and growing authority, not only among blind people but with a whole bevy of professionals, rubbed off on the programme. Thena was always very careful to name it as the primary source for the information in the programme. The two achieved a dual iconic status and the word went round: Attack *In Touch*, and you mount an attack on the blind people of Britain. It was a very clever ploy. Touch wood, it's still working.

If you add to that an established and revered regular presenter, David Scott Blackhall, and an injection of young blood, of which I was only a small part. It has to be said that *In Touch* was a tiny but very secure bit of the BBC in which to find yourself.

When I joined the team while still active with Solent, my only qualification was my blindness. I knew nothing about 'blind politics'; about the large charities which dominated blind welfare; the huge resources some of them commanded or how they were run. I knew little of the structure of social services; about rehabilitation techniques; and the psychology and literature of blindness. Everything I knew was based either on my own experience or on the anecdotes of others. That might suggest shocking ignorance, but one of *In Touch*'s strengths has always been the extent to which it is the voice of individual blind people. It has never been in thrall to any organisation, however worthy it might regard itself, or to the latest fashion spawned by social workers. As time went on I learnt more and more about the world with which I was dealing for the first time as a journalist. To start, though, I was happy enough to have found a niche with a visible ladder to climb as a BBC presenter.

One of the things I quickly discovered was that blind organisations were populated with sacred cows, at whose stolid self-satisfied flanks it was fun to flick with knotted towels. The Royal National Institute for the Blind, the Guide Dogs for the Blind Association, the Blind Ex-Servicemen's Organisation known as St Dunstan's and the newly formed Talking Newspaper Association – all seemed deeply convinced of the good they did, and the enormous gratitude due to them from blind people for their work. Their officials seemed rather less conscious of the fact that the organisations furnished them with safe jobs, reasonable salaries, enormous public approval and far less accountability than would be demanded in business, and that if it weren't for the existence of blind people they would be out of a job. It swiftly dawned on me that pricking the self-importance of such organisations would be fun, would further my career, and might even do some good.

These organisations didn't listen to their customers. The idea, for example, of majority representation of blind people on their committees was just a pipe dream – many are still nowhere near it. Our most consistent target was the RNIB, not because it was the worst but because it had a finger in just about every blind pie. With hindsight I realise its problem was that it tried to do too much with too little. In fact, it attempted to do everything: run schools and residential homes, advise on employment, campaign on eye care, act as a Braille publisher and produce everything in the way of equipment from Braille writing-machines to gadgets to stop your milk from boiling over. The general attitude was that what the RNIB didn't know about blindness wasn't worth knowing, and it was delivered in a patronising tone of voice which left the recipients in no doubt who was boss. The fact that many of the people who ran their departments were themselves blind guaranteed no greater understanding. The reverse was more likely. No one can patronise poorly informed blind people with more conviction than those smug in the knowledge that they have 'overcome their disability'. In reality the RNIB was strapped for cash, often outsmarted in the fundraising game by more instantly loveable organisations like the Guide Dogs. It was delivering a low-grade service which blind people were supposed to tolerate because they had no alternative. As a result, much of my early reporting on *In Touch* was made up of steady sniping at second-rate service, poor standards of delivery of equipment and the refusal of the RNIB to make itself more democratic.

Some organisations presented an even more tempting target. St Dunstan's, to whom the word democracy was a totally alien concept, particularly exercised us. Founded during the First World War to provide for the many servicemen blinded in action, it promised blanket welfare care all the way to the grave and, on the whole, delivered. It had little excuse not to! With a surefire cause with which to raise funds, St Dunstan's far outstripped the RNIB in terms of wealth, even though by then the number of people it needed to serve had dipped below the 1,000 mark by the eighties. It seemed outrageous to us that they'd guarded their money with such fervour, protecting with absolute rigidity the principle that people could only benefit from the organisation if they could prove beyond all doubt that their blindness was as a result of life in the services. One classic example involved a man who was blinded as the result of a bombing raid on a Royal Navy ship in Dartmouth during the Second World War. There was no doubt what had caused his blindness but because he was technically working on board as a civilian draughtsman his claim for all the benefits St Dunstan's could offer was turned down. He was not alone. In the end, despite all the typical arguments about opening flood gates and protecting the interests of their bona fide beneficiaries, St Dunstan's capitulated, though of course they said it had nothing whatsoever to do with *In Touch*'s interest in the case. We did not need the credit as long as he got the money. What was so striking was the outrage these organisations felt. After decades of uncritical approval they were being subjected to the kind of accountability which should have been automatic for any organisation handling millions of pounds originating from the general public. In the case of St Dunstan's, the attitude persists even in the nineties. When we dared to examine why they were selling off some of their holiday accommodation a couple of years ago against the wishes of some St Dunstaners, their director Sir Henry Leach felt it appropriate to write to his old service chum, then Chairman of the BBC, Duke Hussey to call us off. To the credit of Mr Hussey, no calling off took place.

This total horror at any criticism was certainly a common feature of organisations working with blind people. The attitude seemed to be that blind people ought to be grateful for just about any level of service because the work was done for a charity. One of the biggest storms we created was suggesting that the standard of reading on taped versions of newspapers for blind people was abysmal and practically impossible to listen to.

Everyone thinks they can read to the blind. It's rather like scented gardens, one of those lovely ideas which we've never been consulted about. The talking-newspaper movement was a splendid idea based on the simple notion that your local newspaper on a cassette could keep you in touch with your local community. I applauded it, covering their inaugural meeting when they established a national organisation, although even at this early stage they were arguing bitterly among themselves about their aims and objects. Although it's a great idea, that doesn't mean that people should have to listen to an account of the East Thanet rural district council's proceedings read in a monotone on a low-level recording punctuated with the reader's personal opinions or an account of her Aunt Dot's latest hip operation. We suggested that standards should be drawn up and that prospective readers should be auditioned and trained. If they couldn't read properly they would be kindly but firmly asked to do something else. It caused a great storm at the time but all these things became reality.

These spats were nothing compared with my head-on

collision with the Guide Dogs for the Blind Association. Of all
the blind organisations, the Guide Dogs seem to feel themselves most firmly beyond reproach. An endless succession of
those luvverley, cuddly doggie-woggies, posing in their selfless
service to the incompetent blind, had amassed them a fortune.
The British public, prepared to believe that the brains in a
dog/owner combination emanated not from the physics graduate but from the golden retriever, lavished money, silver
paper and bottle tops upon them with gay abandon. It never
seemed to occur to anyone that, while the RNIB was struggling to provide a huge range of services to hundreds of
thousands of blind people with a fraction of the money, the
number of people who could or wanted to use a guide dog was
at that time less than 4,000. As far as I was concerned, it was
the most blatant example of raising money because you could,
rather than because that was where it was most needed.

At the very least guide-dog owners could expect a tip-top
service equivalent to the best money could buy. When we
began to receive a steady stream of letters and calls from
people who said they were dissatisfied with the service, my
interest naturally quickened. By the early eighties the charge
was that the quality of guide dogs was declining, that owners
weren't listened to when they complained, and that all faults
were blamed on bad handling by the owners rather than poor
training at the outset. It was, in short, a dog-orientated rather
than people-orientated organisation.

Satisfied that we had three strong cases with which to
make these points I went ahead and produced a very critical
report. I wrote to the GDBA with our findings and asked for
their comments. (We had not approached them sooner because
owners were clearly worried they would be pressurised not to
talk.) The outrage was palpable, the implication clear. How
could we dare impugn the name of an organisation which was
a national institution?

But impugn we did. Despite the mother and father of a row, the GDBA appeared on the programme and fought their corner. Although they denied everything and admitted nothing, in the succeeding years many of the points we were making have been addressed. The battle goes on.

Not everything on the programme was quite so highpowered. Much of *In Touch* was about solving everyday problems of coping with being blind – choosing clothes which match, crossing a room without turning your shins into craters of the moon, making a cup of tea without scalding yourself. For the first time it made me look at the lives of *other* blind people. At first I thought this was a growing-up experience I could have done without. My stance – the stance of many young blind people – was that blindness is a nuisance which should not be dwelt upon. To find myself interviewing recently blind people for whom these things were not dismissable trivialities but major hurdles and a source of grief was challenging. Still in my twenties, I had to ask myself how I liked my peers hearing me discuss in minute detail the best way to apply butter to toast, or how to arrange blocks of wood so that you could mow your lawn in straight lines. It hardly stood at the cutting edge of political debate, or in line with the attitude which said that blindness was just a state of mind.

Gradually my indignation about the situation of people without my advantages grew. I became outraged that only 25 per cent of blind people of working age had a job. I began to realise that, because of fear and ignorance of blindness, many people who began to lose their sight were hounded from their jobs or talked themselves into leaving work before anyone had really thought of ways of making it feasible for them to carry on. While feeling that I had not been much discriminated against, it was becoming clear that many people were not as robust and allowed themselves to become the victims of other people's preconceptions. Sometimes blind people are each other's harshest judges. It's easy to fall into the trap of which we accuse other people, thinking that we should all be alike, and that because we can do something without too much trouble every other blind person should be the same. *In Touch* cured me forever of the myth that there is solidarity in disability. On the contrary, there is often a great deal of self-satisfaction at having 'overcome' rather more successfully than one's neighbour. I'm afraid it's true that 'the blindhood' is just as fragile and as backbiting as 'the sisterhood'.

Whatever my reservations, fronting a programme like *In Touch* had some huge bonuses.

As a voice presenting any Radio 4 programme, you reach the ears of people with programmes of their own. 1975 was a year of enjoyable firsts for me: my first piece on the *Today* programme, my first report on the six o'clock news and, towards the end of that year, an invitation to research and introduce a series of my own. It was to be based on interviews with people who had reached turning points in their lives: first job, living away from home, marriage, retirement. It was offered on the basis of a reputation I was beginning to develop as an interviewer who could gain the confidence of people and probe beneath the skin yet allow them to feel comfortable enough to talk frankly about their lives. It was a reputation, I was told, upon which a career could be founded. Maybe a salary and a pension weren't essential after all.

Then, out of the blue, BBC Television came knocking on the door again. Apparently I had now reached the dizzy heights where I required not just a three-minute bash but the full thirty-minute profile. In between getting a daily humorous column on Solent's afternoon show, buying our first car for £50 at closing time in a pub and getting a regular slot on Radio 2's *Charlie Chester Show*, much of 1976 was spent filming for *See It My Way*.

At this point I made a strange discovery. I liked television, and it seemed to like me. Apart from the vaguest ambitions, I had always assumed that the problems of a blind reporter breaking into telly would be insurmountable. The difficulties were obvious enough: writing to pictures you couldn't see; moving naturally; establishing the right eye-line. *See It My Way* began to change my view. Admittedly, it was a film *about* me rather than *by* me, but its producer, ahead of his time in recognising that a film about 'the amazing blind reporter' made from his point of view, could turn out to be extremely patronising, gave me my head. I chose most of the subjects and venues, planned the shape of the programmes and wrote the scripts. I learnt from this that writing to pictures which you had asked to be shot was perfectly feasible. It was simply a question of knowing their order, which in turn dictated the logical sequence in which to tell the story. Far from finding writing to pictures a constraint – a problem for many people switching for the first time from radio to television – I found it a pleasing and challenging discipline. Wordy by nature, it was fun to have to concentrate a description of a football match into the twelve seconds for which we had decent pictures.

We filmed my first foreign trip for *In Touch*, a series of interviews in Belgium and France, as well as my trips to Birmingham to do the *Charlie Chester Show* and how I would do a story at a crowded venue like the Southampton Boat Show. But it wasn't just about work. I was filmed following my passion for Southampton Football Club at the Dell, and there was a major sequence filmed at home.

Some of the strongest images in the film were of the children. I was shown playing football in the garden with Tony, then four and Robin, almost three, then bathing them afterwards and, in the final shots of the film, holding day-old Cathy, the latest addition to the family. Always strong-willed, even as a foetus, she had dictated the completion date of the film. Despite Jo's horror at the idea, as soon as he discovered she was pregnant the producer was determined the new baby should feature strongly. He was told with enormous force that he could forget any notions of filming the birth, but a huge bouquet of flowers and the subversion of the nursing staff managed to weedle him into the maternity ward. I have to plead guilty too. By now I was proud of what I had achieved by breaking into radio, but I was prouder still of my growing family. I was absolutely determined that in any film about me they must be centre stage.

11

Family Fortunes

People have children for all kinds of ignoble reasons: to satisfy the needs of their parents; to ensure there will be someone to look after them in their old age; sheer carelessness; or plain conformity. I have the uncomfortable feeling that I had mine in order to boost my flagging ego.

Jo and I ended up having four children. It would be comforting to say that we fell into that extremely suspect group of people who claim to 'like children', a claim as daft as saying you like thirty-eight-year-olds. Even if such a sweeping generalisation had any validity it wouldn't be true in my case. Every encounter with other people's children before the birth of my own suggested that I didn't like them and they didn't like me. Babies suddenly finding themselves placed in my clumsy embrace would instantly scream; toddlers would wriggle out of my less than enthusiastic grasp at the earliest opportunity; and older children seemed to regard me either with frank puzzlement or sullen indifference.

So why this rush toward frenetic procreation, undoubtedly

more at my instigation than Jo's? I conclude that I did it because I could. Having children is an indicator of normality which society respects and takes seriously. In terms of my dealings with other people being blind had been composed of a series of small but corrosive embarrassments, situations which make you look like an idiot though you know you're not. You might have trouble peeling a potato, or changing a light-bulb. Or you're frequently lost or disorientated and need help. Every time you enter a shop or join a bus queue or go to register your vote, you know you can't do it alone. You must enlist the assistance of another human being. People like me spend much time saying and pretending to ourselves that we don't care about such things – but we do. It unmans us, and affects the way we are seen by other people. We are not regarded as providers, but takers. People very rarely ask me for directions, or for advice in filling in their tax forms, or to help carry their bags. I still find myself on trains being pathetically grateful to have the chance to hand out information on connections, timetables and the best way and the best day to get from Taunton to Leamington Spa. Quite simply blind people suffer from a dearth of giving.

The surefire way of being certain there's always someone on hand every time you need to be needed is to create your own ready-made family. That way you can raise them from the start to regard blindness as an unfit subject for sympathy, to think of you as a regular supplier of money, advice and shelter and to serve as the suitable receptacle for a good kicking whenever a regular supply of money is not required. In other words, you are treated in the same way as every other parent expects. Two for the price of one in fact – the badge of achievement bestowed by fathering children and a built-in repository for all my unused altruisms. Poor kids!

Blind parents are supposed to be obsessed with whether their children will also be blind. It barely crossed my mind.

I dismissed it with the comforting thought that blindness, so far, hadn't been so bad for me and that if anyone could help them avoid the pitfalls I was the man. For some reason Jo bought into this ultra-robust line of argument, adding that, if she was prepared to marry a blind man, why should she be so concerned at the prospect of giving birth to blind children. Neither can I claim to have thought about the cost of such an event for the National Health Service. We relied for information on its likelihood from the advice given to my brother Colin and his wife when they were thinking of starting a family. 'One in four' were the odds Doctor Ladbroke's offered. So far they'd had two daughters, Karen and Nicola, both sighted. Taking this into account, along with the fact that my parents had been told there was a million to one chance of my being blind and the fact that Jo was already pregnant, we decided not to worry. We steamed ahead.

The result was the happiest ten years of my life. From the birth of my oldest son Tony to the departure of my foster daughter Fiona, the children were the centre of my life, my entertainment, my hobby, my responsibility, my purpose. During this time considerations of career and financial success were secondary. I might not be uprooting any trees in the media, but it was more important I was there at breakfast time to listen to their chatter and, when the time came, walk them to school, and then usually there again at suppertime, to bathe them, put them to bed and read them a story. I was no prototype New Man. Having these children was a minor obsession and I determined to do it properly.

We had little time to plan being good parents. One minute, so it seemed, we were standing nervous as kittens outside the first front door we could really call our own; the next Tony's birth was upon us. He was premature in two senses, earlier than we'd planned, and then he compounded it by speeding up the biological process too. Jo, always very sanguine about medical matters, mentioned casually one morning that she was feeling a few stabbing pains but she assured me it was nothing to worry about. By the time I reached Radio Solent she was already in hospital. When I came home that evening they were talking worriedly about caesareans and inducing the birth.

I suspect that, like us, many first-time parents are protected by their naivety. Ignorant of the things that can go wrong you tend to let the medical team take over, assuming they know what they're doing. By the time you realise any different it's usually too late anyway.

I was unprepared for the rather new trend of fathers being present at the birth. Brought up on the Doctor Finlay-like tradition of fathers anxiously pacing the waiting room, I was totally unready for my close encounter with the birth process. When it became clear that the main event was at hand and that Jo was being whisked off to the labour room, I stayed where I was, thinking I'd be there for the evening. 'Come along then, you too,' said the brisk, no-nonsense midwife. Totally unexpectedly I found myself witnessing the start of a new life.

I am very glad I was there. At least one of us was awake when our first son was born. Jo was being quite heavily sedated and she developed the rather disconcerting habit of dropping off to sleep between contractions. Jerked awake by a spasm of pain, she would ask me a question and then nod off again before I had time to think of a reply. Her most devastating performance came after the birth itself. 'What is it?' she asked. Before they had time to tell her that Tony was a boy, she was fast asleep again.

However many times it has been described, it is still an extraordinary feeling. An action of yours has led to the creation of an independent life. It feels dangerously like arrogance, but nevertheless it is an intoxicating and unforgettable moment. It's certainly the closest I have ever come to a mystical experience. I held the tiny bundle briefly – he was only five pounds – then left the hospital at 1.00 a.m. with Jo now in an uninterrupted slumber. I walked on a cloud through the new maternity wing with the refrain beating in my head, 'I've got a son, I've got a son.' For the first time being grown-up meant something.

My elation was also premature. Either out of kindness or cowardice, nobody had explained to us the kind of problems Tony was likely to face as a premature baby. Only the following morning, when I rang to see how they were, was I told in typical hospital fashion that 'Tony is having a few little problems breathing on his own'. The nurse might have thought this a little problem; I thought it was quite a big one. I was up at the hospital right away.

Either out of stupidity or wishful thinking I was unaware that Tony and the staff were fighting for his life. Jo wasn't given the full facts either. One memory conjures up that day for me – the periodic ringing of a bell.

'Some poor kid's going through it,' said Jo. 'That's a security blanket. The baby lies on it and the bell rings when it stops breathing.'

Little did she know that the baby on that blanket was ours. I finally went home feeling numb. It's hard to grieve for someone you haven't met yet. You grieve for your hopes.

We had no clear explanation of what was wrong, just that 'premature babies do these kind of things'. The following day he had lost one whole pound of his paltry five. Then he turned yellow; he had jaundice. This apparently was common in premature babies. After that he simply stood still. He got no worse, but neither did he get any better. He didn't gain weight and he still had trouble feeding. After a week, Jo should normally have been able to bring him home, but we were told that this was too risky. They wanted to continue to monitor his progress, so Jo came home alone.

234

It was eerie. We had a child, yet we didn't. Jo had gone through the process of giving birth, but we had been returned to the status of a childless couple. And amid all the worry about Tony's survival I felt cheated! This huge experience, which was to have changed my life and given it purpose, had been snatched away. Somehow it wasn't real. And it wasn't grown-up. If I'd been really grown-up this couldn't happen. Grown-ups don't have their babies taken away. They fight for them to the death!

It was irrational but I can remember we both felt totally lost. Tony was born just before Christmas. Throughout that holiday we felt we were missing out on the irreplaceable experience of our first son's first days.

After a month he had still not improved. He'd gained hardly any weight and his progress was static. Finally the hospital made a decision. They grudgingly allowed Jo to bring him home – only, they said, because of her nursing experience.

He never looked back. Do tiny babies sense the awful sterility of hospitals? From the moment he was brought out of that stuffy atmosphere, with its mixture of unpleasant smells, and welcomed into our new airy flat, he seemed to open like a flower. Jo knew little about babies but had loads of common sense. My mother, heroine of the upbringing of two blind children, was on hand, and Tony and I took to each other like ducks to water.

I remember vividly arriving home on Tony's first day of freedom. As I came through the door I was greeted with the splendid sound of tetchy infant grizzling. Jo handed him to me without ceremony.

'I've just fed him. He's eaten it all but I think he's got indigestion. See what you can do.'

To my own astonishment I tossed Tony across my shoulder with his head pointing down my back and patted him gently but firmly. He belched furiously. A warm rivulet of saliva enriched with natural goodness ran down the back of my neck. I welcomed it like a pint of foaming bitter. Tony promptly fell asleep.

He turned out to be a happy, self-contained child. Possibly because of his slow start he was initially rather dozy and could have slept for England. This meant we were spared the agonies of the interrupted nights so many parents associate with their first child. Bowling along blissfully unencumbered by the theories of Benjamin Spock, bringing up baby was a joy. He even interfered very little with our social lives. I was now playing piano regularly at night, and the landlord of one of my pubs had a twelve-year-old daughter. Recognising a ready-made babysitter we would wrap Tony up warm, pack him down in the well-sprung old-fashioned pram and transport him through the twilit streets of Winchester. We would often wheel him home again well after midnight, transferring him, blissfully unwaking, from pram to cot.

Tony's sang-froid extended to other aspects of life. Our flat had only one bedroom, which meant that until he was eighteen months old his cot was placed beside our bed. This inevitably meant that his education in some of the basic facts of life was as premature as his arrival. It was common for us to emerge from the delights of morning love-making to find Tony bobbing animatedly up and down at the end of his cot with a huge grin on his face. He was a very polite and considerate voyeur, never making rude comments about technique and appearing, on the whole, to applaud our efforts.

Very small babies are not entertaining toys for blind men. They don't move much, make only desultory and uninteresting conversation and leak unpleasant and unmanageable materials from both ends. The fun really started for me when he began to move, particularly because he did it in a very odd and individual way. Tony's preferred method of propulsion

236

was not to crawl like most babies but to haul himself along on his back, using elbows and heels to achieve momentum. Guests would watch this performance with astonishment, particularly because he travelled at such lightning speed. The difficulty with this – although it never struck me as being too much of a problem – was that he couldn't see where he was going. Sporadic forays across the living room were inevitably halted by a smart crack as Tony's head came into contact with the far wall. He never cried when this happened, but he became extremely frustrated because he hadn't yet mastered the art of turning round. Once he had been manually reversed by an acolyte, he would happily patter off to do the same thing at the other end of the room.

At some point Tony did decide to leave the crabs, turn over on his front and join the human race. This was the signal for Tony's and my real companionship to begin in earnest. Our voyage of discovery took us all over the flat. I had been desperate to have children in order to have the chance to teach. We lived on the first floor, so lesson one was mastering the stairs. His predilection for travelling backwards came in handy at this point. We spent evening after evening inching up and down the staircase, negotiating the narrow bend at the top, securing each step Bonnington-like with our back feet before moving down to the ledge below. Tony, at heart a careful child, took this very seriously and was prepared to indulge my preference for the gradualist approach.

Then we could move on to the wider vistas of the doctor's surgery below. This was a surprisingly fruitful playground, and an ideal if unlikely venue for an embryonic form of football. We carried my rattling ball down there every night when I came home from work, and had enormous fun threading it through a labyrinthine network of tables, chairs, sofas and other rather more delicate medical equipment. The game gradually became longer and longer and evolved into a strange

mixture of football and lacrosse. It became increasingly difficult to interrupt them. Reasonable requests at around nine
o'clock for Tony to be brought up for his bedtime were
greeted with gales of mirth and the sound of Tony on hands
and knees beetling off in the opposite direction in pursuit of
the ball. We never broke anything valuable, miraculously, but
I suspect that some of the furniture placements caused doc-
toral consternation in the morning.

Our juxtaposition to a rather smart medical practice created other stresses and strains. Tony's large pram in the
vestibule apparently did not sit well with the ambience they
were trying to create. Matters came to a head one day when Jo,
coming home but discovering that she'd forgotten her key,
stepped daintily through the open surgery window only to
find herself in the middle of a rather intimate medical examination. It was mutually decided we should move on.

In quick succession we acquired our first council house
with a garden, a stray dog and son number two, Robin. From
the start it was obvious that Robin was very different from
Tony: noisy, demanding, gregarious, he was by turns ecstati-
cally happy and spectacularly miserable. Lulled by Tony, we
quickly tasted the joys of those interrupted nights and learnt
that if Robin wanted something, he wanted it NOW. Once he
had what he wanted he displayed enormous charm and a loveable nature. Coupled with this, he was a child in a hurry. He
walked early, talked early and seemed most in a hurry to get
into Tony's life. He idolised him from the start. As soon as he
was able to totter along, he followed him around like a
shadow.

By now our games had acquired the sophisticated breadth
which can be achieved with a two-year-old. To sliding down
the stairs and surgery football we added endless talk, not that
I was getting too many replies. Tony, Einstein-like, did not
deal in individual words. He was waiting for the fully fledged

sentence to come along so that he could express himself properly.

When the two of them melded together as a unit – 'Tone 'n' Rob', 'the boys', 'the kids' – my pleasure in them was fully realised. Rob's arrival added a physical dimension to Tony which might otherwise have lain unused. His rather gentle and emergently intellectual nature toughened under the need to cope with Rob's robust brashness. As they grew everything became a game; and to the bikes, trolleys, sledges and roller-skates of other children they brought and added elaboration, an almost Brunel-like complexity. Every game had its rules which had to be followed to the letter. Tone 'n' Rob couldn't just go out to play. They had to construct at the same time. They quickly graduated from dens in the garden to multi-layered living systems with intersecting tunnels and passages running off each other at bewildering angles. They claim the housing estates they grew up on are still dotted about with their microcosms of seventies boyhood life. Judging by what went missing from our house at the time, some of them must be very well stocked. In years to come anyone wishing to research late twentieth-century domestic cutlery and gardening tools should head straight for whatever's standing on Winnall and Stanmore housing estates in Winchester.

Tony's analytical mind allied to Robin's get-up-and-go was a nearly unstoppable combination that sucked in the other kids in the street. Nevertheless they seemed to prefer working with each other in isolation, the inscrutable captain and his able lieutenant, striking up a relationship which seemed telepathic.

Robin trusted Tony implicitly and would have followed him anywhere. One Sunday evening, after it had been suspiciously quiet for too long, we went out to the garden shed to discover Robin sitting totally still while Tony systematically painted him with grey emulsion. Every available square inch of skin had been covered. A swift visit to casualty did not succeed in removing it all, and we were still getting it off after many scrubbings weeks later. Years afterwards Robin found a revenge of sorts when an equally passive and obedient Cathy assumed the role of a statue while he cut off her beautiful long hair.

People often ask me if I wish I could see my children. I know many people who have been born blind feel this way. This puzzles me. In the only sense that seeing means anything to me, that is, in being able to conjure up a satisfying and realistic picture of them when they're not there, I can *see* them. Twenty years on I can still call up an accurate tactile picture of Tony aged six. A long angular face with very small features, only partly known as boney because it rhymed with Tony. Robin, much flatter faced, with my small, plump hands and a frame which looked, misleadingly as it happens, as if it could stop a runaway train. Cathy diminutive, almost doll-like, with disproportionately large ears. Playing with them, bathing them, putting them to bed daily, those touch-memories are etched deep into my consciousness. In this paedophile-obsessed, father-suspecting age, it's interesting to speculate just how blind dads are supposed to have a suspicion-free relationship with their children.

While the boys were small my blindness rarely prevented me from getting involved in their physical lives. At this point I could still run as fast as they could in familiar surroundings, kick and throw a ball, push them on swings or weigh down one end of a seesaw. Admittedly, my physical efforts were not always helpful or effective. Paddling one afternoon in Winchester's famous water meadows, Jo suddenly yelled out 'Good God, Rob's swimming!' As Robin was less than one year old at the time, my over-active protective instincts were immediately up and running. 'Is he all right?' I yelled, plunging in after him, across the uneven gravel and stones. He, in fact, had been perfectly fine, swimming like a crab – until I planted my foot firmly in the small of his back and sent him straight down into the river bed. He emerged, coughing and spluttering. For some reason he wouldn't go in again for the rest of the afternoon. Typically though, Rob wasn't deterred for long.

It was odd, too, that out of one blind and one sighted parent, I was always the one who would perform the daredevil stuff with them. When Tony had a sledge for his eighth birthday it was me who rode shotgun with them, eventually piling Rob and myself into a brick wall at the end of a particularly steep slope. Despite a few cuts and bruises we survived. At fun fairs I was the one who took them on the roller-coaster or the Mexican hat. Just watching us made Jo feel sick. And when as a teenager we took Robin to Florida he was still insisting that I should accompany him down the so-called 'kamikaze' water chute at Orlando's 'Wet 'n' Wild' complex. After hurtling and eventually somersaulting down an almost sheer water slide, I had to persuade him to do it a second time. Jo contented herself with the tart observation that, as I couldn't see it was two hundred and fifty feet down, it was hardly surprising that I wasn't scared.

Even some of the more ordinary things were pretty hair-raising. Until Tony was almost five we had no car. I used to walk the boys all over Winchester, even when they were quite tiny. With my only recently honed mobility skills this now terrifies even me. From a young age I relied on them to use their eyesight sensibly, but we survived. Everything was turned into a game. One regular walk led past the 'big school' to 'play school' and required us to cross a horrendously fast and busy main road heading for Southampton. Before that ordeal, though, many rituals had to be tackled. The main purpose of the walk was not to get to school but to play the 'blue car, red car, green car' game. Every self-respecting parent knows this time-honoured game is won by the person whose chosen car colour passes most often. Mysteriously, my colour always ended up in very short supply. We then reached a point in the journey where, because of a series of low walls, it was possible to travel some distance without having to touch the ground. This ritual had to be religiously observed before we diced with death on the main Winchester to Southampton road.

As they grew older the chore of holding my hand became increasingly irksome. The boys would squabble about whose turn it was to 'guide Daddy', and who could run free. My belief that I was holding their hand to keep them safe was clearly at odds with theirs that they were essential to my being able to put one foot in front of the other.

We must have made a bizarre sight tramping around Winchester but on the morning of Jo's driving test we decided to make a virtue of our conspicuousness. I was due to take the children, then aged five and three, to the dentist. The Winchester test-drive route is well known to local inhabitants and we contrived to be seen no less than three times by Jo's examiner as she drove him round the course. I'd told Tony and Robin to keep a keen eye out for Mummy. On each occasion, as we carefully stumbled up the road, they waved furiously as a reminder of how necessary a car was. She passed first time.

But for all this physical derring-do, our nightly bedtime ritual most vividly conjured up our closeness at this time. It consisted of three parts. First, bathtime. This was an extremely wet affair with most of the water usually ending up outside the bath. Just before Christmas, one year, the dining-room ceiling actually began to collapse because of the amount of water regularly deposited on the bathroom floor. After the bath came the magical part, the bedtime story.

Obsessed with books myself, there had never been any question that I would read regularly to my children. The only issue was whether enough children's books in Braille were available. In the early days I didn't bother about real books anyway. I just dredged my memory to retell old favourites like *Goldilocks and the Three Bears*. They were more enacted than retold, with actions and voices, and the pièce de résistance of the *Billy Goats Gruff* coming when the wicked troll was finally butted into the river. To be sure of a really good laugh, at this point it was necessary to hoist myself up above the top of the boys' upper bunk bed – the parapet of the bridge, you understand – and in butting the troll I hit my head on the ceiling. It dawned on me that no great subtlety was required to keep children amused.

After that I started to try to build up a collection of books. I realised how few you could actually buy. The biggest supply of Braille books came from the library but, with just one small section being read every night, library books were inadequate. You would have to send them back before you had finished them. In any case, the essence of children's stories lies in repetition, being able to go back to them whenever they are demanded.

Such books were available but it meant that, like it or not, Tony and Robin were fed a rather strange mixture of early literary influences. Because most of the books were old, they included *Grimm's Fairy Tales* in their original and grimmest versions, *Rikki-Tikki-Tavi*, *The Wind in the Willows* and *Winnie the Pooh*. Not by nature an old-fashioned parent, I might have wanted to mix this up with modern children's fiction, but it was not possible. They were force-fed the literary classics.

Nowadays the business of blind parents reading with their sighted children is taken very seriously. One school for blind children has built up an impressive collection of hundreds of books which juxtapose print and Braille text alongside each other, with pictures added. It's a splendid development and I would have loved to be able to use it. But we did okay: me standing up with the battered unfashionable looking Braille books placed on the top bunk, the boys curled up there too, screaming with mirth at old unexpurgated fairy stories of breaktaking political incorrectness.

We reserved our particular reverence for the story of the apple barrel. It's an example of Jacob and William Grimm's work that is not much read in the classrooms of today, which is something of a sadness. Yet again, stepmothers get a bad press. It tells of a little boy who helped himself from the apple barrel once too often, whereupon a slightly irritated stepmother slammed the door on his head, decapitating him. We all thought this gave the story a pretty jaunty start, but better followed. Realising that her actions might not be popular with the rest of the family, she stuck the head back on and propped the little kid up in the corner. Sister came home, said hello to her brother, who naturally enough ignored her. 'How rude your brother is,' said stepmum. 'Go and box his ears.' At this point his head fell off and the sister was blamed. The first time I read this to the boys our screams of delight were such that Jo came up to see whether murder was being committed. It never failed to please.

The final ceremony, the last compulsory trip to the loo, was surrounded with its own rules and regulations. The journey had to be made on my shoulders. Tony sat circumspectly astride but two-year-old Robin insisted on standing upright on them. However gently I undertook these trips, Robin would sway violently from side to side. He usually toppled off at least once. It didn't matter. He had out-dared his brother, and went to bed happy.

Into this competitive, obsessive and essentially male environment emerged our third child. Jo had made it known that she could do with a little female solidarity around the place. I'd always imagined I wanted lots of kids but I was now very happy with my lot. I had my gang. The rules were clear and understood. Why rock the boat? But Jo was insistent that we wanted a girl, and I was happy enough to go along.

Cathy has always insisted, and I am inclined to agree with her, that she got a raw deal. She did *her* bit all right. She popped out on cue, very much the wanted girl, a placid baby and very much exhibiting traditional feminine attributes from the start. It seemed hard for Cathy to find a comfortable spot in this well constituted male hierarchy. Circumstances were against her. She was not the first born and therefore did not benefit from being treated as unique. She was not the close-following second, able to hang on to the coat tails of the first. She would not have wanted to. Following has never been Cathy's style, nor competitiveness, whether academically, in sport, or anything else. It was evident from as early as play school that Cathy liked to make her own rules, not play to anyone else's.

Other factors worked against her. For instance, although she was very much planned and wanted, I think Jo would be the first to admit that the archetypal mother–daughter relationship is not quite up her street. In some ways closer to her brothers than her sisters or her mother, Jo, at heart, is not into gossip, dressing up or cosy sisterly chats. She is much more the commonsense fixer, and her ability to mend bicycles, fit batteries into malfunctioning machinery or improvise a sledge from a piece of hardboard or a polythene bag helped her fit much better into the rambunctious male bear pit into which our house was developing.

This all coincided with Jo's feet becoming itchier about getting back into nursing and with the arrival in early 1977 of foster daughter Fiona, an event which must have diverted attention which would otherwise have been hers. I tried to include Cathy in the games and readings but the three-year gap between her and Robin meant that someone more senior was always making the decisions. I can see that there were far too few occasions when she was the centre of attention, or the arbiter of choice. The result was that, as soon as she was big enough to impose her will, she sought solace outside the immediate family.

Fortunately an admiring covey of grandparents were on hand to fill some of the gaps. Both of my parents adored Cathy, the daughter they had never had. She spent at least as much time in their house as she did in ours. Dad, in particular, who could be abrupt with children, hit it off with her from the start; whereas the boys had learnt to treat him with respect and not a little awe, Cathy showed no such caution. On one occasion when she can have been little more than three, Mum wasn't feeling particularly well, but Dad happened to ask her absent-mindedly, 'Making a cup of tea, duck?'

Cathy was on her feet instantly, standing in front of him, finger wagging. 'Don't you know Nanny's ill?' she said imperiously. 'Go and make it yourself.'

He meekly departed.

Cathy developed another ploy for gaining attention. Shortly after her third birthday we moved house, and soon afterwards she started to disappear for increasingly long periods. Initially puzzled and worried, we began to be told by several older people on the estate that Cathy was regularly dropping in on them. She had apparently set up her own visiting service for old ladies, and had virtually drawn up a rota. In particular she had set up a second home in the house of the leader of the local Brownies, and had an enormous collection of dressing-up clothes. Cathy went round day after day to indulge the interests that weren't being catered for at home.

All families experience their own difficulties with dynamics; but my blindness had very little part to play. People are often very curious about the problems of blind people bringing up children. Though Jo could see, she didn't do all the work. We were able to divide tasks up so that the jobs which needed eyesight, such as drawing and painting with the children, could be done by her. I concentrated on things that required talking. We complemented each other particularly well.

Discipline was possibly a problem, not because I couldn't see, but because I'm not very keen on it. If the children were rarely punished it was not because I didn't know what they were doing but because I rarely thought punishment was the appropriate way to deal with their behaviour. If anything, I think I was rather better informed about what my children were doing and thinking than most parents. I was an inveterate and unashamed spy, with eavesdropping my principal weapon. Used to listening to gain information, I would crouch at keyholes, stand out of sight behind closed windows, or sit pretending to read a book under the trees at the end of the garden. It took the children a long time to absorb the fact that because I couldn't see them it didn't mean I couldn't hear them. I very rarely used the knowledge gained to interfere. I simply worked on the basis that knowledge was power, and that it was better to know than not to know.

One evening I had finally carved out some time to read to Cathy from the book of her choice. Not interested in the doings of *Ramona the Pest*, the boys went off to play and inevitably they were soon squabbling. My attention was diverted away from the exploits of Ramona to monitor their argument's progress. As they half fell, half wrestled their way down the stairs, I knew instinctively that matters had reached the point where intervention might avert a disaster. I also knew how often Cathy's needs were abandoned to sort out the boys. I pressed on. When the front door was yanked open I half rose to my feet. Before I could even reach the top of the stairs, it slammed, there was a shower of glass and Tony had a four-inch gash along his wrist. Result – another night in casualty.

People love to ask how my children reacted to my blindness. This is very hard to answer because they don't tell you. I always liked to think that my own genuine lack of concern and my willingness to give straight answers to straight questions would stop it being much of an issue but that makes the fundamental mistake of thinking your children will see things the way you do and the way you want them to. I'm sure they were teased by other children about the fact that Daddy was blind, but interestingly, from what they've said since, I get the impression that they were more upset by the stupid attitudes some *adults* took towards me. It's embarrassing for children to watch the father they take seriously treated and talked to as if he were the six-year-old, and puzzling when he doesn't react by putting the guilty party in their place. It is difficult to explain that this is not a battle you can afford to fight every day of your life.

On one occasion though I do know how other children reacted. Cathy asked me one morning if I was planning to be at home that afternoon. Thinking she was up to something and hoping for the answer 'no', I said with some relish that I would be in all day.

'Good,' she said with some feeling.

Puzzled, I asked her why.

'Well,' she said with typical Cathy solemnity and directness, 'Angie Britton wants to come round. She's a bully but she's scared of you 'cause you're blind, so,' she went on with impeccable logic, 'if I tell her you're here, she won't come.'

In future, on the rare occasions when Angie did venture in, I worked particularly hard at my most menacing Blind Pew impression. It was a unifying point between Cathy and me.

If anything I had too much, rather than too little confidence in my parenting ability. This led us to the fateful step of fostering Fiona. I'm still not really sure why we did it. It's the question they continually asked you while you're being vetted. The final catalyst was a television programme Jo and I watched together, but I suspect that it was an idea waiting to happen. When asked we muttered vaguely about both having been sent off to boarding schools and not wanting other children to grow up in institutions. We said it seemed wrong that we had room in our family while thousands of children still lived in children's homes. And to me there seemed something almost indecently tidy about having two healthy boys two years apart (Cathy wasn't on the scene when the process began). It almost invited a knock on the door from Robert Robinson with an invitation to appear on *Ask the Family*.

Whatever they try to tell you, the vetting process to become foster parents is haphazard. You're a human being. The social worker's a human being – how could they be anything else? Luckily we had a good relationship with ours. They vet both parents together, then apart; to make sure, I suppose, that one partner isn't bullying the other into giving consent. Our social worker Dave conducted most of my vetting in the pub. The fact that I could recite England's 1966 World-Cup-winning side and drank my whisky neat were good indications that I was up to the job. There had been some question as to the suitability of a blind man as foster parent. This objection appeared to dissolve when it was realised that (a) I was a respected broadcaster (*clear* evidence of parental solidity) and (b) Jo was a nurse, which *clearly* meant she would take charge of all the child's physical needs. Two healthy, happy, obviously well-looked-after toddlers may have swung the deal.

One winter's evening we arrived at a Basingstoke children's home, looking over and being looked over by Fiona. My first impression was of a chunky, confident ten-year-old who didn't stand on ceremony. After we'd been there only five minutes or so she grabbed my hands. 'Let's go and see the donkey,' she said, marching me to the end of a rather overgrown garden.

'You can feed him if you like,' she said, as if I were the ten-year-old and she the prospective parent.

She briskly uprooted a handful of grass.

'Just hold your hand out flat,' she said, ''e won't bite.'

I put out my hand and with a snort he lunged for it. This donkey had clearly not read the script which said he should be giving rides on Blackpool beach and carrying the odd message of peace and goodwill to Jerusalem. Fiona grabbed my hand again and we took three swift paces backwards.

'I don't think he'd bite,' said Fiona judiciously, then, 'but he might.'

After less than half an hour's acquaintance some important points had already been established: directness and a mutual physical ease which, under the circumstances, was surprising. Children are usually more relaxed with blind people than adults, particularly when some parent is not around putting the fear of God and years of ill-informed prejudice into them. What you don't expect them to know is the right way to help unobtrusively, how to guide for instance. Fiona seemed to understand this instinctively.

After three or four meetings and visits to our house, both sides decided to give it a go. It probably wasn't a long enough apprenticeship, but in the end you have to decide these things on instinct. No waiting period would guarantee success.

Fostering is not a fairy tale, and it is rarely, if ever, love at first sight. I can't speak for Fiona but it wasn't long before we realised that we'd taken on a challenge, the magnitude of which we had substantially underestimated, not because we weren't warned – no one said it would be easy – but because you can never be prepared for it.

It might have helped had we been given, as we should have been, more hard information about Fiona's past. What we saw was a little girl in a children's home with two older brothers who also needed a family. We knew Fiona's mum had died when she was a baby, but her father was still alive but couldn't or wouldn't cope. We certainly did not know that Fiona had had fourteen short-term foster homes before she reached the age of three, and that earlier attempts to place her long-term had foundered on her eldest brother's resistance to having the family split up. The fact that Fiona already had a natural family was something we quickly learnt we could never afford to ignore, however much we might want to incorporate her into ours. The notion of Fiona Robertson as a White clone was a non-starter.

It started well. Fiona is, by nature, direct, enthusiastic and affectionate, a strong basis for a relationship. When she first arrived she was good, disconcertingly good, in Saki's telling phrase, horribly good. This is apparently a fairly common phenomenon. Children placed in a family feel they've been set a test. If it's somewhere they like or prefer to previous homes, they're terrified that any bad behaviour will result in them being sent away. And so, liking it well enough, Fiona, at home at least, was angelic.

The single factor that ensured Fiona stayed long enough to give us a chance was Cathy. The fostering process is often a long and torturous path. At one stage we so despaired of our own local authority finding us a child that we applied to the hard-pressed London boroughs. We also decided that the gestation period for Hampshire Social Services was long enough in which to produce a baby of our own. By the time Fiona arrived, Cathy was already six months old. Our attempts to escape the symmetry of two boys resulted in a symmetrical family of two boys and two girls.

Fiona doted on Cathy from the start and did her best to help Jo with her. The problem was that institutions, however benevolent, do not engender initiative. Not long after she arrived Jo asked Fiona to prepare Cathy's bath. She disappeared upstairs for some time. Not wanting to be standing over her, after a while Jo nevertheless thought she'd better go and see what was happening. She found Fiona standing solemnly beside the bath while Cathy gurgled happily on the floor. Fiona was looking perplexed. 'I've put the plug in,' she said. 'Shall I run the water now?' Fiona was not stupid – far from it. She was simply unused to being allowed to make decisions for herself, however small.

Looking back, I can see our family must have provided a dreadful culture shock for her. Products of the sixties, even when the children were at an early age we believed that all decisions should be fully discussed. Their opinions were sought on everything from the colour of their bedroom wallpaper to where we should go on holiday. This provided Fiona with endless agonising decisions. Where she came from there had been far too many opinions to bother about the views of individuals. If you didn't like it, you lumped it.

Fiona did not remain an angel, but neither did she become a devil. Certainly at times she was difficult. We expected that and, quite apart from her background, she was becoming a teenager. But we never regarded her as beyond our control at home. Our problem was that once out of the house, around the local estate and at school, it was a very different story. Released from the shackles of foster parents too irritatingly liberal to yell at, Fiona seemed to return to methods with which she was more familiar and which had served her well at the children's home, including swearing, manipulation and fighting.

We remained in ignorance about much of what went on in the neighbourhood as Fiona began to flex her muscles. Not much given to gossip, the whispering campaign which was beginning to gain momentum was passing us by. Fiona's problem was that, despite our stand-offishness, we were well known. Local blind boys who make good find it hard to go unnoticed. Suddenly added to our well-established family, a ten-year-old with a colourful vocabulary and a handy pair of fists could not hope for anonymity. She was an outsider and made to feel it. In the end Fiona's exploits penetrated even our preoccupied isolation. One day she was brought home held firmly by one ear by an irate neighbour who informed us that our fucking, sodding daughter had sworn at his bleeding, fucking wife. Fiona, tearful but markedly unrepentant, maintained, almost superfluously we thought, that his fucking wife had sworn at her first. She may well have had truth and justice on her side, but emotions were mounting. Late one night I received a telephone call from a woman who refused to give her name who said that if we didn't get Fiona off this estate she would 'see to it that we did'. Fiona, it appeared, had been bullying her granddaughter. When she refused to come round and discuss it, I'm afraid I lapsed into some of Fiona's choicest phraseology myself.

What I found profoundly depressing about these increasingly frequent encounters was the total lack of tolerance shown. People weren't aware of all the details of Fiona's history, but they knew enough to realise she'd been given a rough time, yet repeatedly throughout Fiona's time with us, neighbours, teachers and police officers seemed steadfastly determined to ignore her many good qualities.

We knew, for instance, that Fiona was fiercely loyal. Having accepted our family, she was immensely protective of us. Much of her trouble arose when she pitched in on the side of one or other of the boys. As their assailants were usually much smaller than her, Fiona would wreak her version of family vengeance by sorting out their older sisters, or even their brothers. If anything the boys on our estate were more nervous of Fiona than the girls.

There is another picture of Fiona, the one most often seen at home. Gossipy, affectionate, impulsive, generous with meagre resources and, as the effects of institutionalisation wore off, increasingly self-reliant. As the adults stood around flapping, it was Fiona who bandaged up Tony's arm the day he put it through the glass door. When we returned from casualty, it was Fiona who had temporarily blocked up the window with hardboard. It was Fiona who joined the army cadet corps and the local swimming club and took herself off to learn aikido. She found her own job at thirteen and kept it even after we abruptly parted company.

That came later. For the time being, for all the problems, we were feeling rather smug with ourselves. Or I certainly was. We knew that everything wasn't perfect, and that Fiona sometimes bullied the boys to get her own way. Sensitive Tony sometimes had difficulty accepting her rough and ready ways (although stupidly we didn't realise how much he resented the loss of his status as oldest child); on the other hand for Robin, those rough and ready ways were all too attractive, and tempting to imitate. And when Cathy and Fiona, divided by ten years in age, shared a room, tension was bound to result.

I thought I could cope. My job was developing true enough. I was beginning to have to travel around more and more. But my focus was still very much my home. I was very proud, maybe a little too proud, of my growing family.

12

Have Stick, Will Travel

I have sometimes wondered what I would do with all my excess energy if I didn't have to travel. Getting around when you are blind is enormously taxing and uses up large reserves of initiative, patience, tolerance and sheer hard toil. I reckon that most blind people have already done a good day's work before ever they make it to the office or the factory. Perversely, though, since that first ill-fated trip to the local shops aged eight, planned like a military campaign but ending in disaster, I have come to love travelling. I don't mean lying on golden Hawaiian beaches or strolling around the world's finest museums or art galleries or even talking to fascinating locals in foreign downtown bars. That is relatively boring compared with the sheer joy of just moving around, negotiating idiosyncratic buses and trains, planning routes and connections with meticulous care, using your knowledge of road systems to work out car journeys for your drivers. It is, I suppose, the joy of being an expert.

The picture changed for me while still at Worcester, when

a craze for hitch-hiking swept through the school. Along with many other youngsters in the sixties we suddenly discovered that by standing at the roadside and sticking out our thumb the world suddenly became our oyster. Needless to say the school authorities tried to ban it, but it proved a rather stubborn plant to uproot. Most boys only used it for short trips out to country pubs or to see rurally based girlfriends. Typically, my first attempt was a 250-mile round trip home and back in one day.

It was a partial success. I and the totally blind friend who came with me almost gave my mother heart failure when we turned up out of the blue. She was cleaning out the larder shelves when we arrived and nearly fell off a pair of steps as we suddenly appeared tousled and covered in oil from a rather grubby long-distance lorry. I incurred the wrath of my father for scaring her half to death, and on the journey back we had to drop into a police station and enlist constabulary help when it became clear that at ten o'clock at night we weren't going to progress much beyond Chipping Norton without someone else's clout.

The success came when I realised that, far from being a daunting place, the rest of the world was only a thumb away. I stopped thinking in terms of the next lamppost, the next curb down, the next confusing intersection. My horizons broadened at a stroke, taking in cities, counties and countries. Paradoxically the macro picture was much easier to deal with than the micro. Crossing the public bar of the Dog and Duck without making a prat of myself was genuinely difficult, but there was absolutely nothing to stop me hitching lifts across Europe or catching a plane to New York. Precision is required for travelling on a small scale, but on the grand scale you only need to be heading in the right direction. Even now I feel far more comfortable zooming off to an unknown city on the other side of the world that I do going shopping in my home town on a Saturday morning. For a start, no one you know sees your mistakes.

Having lost my hitch-hiking virginity, over-indulgence followed. Five of us with only one half decent eye between us decided to hitch around Devon and Cornwall in the following summer holidays. The results were uproarious and enlightening.

The thing we realised very quickly was that being blind was a good hitch-hiking card, but being part of a group of five was a very bad one. Picking up one blind person feels like an act of mercy. Picking up five, even assuming you have a vehicle large enough, feels like a lifetime commitment. Hiding two in the hedge sometimes worked, but left a sour taste in the mouth. We soon learnt to split up. Many of the people who picked us up couldn't believe their eyes and seemed to have only the haziest notion of the purpose of the white stick.

'Does it operate by radar?' I was often asked.

One bloke thought it was some kind of radio receiver sending navigational messages from the ether. They were only about thirty years ahead of their time; scientists are just beginning to use satellite technology. Others clearly thought we weren't really blind at all, and that the stick was just a ruse to engage their sympathy. After a few encounters like this I began to make it a point of honour not only to bang my head as I clambered in, as some kind of guarantee that I was the genuine article, but just in case they remained unconvinced I would bang it again on the way out to improve the chances of the next blind hitch-hiker they encountered.

I also realised on this holiday that the contract a hitch-hiker makes with his lift is a complex one. You get the ride but in return you have tacitly agreed to be bored to extinction by their appalling right-wing views on race and youth, their exotic religious beliefs, the faithlessness, shrewishness or bizarre sexual practices of their partner, and the over-weaning fascination of their job which they have usually been engaged in for over thirty years. When the dangers of hitch-hiking are preached to young people this is an aspect too frequently ignored.

I once hitched a lift with a man whose idea of an amusing journey was for me to guess his profession – a kind of mobile *What's My Line?* It took me from the University of Kent to the outskirts of North London to work out that he was the man who made the flags British Rail guards used to wave off trains. Once, simply in the interests of making conversation, I asked a man to explain the strange clanking noise issuing from the back of his lorry. He settled himself back with a contented sigh. I knew I'd just made a very big mistake.

'I bet you'll never guess,' he teased.

It wasn't long after the British Rail flags incident. I declined to play that game. He was clearly disappointed, but decided to make the best of a bad job.

'Well,' he said. 'I travel in urinals.'

I might have known. He delivered them to pubs, clubs and schools all over the country and was one of the nation's foremost experts on the subject. Between Leeds and Northampton I had my education completed on the subject of the most effective flushing systems, drainage and arguments within the industry about the best height for splash guards. Moral: Never ask a question.

The West Country holiday was an early preparation for this kind of thing. I was heading for Plymouth one afternoon – by this time I'd learnt the value of hitching alone – when I was picked up by a man who at first seemed a model citizen for a lift giver; his views on sex and religion wouldn't have got him locked up. Conversation was going along pleasantly enough when he suddenly paused and said, 'I wonder if you wouldn't mind just handing me a little square box you'll find in the glove compartment.' I was still green. I asked a question.

'What's in it?'

'Oh, just a few pills I have to take.'

He saw my quizzical look. I still hadn't learnt. 'I take them because of my blackouts.'

Suddenly in my imagination we seemed to veer across the road. I must have gone a funny colour.

'Oh, there's nothing to worry about at the moment,' he said with total confidence. 'You see, I had one last week.'

I knew enough that blackouts didn't work on a quota system. He was to fork left at the next turning. Bugger Plymouth, I was going right.

In the case of the farmer with the rabbits the boot was on the other foot. This time we were hitching as a group and had been standing by the roadside for close on an hour without the glimmer of a lift. Then a van slowed down. A number did that. They would slacken their pace as they approached you, glide past and watch you, faces brightening as you came hammering along the verge towards them. Just as you reached them they would accelerate away, sounding their horns and shouting obscenities through the window. An old country sport, presumably.

This van was a genuine stopper. As we huffed up to it the driver opened his off-side door, but before he had a chance to open his mouth there was a rustling, scuffling sound and the roadside suddenly seemed to be crawling with wildlife.

'Dang rabbits,' shouted the farmer.

He had been taking them to market but hadn't bothered to secure them properly. Suddenly perceiving an unexpected glimpse of freedom they were off to explore the highways and byways of Devon before they ended up in a stew. Realising that we were the main cause of the disaster we did our best to help, in the process of retrieval crawling around on the muddy verge making what we judged to be rabbit-coaxing sounds. Fortunately they were not your Ramboesque

Watership Down-type rabbits, but more effete hutch-dwellers. After twenty minutes or so we had rounded up most of them and the farmer seemed to have lost interest in the rest. He finally climbed back into the van and was about to drive off when he remembered why he'd stopped in the first place.

'Where're you going, lads?' he asked half-heartedly.

We told him. It turned out that fifty yards up the road it forked. He was going left. We were going right. Another good man lost to hitch-hikers forever.

Some problems stemmed not from dodgy lifts but dodgy eyes; only one out of ten eyes operated anywhere near full strength. Most evenings ended in the local pub. Finding our youth hostels, tucked away up country lanes or in isolated glades, often proved something of a challenge.

The night we stayed in Tintagel, Hoppy, proud possessor of our one eye assured us as we set off home, full of confidence inspired by Cornish ale, that he knew where we were going. Thirty minutes later, even though it had only taken us five minutes to reach the pub, he was still bullish. To bolster our confidence and as evidence of his elevated one-eyed status he insisted that he was following a light. Impressed, we plodded on in his wake. When he stopped very suddenly we all shunted into him, practically knocking him off his feet. In a shaky voice, he said, 'I think that's a cliff edge in front of me.' The effect of Cornish ale abating rather suddenly, we became for the first time aware of the sound of the sea. Hoppy, it appeared, had been leading us toward the welcoming gleam of a lighthouse.

Holidays and school ended, but hitch-hiking did not. For the next few years of relative poverty it provided me with my staple method of transport. It runs like a thread through those years: thumbing my way back from York to Winchester when the going got tough; that fateful journey from the University of Kent to doorstep Radio Solent; even after I started work, when trains, buses, taxis and scrounging lifts from friends proved fickle, I was still not above resorting to my old ways. I had by now become much more adept than in my Cornish days. With what was now deemed my unfair advantage of that magic stick I became something of a byword for completing journeys more quickly than can be achieved by any other form of transport. My pièce de résistance came when Jo and I went back to York to visit old friends. Still strapped for cash we agreed that she and Tony, then aged about three, would go back to Winchester on the train while I would hitch. I was secretly rather glad to be back on the open road.

When she reached Winchester I was waiting for her at the station. I'd already been home and gone for a lunchtime drink. I was accompanied by our dog, which I had managed to persuade my last lift to pick up from nearby kennels.

Travel for blind people can become an all-consuming consideration. When I began to work for radio 'getting there' was often far more of a problem than what you did when you arrived. It quickly became clear that desperadoes planning to jump from ledges would not hang about while I checked up the times of the number 72 bus. Speed – the essence of good reporting – was not always possible. My most creative solution to this problem was to attend not our morning editorial meetings, but those of BBC Television on the floor below. Having discovered what they were covering on that day, and knowing that transport was required for the crew and equipment, I would then go back upstairs and sell the same story to Solent, my method of getting there assured. It did have some drawbacks. As television takes so much longer than radio I was usually finished and ready to go even before they'd set up their cameras. Usually there was only one solution to this. It would be nothing unusual for me to carry my story back to Radio Solent in the cab of a long-distance lorry. Hardly Richard Dimbleby, but it did the trick.

Even after I began working for national networks I still could not completely kick the habit. One of my early jobs for *In Touch* was a series of interviews in Scotland. I didn't have the ready cash for the fare and advances were not on offer. I solved the problem by hitching up the west coast, conducting my interviews first in Glasgow, then in Edinburgh, and then making my way back down the east coast. However at ten in the evening, stuck in a windswept service station somewhere in County Durham, I realised my chances of getting back to Winchester that night were nil. It was another occasion when I had reason to be grateful for having friends in York.

Working for the network brought the chance of foreign travel, and with it a whole new set of problems to enjoy. Up until then I had led a rather sheltered life when it came to contact with other people's cultures. It had not yet occurred to me, for example, how heavily I relied on my verbal dexterity to talk my way out of trouble, or that in some societies my solutions might not even be considered acceptable.

The language difficulty emerged on my very first trip abroad for *In Touch*. I was to go to Belgium to check out an art gallery and museum which was allowing blind people to touch certain carefully selected exhibits. It may not sound significant today, but this was when in Britain the merest hint of human flesh in the vicinity of a precious artefact would bring the police forces of six counties down on your head.

The job itself was simple enough. Having flown to Brussels I was given the hands-on tour by a rather delectable Belgian curator. The highlight of the interview was our mutual examination of a carved wooden statue representing a naked Nigerian warrior. As I dutifully groped the impressive figure with one hand while holding the microphone with the other, she groped for the correct English terms with which to describe the parts of his anatomy I had currently reached. I could only conclude that she had learnt her English either in a school playground or an army barracks as the terms 'willy' and 'bollocks' – pronounced very prettily – spilled on to my gently whirring tapes. I wanted to be there when Thena Heshel edited it.

My problems really began when I reached my hotel room. Not, at this point, a seasoned traveller I wasn't yet wise in the art of securing vital information. In England, even back then, someone would probably have made a cursory attempt at describing the layout of the room. Here though, defeated by the absence of a meeting point between his English and my Flemish, the porter dumped my bags on the bed with a grunt and departed. Hotel bedrooms are much the same in any language: a bed the size of which can be ascertained by lying across it, a wardrobe with incomprehensible hangers, an armchair, a TV and a phone if you're lucky.

Bathrooms speak with a far more distinctive foreign accent. I approached my first Belgian bathroom with true Anglo-Saxon caution. Bowls and basins were dotted about, some of them set at rather peculiar heights. Their precise purpose was unclear. I decided that exploration of these should be postponed for a future date. It was the summer of '76, and Belgium was as stinking hot as Britain. After a morning spent wrestling with naked Nigerian warriors my crying need was for a bath. Then my troubles truly began.

At first glance the bath looked orthodox enough: taps on either side, plug hole, plug. Without pausing to undress I turned the left-hand tap and was instantly struck in the back by a jet of freezing cold water. Ah! A shower. Without pausing to think I wrenched the tap in the opposite direction. This time I was struck in the back by a jet of boiling hot water. Conclusion: this tap was not on/off, it was circular. I could have lost my nerve at this point, but British sang-froid saved the day. Reaching up above the taps I found a large, imposing and promising-looking control on the shower itself, and twisted it with confident intent. The result was dramatic. The entire shower fell off the wall and into the bath. This could have been an improvement. The water was now going into the bath and not all over me, though it was arriving there by a rather circuitous route. The weight of the nozzle meant that when it landed in the bath it rolled over like a dog and proceeded to spray water at the ceiling.

By now my competitive instincts had been aroused, possibly at the expense of a sense of proportion. I was determined to have what I considered a conventional English bath. Concerned to keep the water within bounds, I tore off my clothes, jumped into the bath and sat on the nozzle. This might have been effective, if uncomfortable, had I not inadvertently nudged the original tap controlling the temperature as I jumped in. Consequently on lowering myself on to the nozzle – and to revert to the language of Belgian museum curators – my bollocks were sprayed with a jet of boiling hot water.

It is not possible to put it better than the late Gerard Hoffnung battling with his famous barrel of bricks: 'At this point I must have lost my presence of mind.' I leapt out of the bath, upon which the dog nozzle rolled slowly on to its back again and sprayed water at the ceiling. I fled the bathroom and summoned help via the phone. When it came we discovered that Flemish was unnecessary. I merely pointed at the devastated bathroom and was rewarded with a series of eloquent tutting sounds. For the rest of the trip I departed from my usually high standards of cleanliness.

On this trip I also experienced for the first time the full trauma of trying to get directions in a foreign language. It's bad enough in Britain. The directions blind people need are a different language in themselves. Not for us elegant clock towers that 'you simply can't miss', churches with weather vanes and 'a funny-looking little house with a crooked chimney'. We need directions you can touch. Railings which make a nice clanging noise when you hit them with a stick; lampposts and telegraph poles we might walk into but at least reassuring us along with the pain that we are heading in the right direction. Most of all we need people who know their left from their right, who can count, and who agree on the definition of 'a turning'. I can't tell you how often 'the third on the left, mate' has turned out to be the fourth on the right. Lack of numeracy and a sense of direction play a part in this, but it's also because most sighted people think of 'a turning' as a road that goes somewhere, whereas to me anything involving a break in the pavement can feel like a turning: the entrance to a school, a garage forecourt, even the drive of a large house. The only reliable solution is to obtain your directions from another blind person who speaks the same language, and that is not always a viable course of action.

Brits also have a tendency towards over-solicitude. Many believe that even though they have only encountered you thirty seconds ago the responsibility of caring for you has passed to them alone. They find it hard to believe that you have somehow managed to carve out a life before they came on the scene and that you will do so again after they've gone. Often unable or unwilling to give you directions and let you go, they insist on accompanying you all the way to your destination or as far as you will let them. Even when as kindly as possible you have shaken them off, you know as you go on your way that their eyes are boring into your back waiting for the disaster that will convince them that they should have accompanied you even unto death. Normally these days a trouble free traveller, I've clattered into many a lamppost far too aware of this self-fulfilling scrutiny behind me.

No one can accuse the French of undue solicitude, but they have a national vice of their own when you can coax them to give directions at all: over-elaboration. My love affair with the London Underground now well and truly cemented, I decided that I would try my luck on the Metro when I went to Paris following my trip to Belgium. Sooner or later of course, I needed to ask for help, which is when I discovered that for the philosophy-loving French the important thing is not to get you where you want to go but to achieve 'the right answer' regardless of its practical effects. The first person I asked thought she knew where I ought to go but just in case decided she'd better call over a friend to confirm it. As they dotted the *i*s and crossed the *t*s in a stream of voluble and to me incomprehensible French a third voice chimed in. By the frequency of the word '*non*' I deduced he thought they were barking up the wrong tree. A violent altercation ensued, quickly attracting others. Pretty soon there were about ten of them animatedly dissecting the Metro map to plot the most satisfyingly ergonomic route to the Gare du Nord. Calculating that in the meantime I had missed at least three trains, I slipped quietly away. Nobody attempted to stop me or even appeared to notice my going.

Ironically in many ways the country where it feels most different to be blind is one with which, notionally at least, we share a language. The United States has genuinely bought into the disability rights philosophy. You can have rights; you can have anti-discrimination laws. Just don't expect any goddamn favours on top. There is an inescapable and rather charming logic to it, but when you've spent all your life in the patronising, charity-based and therefore very ambivalent attitudes of Britain, you can find it a little disconcerting.

I was a slow learner. On my second visit to make a pilot of a television programme for disabled people that we hoped to sell to Channel 4, I was still making gaffes. When we landed at Newark we desperately needed to make a plane connection to Washington DC in about half an hour. It was going to be incredibly tight, particularly with our seventeen separately packed pieces of filming equipment. Airport staff all over the world enjoy taking television equipment to pieces, revelling in the distraught faces of usually unfailingly cocky television directors and producers. They particularly enjoy it in the States.

I decided desperate remedies were in order.

'Let's play the blind card,' I said.

The producer was worried and doubtful. Not about the Americans, but about me. He was learning the sensitivities of disability as a topic. He had hired me in the guise of an opinionated, fiercely independent journalist to make a series about the rights of disabled people. Twelve hours into the project I appeared to be advocating a bit of judicious grovelling.

'Are you sure you don't mind?'

'We haven't got time to mind. Play the bloody blind card.'

The blind card involved shamelessly exploiting your disability for instant personal gain: strategic use of the stick, a stumble, the bewildered look. As you might imagine, it works like a dream in Britain. I'd been using it ever since as a child I realised I could make it to the front of long queues for rides at the fun fair. It is extremely effective, and utterly hypocritical.

But it doesn't work in the States. My slight but discernible stagger as we walked over the threshold of the plane secured our place on a staff-only route which carried us to the front of the line. But flying with Virgin we had still been in the hands of an all Brit plane crew. When we made our sudden and apparently miraculous appearance ahead of all the Americans who'd been with us on the flight we were greeted by a storm of spontaneous booing. I was startled but still bullish; we were at the front, weren't we? The baggage collector, taking his cue from the enraged multitude, then proceeded to dismantle with infinite and exaggerated care every

267

camera, every light, every tripod. The crowd's boos turned to purrs of satisfaction and approval. Needless to say we missed our flight, and only narrowly escaped missing our luggage as well. It was spotted just in time, being loaded not on to flight 174 to Washington but on to flight 147 to Fort Lauderdale. Play the blind card in New York, and retribution will be swift and thorough.

I should have known better. My first visit to the States had almost ended before it began. I'd always been fascinated by American life, ever since I'd set my alarm clock for 3.00 a.m. to hear the invincible Rocky Marciano beat the hell out of our boy Don Cockell back in the fifties. I used to comb short-wave radio, frantically seeking real radio stations broadcasting to real Americans, as opposed to cheap propaganda imitations such as Voice of America or the American Forces Network. I wanted to hear the Hot 100 and the glitzy adverts, which in my childhood made the country sound so different from safe, drab fifties Britain. Nevertheless I was well into my thirties before I made it, somehow managing to persuade British Airways that if they paid my fare I would report, impartially of course, on their facilities for disabled passengers. But my naivety betrayed me. Assuming that BA had made all the travel arrangements, I was preparing to board when someone asked, 'Where's your visa?'

I was genuinely puzzled.

'Visa! What visa?'

There was a horrified pause.

'You need a visa to go to the States. Everyone from Britain does.'

Veteran of one flight to Cork and one to Brussels, this was news to me. Amazingly, I managed to talk my way on to the plane – this was still Britain and I was playing the blind card. Once on the plane I had absolutely no assurance I would be allowed into the land of the free.

It was among the longest seven hours of my life, wondering whether my experience of the States was destined to be two consecutive transatlantic flights.

The conversation at Dulles airport went something like this:

'Where's your visa?'

'I haven't got one.'

'Why not?'

'I didn't know you needed one.'

'Everybody needs one.'

'Americans don't need them to enter Britain.'

'Not the point.'

I tried the blind card, 'I couldn't read the literature. It was all in print.'

She didn't hesitate. 'Not my problem. You should have had it read to you.'

Long pause.

Impasse. I felt I'd reached the point when it was safer to say nothing.

She shrugged. I heard it. Then: 'Do you have fifteen dollars?'

I wondered if we were still having the same conversation.

'Yes.'

'Hand it over.'

'Why?'

'That's the cost of a visa waiver. Enjoy your stay.'

I didn't get the chance to ask why, if a visa waiver could be obtained for fifteen dollars, it was regarded as so important in the first place. If any card got me in on this occasion it was not the blind card but the British card. I think she just got bored with the silence.

Once in I had to learn fast. However independent we like to think we are, blind people need the right help. Getting the right help is all about asking the right questions. In Britain ingratiation is still very much the preferred syntax. Sentences beginning 'I wonder if you wouldn't mind just . . .' or 'I don't suppose you could possibly . . .' still tend to bring home the bacon. Don't try it in the States. Brits may like to think they're doing you a huge favour. Americans want to know what it is you need and fast. 'I wonder if you wouldn't mind just passing that cup' is likely to illicit something like 'I wonder too' and no cup. That's if you're lucky. 'Could you possibly' will probably produce 'It's possible' but still no cup. Preferred options are 'Pass the cup' although 'Pass the god-damn cup' may prove to be quicker. Such directness is fine not to say refreshing once you get the hang of it. After a while I found seeking directions in American cities a positive joy. 'How do I get to Carnegie Hall?' once you've fought your way through the statutory 'Practice lady, practice' brings forth a stream of terse but comprehensive instructions. You might even get a 'Good luck', no armed escort, no eyes boring into your back as you go. Americans have no time for all that. And with the grid system of streets you don't have as much trouble with turnings.

Shops, though, except for the very swankiest, are a night-mare for blind people. Blind American friends who have the money come to London to shop, not because it's cheaper but because they'll get served more quickly, even allowing for the trip. Basically, blind people are supposed to know what they want and where it is before they set foot in an American store. Most assistants don't see it as their job to mollycoddle you. The stock response to requests for help is 'You should have brought a friend.'

And then you meet the exception. This is the blind person's example of that well-known American dichotomy swinging wildly between extreme rudeness and extraordinary generosity. On that first visit to Washington the American football craze which swept Britain in the eighties was reaching its peak. My son Rob would have killed for a Miami Dolphins football shirt, particularly one acquired in the States. So would every American kid his age.

I combed the sports shops of Washington, even shopping in the areas white tourists were advised to steer clear of. Not surprisingly here I found what I was looking for. The guy in the first store I tried had just that moment sold out, but he said he happened to know a rival store had just taken a new delivery. Hesitantly I asked if he could give me directions. 'I'll do better than that,' he said. Despite being on his own he shut up his store and marched me four blocks to his chief competitor. Robin had his shirt, although once again I remained unsure whether the hand had been won by the British card or the blind card.

Such confusions in attitude to service for blind people are legion in the States. Despite aggressive anti-discrimination legislation this still seems to have much more to do with deeply ingrained attitudes. Take the difference in approach between shops and restaurants. American shops are positively arctic, whereas restaurants almost overwhelm you with their eagerness to serve. Go into an English restaurant and ask them to read you the menu and the conversation will go something like this:

'I wonder if you wouldn't mind just reading me the menu.'

'The beef's very nice today.'

'Yes, good. Would it be possible for you to read me the menu?'

'Why don't you try the steak and kidney pudding? My Stan was in here last night, and he said it was gorgeous.'

Bully for Stan, say I. On the odd occasion when you can persuade someone to read from the menu in England the technique is for them to pause lovingly after each item positively daring you not to order it. This, presumably, is what passes for choice.

Not so in America, where choice is a religion. Over there Chuck or Hank or Wayne, having introduced himself as your waiter for the evening, will then proceed to read you the menu in the minutest of detail until you find yourself begging him to stop. Three items in, you just know you're going to order the first dish he mentioned because your brain has gone into food overload. No chance, though. He'll press on with nine kinds of chilli, twelve fish dishes, with sub-divisions and multiple variants of pancake.

On the other hand there are times when the American penchant for thoroughness is an absolute godsend. When you are travelling information for the blind is gold dust and the Americans give it to you in spades. On the Washington subway the driver not only announces the name of the next station long before the train stops; the side on which doors will open; enough possible line interchanges to satisfy the pickiest trainspotter; and still finds time to wish you a pleasant evening. On my first trip I thrilled to announcements like 'This train's next stop is Foggy Bottom. Doors opening on the right. You all have a good day.' Contrast this with the tedious debate continuing in Britain, where London Transport insists that drivers can't or won't be trained to make announcements along with all their other duties and that, in any case, frequent announcements would annoy other passengers. They insist on regarding the anodyne, prerecorded messages they've tried out on a few lines as a daring and innovative experiment. In a city which welcomes 20 million visitors a year we're supposed to believe that people will be annoyed by being told where they are. I don't think so.

For a rather complicated reason blind Americans are not overjoyed and overwhelmed with gratitude with all this special provision. The American National Federation of the Blind, which has a membership of over 50,000, espouses a philosophy that says that special provision for blind people is only acceptable if it can be justified as useful to everybody else. In other words, don't patronise us! Announcements on trains pass that test. They happily argue, as do I, that everyone benefits from being told where they are. The problem arises when transport authorities start doing things such as creating textured, bumpy surfaces to warn blind pedestrians that they are approaching the edge of the platform. That, says the Federation, is patronising. Properly trained blind people don't go falling off the edges of platforms, and to pander to the incompetent is to degrade the rest of us in the eyes of the public, 'reinforcing negative images of blind people'. Hallelujah! Not content with just declaiming it, they actually took the Bay Area Transit service in San Francisco to court, seeking an injunction against them installing any more of the pesky textured platforms.

The problem with this politically correct mantra, if I really need to point it out, is that in the real world blind people *do* fall on to railway lines, having failed to reach the high standards of mobility expected of them by the National Federation of the Blind, or being just plain tired or drunk. I'm not sure I know any blind person who travels frequently who hasn't fallen on railway lines. After a particularly good evening one of my close friends fell on to the line, clambered back up again none the worse, and, it being an island platform, promptly fell off the other side. I've even done it myself in particularly embarrassing circumstances. Towards the end of my school career I kicked up an enormous fuss about being escorted to London by my mother to be put on the train for Worcester with all the other kids as if we were parcels. I pointed out with my usual maddening logic that the London train stopped at Reading and that there was a regular service between Winchester and Reading. This would be cheaper and I could perfectly well do the journey on my own. In truth, even at seventeen I still found it hard to deal with the awkward

parting with Mum at Paddington and the high-octane jollity
of the other kids on the train, most of whom seemed to hate
their families and be glad to be rid of them. I preferred to
undertake the journey in solitary gloom.

The problem with maddening logic is that it doesn't work
too well on a complicated railway station, with a suitcase in
one hand, a box full of records in the other and a white cane
nowhere in sight. The inevitable happened. Changing trains at
Reading, I fell on the line.

This was before electrified rails and there was no train
coming, so I clambered back on to the platform with no major
physical injuries but my dignity in tatters. Waiting for me, as
my head emerged on to platform 7 was a laconic station official
who had been nowhere in evidence when I needed him.

'You fell on the line?' he asked, with massive redundancy.

I almost said no, I'd been down there looking for tad-
poles, but I realised in time the vulnerability of my position
and that this was a man to be humoured.

'Where are you trying to get to?' the inevitable interrogation began.

'Worcester,' I said.

'What's at Worcester?'

'School.'

I was keeping my answers brief but apparently not brief
enough.

'Would you like me to ring them and tell them you're
coming?'

No, I most definitely would not. Clearly any such conversation would inevitably end with making reference to my
unseemly nose dive. Honesty was the only policy.

'Er – actually, that would be a bit embarrassing.'

Still inclined to play the English public school gent I felt
in my pocket and extracted two pounds, one-fifth of my
pocket money for the whole term.

'I'd be very grateful if you didn't tell anyone.'

He took the money gravely, sucked on his teeth for a bit, then pocketed it.

'Well, as you're not hurt, I suppose it will be all right,' he said. 'I'll give you a hand on to the Worcester train when it arrives.'

He was a man of honour. When I reached Worcester there was no gloating reception party waiting for me to say 'We told you so.'

Similarly, some of my American friends would have been only too happy to have been on the receiving end of a little patronage and degradation if it would have prevented them from plummeting on to the line at Foggy Bottom, a sure way of you all not having a good day.

I have attempted to debate this point about special treatment with the mandarins of the National Federation of the Blind. I and others have asked them the difference between the configuration of bumps on a railway platform to warn you about its edge and the configuration of bumps which comprise, for example, a Braille menu in a restaurant, which is approved of. Both surely replace information which is usually obtained by sight with information obtained by touch. Neither pass the test of being useful to *everyone*. 'Ah,' they replied sagely, 'but Braille is the equivalent of a language. It is an aspect of our distinct culture to which we have a right. It's the same as sign language for deaf people.'

If you'll forgive me mixing my theological periods a little, we continue to debate how many angels can balance on the head of a pin, while American blind people continue to topple on to the line at Foggy Bottom like the Gadarene Swine. I suppose equality always carries a price and demands a few martyrs.

The Federation had not confined its angst to the railways. They've also had a long-running battle with American airlines, which developed a policy of telling blind people that there were certain seats on aeroplanes they couldn't occupy, specifically those close to emergency exits. Blind people, it was argued, would not be able to play a full part in helping those who needed assistance to get out of the plane in an emergency. The Federation rose up as one, arguing that this was discrimination of the most blatant kind. There was no system to vet other passengers for their suitability as rescuers. People were not excluded from these seats because they were physically weak, prone to panic, likely to be as drunk as a skunk or just mean-spirited enough to make sure they escaped first. These were telling arguments with which I have much more sympathy. When the airlines refused to change their policy, Federation members lay down on runways to prevent planes taking off. The battle still rages.

Once the transatlantic bug had bitten, splendid stories like these and the willingness of Americans to engage vigorously and publicly in provocative debates forced me to return to the States several times throughout the eighties. At one time, when the glamour was still winning over the tackiness, I even considered uprooting myself and launching myself as a broadcaster there. Infatuation must have been running at a high level. Given the absence of almost any demand for intelligent talk radio in the States this was an idea best purged from my system before it ruined my career.

At least American disabled people were having a bash. With the black civil rights movement as a blueprint, and with a hardcore of disabled Vietnam veterans furious that they had ended up in wheelchairs in the pursuit of a pointless war and yet without the legal right to enter into the local library, the movement in the United States had some balls. Throughout the seventies and eighties a raft of legislation was forced through Congress demanding access to just about everything: buildings, public transport, employment, education. When the movement didn't get its way or felt a promise had been reneged on, all hell broke loose. In America the highly effective publicity tool of wheelchair-users chaining themselves to buses found its first expression. Disabled soldiers routinely crawled up the steps of the war memorial to make their point about lack of opportunity. When the government seemed to be dragging its feet about its legislation a group of protestors in wheelchairs and on crutches, and with one of their leaders in an iron lung, took over the Federal building in San Francisco and occupied a floor for over a month. Television pictures of California State Police attempting to manhandle them out of the building aroused public outrage, and disabled activists realised that in making the authorities look stupid and mean at the same time they had unearthed a very potent political weapon. By the eighties they were well on course for a comprehensive civil rights legislation on a par with that achieved by the black movement they had so blatantly imitated.

In Britain disabled people were at least twenty years behind. Arguments about rights were largely confined to obscure discussions in frowsty learned journals. Protests had not yet made it on to the streets. A polite enquiry whether anyone minded most awfully if we had a flag day was about as revolutionary as it went. Disabled people were still having trouble fighting off Lady Bountifuls and acquiring their own organisations, never mind having the temerity to demand to sit next to her in a restaurant. The first wheelchair chained to a London bus was still a decade away. The charities held sway and I was barely aware of disability politics, let alone what I thought about them.

Any discussion about travel cannot ignore the extraordinarily sentimental and silly attitude of Britons toward guide dogs. I suppose the reason it makes me so mad is the assumption that the intelligent and decision-making partner in the combination of dog and blind owner must be the *dog*. Despite daily evidence about the massive stupidity of dogs, people are still prepared to believe that they're brighter than blind people. This applies however erudite or successful the blind person. For years David Blunkett could not appear on *Question Time* or *Any Questions* without some fatuous reference from the presenter to whichever of his bloody dogs happened to be curled up beside him at the time. The implication seemed to be not only could David not have reached the studio without Ted or Lucy, but if the questions proved too tricky the dogs could be called up for their expert opinions. Given the marvellous view his dogs had of parliamentary life lying largely ignored at his feet, I have considered writing a political column signed 'Blunkett's Dog'.

There have been times when my indignation about this has boiled over at the assumption that, though there are almost a million blind people in this country and less than 5,000 of them use guide dogs, it is nevertheless almost a crime to appear in the streets without one. I can't tell you how often I have answered the question: 'Why don't you get a dog?' The answer is simple: because you have to train with them in residential conditions far too reminiscent of blind schools for my liking; because they can't real rail indicator boards or restaurant menus; because you look a fool carrying them up and down escalators on the London Underground; because unlike white sticks they deposit shit all over the place; and because they would divert attention from *me*. There is a belief that they attract women. In my experience even this is a myth. Women drool over the guide dog, it's true, but there is absolutely no guarantee that at any point this affection will be transferred to you.

On one occasion I confess to having let my irritation at these preconceptions get the better of me. It was at the end of a day, and I had just pushed and shoved my way off an Underground train at Waterloo. As I set off towards the mainline station a guy took my arm. At the end of long days I'm very happy to let someone else do the steering. But then he uttered those fatal words, 'Where's your dog then mate?'

I don't know why, but some demon must have possessed me. I dropped his arm as if it were red hot, threw up my hands to cover my face and said, 'Oh my God, I must have left it on the train.' He didn't wait to ask any more questions. He was off, pausing only to yell over his shoulder, 'Don't worry mate, I'll soon have it sorted out.' I stopped, appalled. I knew I had started a large unstoppable juggernaut rolling down a hill. I could still escape. I was close to the escalator. It would be the work of a moment to dash up it and lose myself in the crowds on the mainline station's concourse. But curiosity led me back towards the Underground platform I'd just left. When I got there, much incomprehensible shouting was going on, but as soon as he saw me my original benefactor bustled up with the air of a man who'd averted World War III.

'It's all right mate,' he said.

Apparently the thought of a sacred guide dog hurtling unaccompanied toward the Elephant and Castle had been too much for all concerned to contemplate.

I was told that the power on the whole of the Bakerloo line had been switched off. They were radioing ahead to the train and my dog would be returned to me. By now other officials had arrived and were clucking reassuringly. In the end I had no choice.

'Umm, I don't know quite how to tell you this,' I said, 'but I haven't really got a dog.'

There was a very puzzled silence. Someone half asked the obvious question, 'So why – why did you say you had?'

Another realisation dawned. I couldn't say I hated the bloody things. I'd be locked up, not for wasting London Underground's time but just for hating guide dogs. Once again I only had once choice, didn't I?

'Because – because I've always wanted one,' I said in a rush.

There were more clucking sounds, but apparently this was the right answer. It was believable that a blind person deprived of his inalienable right to a guide dog might behave in this irrational way. I had suddenly conferred upon myself the slightly indignant sympathy bestowed on a baby-snatcher. The guards got the commuters on the Bakerloo line moving again. There was a little desultory talk about taking me to London Transport Police, but their hearts weren't really in it. I was allowed to slink away to mourn my sad and dogless state on the 7.30 back to Winchester.

13

White's Last Stand

Jim Moseley was having his lunch when he told me my father was dying. A typical journalist, I had salted away the surgeon's home phone number from a previous encounter. When I wanted the truth about the tests my father had been having on and off throughout the summer and about which everyone was being particularly reticent, I decided to catch him on the hop. Ambushed between dinner and dessert, he told me that my father's cancer was affecting both his bladder and his bowel and that the successful treatment of one would almost certainly aggravate the other.

Reflexively putting the right questions amid my shock, I asked if this meant we should leave well alone. He thought not.

'If we do nothing, it will be a year, two at the most – and painful. If we operate there's a chance he could have as much as five years and not experience so much pain.'

I digested what he had said. Whatever we decided, he was going to die soon. I was going to lose him.

We had known for some time that something was wrong. My father had known for longer. Pathological about illness, his own and everyone else's, like so many people he had brushed his symptoms aside. He joked about his difficulty going to the loo, publicly blaming increasing age, privately praying it was only a dodgy prostate. When a painful attack finally drove him into hospital, he came out joking about pissing broken glass, but the cycle of tests, non-committal answers, more tests, more evasions had begun. As had the complex game of trying to work out just who was protecting whom from what. My impatience with this process had landed me with the job of working out what to do with the worst news I could imagine.

It coincided with something of a trough in my career. It wasn't that it was going badly, just that it was going nowhere. I was still beavering away at Solent, Mr Versatile, having a go at most things but without a real profile. I was still presenting *In Touch* on Radio 4, which in a very specialist field was establishing a good name for me but was not causing plum offers to come flooding in. I seemed to be acquiring an unwanted reputation for worthiness: a series for Continuing Education Radio on fostering children (thank you, Fiona), and another for the same outlet on new directions in nurse training (thank you, Jo). I was destined to regurgitate the lives of my nearest and dearest, but nothing else was catching fire.

Similarly my love affair with the children was beginning to wear a bit thin too. I didn't love them any less, but as they grew older I felt less pivotal, less necessary, less infallible. I was learning my place in other independent human lives. Jo spotted it too. One evening she said in the middle of one of those domestic heart-to-hearts, 'Time for you to stop hanging around those kids. You've given them what you can, it's time to start looking after your career.' I knew she was right, but my habits were ingrained. I didn't know where to start.

Jim Moseley's news drove all thoughts of career development from my head. I carried on working, of course, but stopped thinking about it. My zeal to be first with the news left me firmly with the responsibility of deciding what to do with it. I became the family's news manager and spin doctor; ferreting and chivvying out information from those unwilling to give it, then trying to decide who knew what, who ought to know what and who knew but was pretending they didn't. I came to the conclusion that in such situations most people are aware of most things. The only decision is whether they want to talk about it or not. It kept me occupied. It was my way of dealing with it. It was the position I was to occupy until Dad's death a year later.

I knew the truth for a long weekend before Mum and Dad found out, with only Jo to share the knowledge. All my instincts for openness made me want to tell them. Deeper instincts told me that they wouldn't want to hear such news from me. At thirty-four I was still the little boy. It was their job to protect. In any case, in order to believe it and to think how to deal with it, they needed to hear it from someone their generation would regard as 'in authority'. It was a bizarre weekend: knowing and not saying but I was grateful for the cop-out and there was still a corner of my mind which could say if they don't know it's not yet true.

After they heard the news they took it like all the downs in their married life, with stoicism and with an instant determination to 'fight it'. They had only ever fought on the small things in life. Over the big things – the birth of two blind children, the failure of Dad's business in the early seventics, the death of their own parents – they had always stood together.

The first stage in 'fighting it' was agreeing to have the surgery that was necessary. I don't know to this day whether they were totally frank with Dad, whether they told him as they had told me that this was a holding operation, a pain reliever and that the prognosis was bleak. My impression is that they gave him some hope and that he decided to cling on to it. He hated the thought of surgery but he hated the thought of death, of not being there, even more. It started with the phoney war. There are many statements of intent. Strategies are laid out, alternative plans are examined, yet nothing seems to happen. He was told he needed a course of chemotherapy, which would reduce the cancers to the point where they were operable. This he endured, not suffering too badly from the side effects they said might occur. It took months. During this time it felt as if you were fighting an unseen enemy using weapons you could not rely on.

The waiting period had one advantage. It gave me a little time to mend fences with Dad which if not exactly broken had been rather badly trampled from time to time. I wouldn't say that we had grown apart, but the closeness that had developed over the constant separations of boarding school couldn't be sustained when we lived a couple of miles apart in the same city. Perhaps by seeing each other on a regular basis we became far more aware of each other's faults and learnt to take each other's good points for granted, a process many fathers and sons deal with during the growing-up years. As time went on I found him increasingly set in his ways, a bit crabby and on some pet issues less tolerant than the father I had put on a pedestal. In turn I think he often found me bumptious and scornful of attitudes I regarded typical of his generation. And he also thought I was overly indulgent to the children. There was always a deep love there, but one which was sometimes disfigured by petty disagreements and the occasional major row. After one of his diatribes, which began as a polemic against neighbouring kids playing on his precious lawn but ended as a salvo against all modern youth, I exploded. I accused him of sounding like all those narrow-minded, bigoted, hard-faced people I remembered him preaching against when I was young. Then, fuelled by the row and a few drinks I dare say, I uttered the fatal words.

'Go home, old man.'

The phrase, hanging in the air between us, was deeply regretted immediately. I knew that most of the time he was none of these things, just tired and exasperated. I also knew that above all he hated the idea of growing old both physically and mentally. I could not have said anything more hurtful. At our next meeting we patched it up, but it remained an obstacle between us.

When he became ill I realised too late that much of the crabbiness and tiredness had almost certainly been caused by a combination of the early physical symptoms of the disease and his unshared worry about it. Fortunately we had what some parents and children don't have, time to put it right. It was not a time of huge confessional or profuse expressions of love. Even had it been our style, it would have been impossible, because it would have meant having to acknowledge the possibility of his death, something he wasn't prepared to do. The trusting, humorous and comfortable relationship with which I'd grown up but which I had somehow carelessly allowed to lapse was re-established. We joked. I confessed my still unfulfilled ambitions. We talked as before about everything – politics, religion, science – about everything, that is, except the one thing on both our minds. Desperately anxious to talk about its implications myself, to help me come to terms with it, I tried to raise the subject on a couple of occasions. Knowing his views about religion, for instance, I wanted to know how far I should take his contempt for clergy and the obsequies of death. Did he really want to be buried in the garden, as he'd often half joked? I would have been more than happy to take on the establishment to make it happen. He wouldn't engage. On one occasion, although we were in a pub at the time, he broke down in tears. Afterwards he blamed the lowering effects of the chemotherapy but we both knew that for him to talk about it was to admit its possibility, and that he was not prepared to do. The nearest he came was the night before he went into hospital for the big op. As we parted he touched my arm. 'Take care of your Mother, if . . .' He got no further. He couldn't, but at least he'd said it.

After one brief spasm of hope the omens after the operation were never good. Towards the end of the day of the operation, during which the Falklands War started, unnoticed by me, I had a phone call. Jim Moseley sounded as triumphant as I've ever heard a doctor.

'Got the bloody thing,' he yelled presumably referring to the cancer. 'It was like getting a cat out of a tree, but we got it.'

His enthusiasm was infectious, and I allowed it to fuel my hope.

The following day I went to see Dad. My mother told me later that when I walked into the ward his face lit up and he said, 'Now we shall get some answers.' I think it was his first acknowledgement that, as a fixer at least, I had come of age. If only I could have lived up to my billing. But neither then nor afterwards did I repeat my initial success of extracting information from the medical staff. We met a wall of silence. Maybe, as they claimed, they didn't know at that stage whether the operation had been successful. Maybe they knew that my father didn't really want to know if the news was bad, and had me rightly tagged as a compulsive communicator. Whatever the reasons, I could make no progress either then or in the months to come.

On that first night he seemed very weak and distant, but that was hardly surprising. Over subsequent days and then weeks there was hardly any perceptible progress. They kept reminding us that it had been a major operation, and that such procedures were a massive shock to the system. For a long time he would remain extremely tired. I could accept all that, but something deeper was nagging away at me. It was him; the man himself. He was different. It was not just weakness, something seemed to have disappeared. It was as if they had gone in to extract the cancer and removed part of his personality at the same time.

Mum was spending every day at the hospital. Jo and I were going in most days. One Sunday afternoon I got a phone call at home. He had taken a sudden turn for the worse. Emphysema had set in and he was delirious. When we got there it was clear they didn't expect him to last the night.

He did. He lay unconscious, uncommunicating for most of the following day. Toward evening they told us that he now had a thrombosis in the leg and that they would have to do a below-the-knee amputation. We were horrified. The man was dying, for God's sake. What was the point of chopping bits off him? They said that if they didn't gangrene would set in. We accepted it, as you must.

Miraculously he came through that and the following night, another one they had confidently predicted he would not survive. All these memories are strangely interlaced with the events of the Falklands War, which was now in full swing. On the day of his relapse the *Belgrano* was sunk. On the morning of his second predicted demise the *Sheffield* was bombed in retaliation. Dad, obsessed by news and interested in the mechanics of war, hovered between life and death, oblivious to it all.

Then something bizarre and unexplained occurred. I had mentally said goodbye to him, but he began to come back to life. At first it was imperceptible: a pressure on the hand; his eyes following people round the ward. As we went to leave he very clearly waved to us and tried to say goodbye. It was the first word he'd uttered for four days. The doctors were bluntly baffled. They had removed all treatment, all drugs. And from that moment, so it seemed, he had begun to rally. Always suspicious of pills and potions, it was almost as if his body was having the last laugh. We wondered if it was just a temporary phenomenon, but the rally lasted. A week after the emergency he was sitting up in bed talking more strongly and more coherently than at any time since the operation. We seemed to be in the presence of a medical miracle (or rather a non-medical miracle).

We were now faced with a quite unexpected dilemma. Months earlier, before Dad's illness had been diagnosed, we had booked the family's first ever foreign holiday, arranging to go to Corfu with friends who had two daughters the same age as Tony and Robin. The holiday had been hugely anticipated. While Dad appeared to be dying it looked as if the holiday would coincide with the time that Mum would need us both. When he began to recover the problem remained equally delicate. We couldn't tell how long the recovery would last. Even if it were to continue, being away for this crucial fortnight seemed inconceivable. Yet as the recovery carried on, it felt to me that to cancel went against the spirit of the sort of man he was. One answer would have been for the rest of the family to have gone without me. While leaving the decision entirely up to me Jo made it clear that my not coming would spoil it for the kids. In the end we went, having made all the arrangements for a hasty return should the situation change.

It turned out to be a wonderful holiday, somehow intensified by the knowledge that it could come to an abrupt end at any moment. As it was, we were kept informed on rather erratic phone lines by an uncle who worked for the Post Office. Dad's progress continued to be satisfactory. We returned tanned and relaxed to a momentous event. He was allowed to spend a day at home, his first time back for ten weeks. Seeing him sitting in his small beloved garden was something I'd never expected to witness again. He wasn't up to going to the pub, but we returned at lunchtime with a pint in his favourite glass covered in clingfilm. We could of course have brought him a can, but it wouldn't have been the same. That day it was very clear how weak he still was. When he came home the following weekend it was to begin a brave, dogged but ultimately hopeless fight.

As we watched helplessly throughout the summer we were engaged in another desperate battle of our own. The situation with Fiona, now fifteen, was beginning to unravel fast. It was not a sudden event. We had been trying to paper over the cracks but we seemed to be on a collision course – one too many irate parents on the phone, one too many summons to the school and then one too many policemen at the door. The occasional fight in the street had degenerated into street fights. As often in these cases, the facts were never fully established but they landed Fiona in court. She seemed at this point to be consumed with a kind of rage and a determination to force us to give up on her. We, in turn, were filled with despair, recognising that after telling Fiona over and over again that she was as much a part of our family as any of the other children, we were about to do something which we would never have contemplated with any of the others: admitting defeat. Defeat from a mixture of anger, tiredness and a fear of the effect of the mayhem on the rest of the children. Unwilling to have Fiona think we regarded her as a problem, we had probably made too little use of social services and foster-parent support groups. Cosy evenings over coffee discussing bed-wetting, sibling rivalry and the size of the foster-care allowance had never been our bag. We now made a belated cry for help to be told that Fiona was just 'going through the normal teenage difficulties'. That's probably what they told Bonnie and Clyde's parents. During one of Dad's periodic returns to hospital we had one final cataclysmic door-slamming row, one more running away, one more policeman's knock at 3.00 a.m.

Fiona, apparently still not wholly convinced that she wanted the ultimate break, had been picked up loitering outside Winchester police station, not the most daring bid for freedom ever made.

If she wasn't sure, we now were. We told social services we had reached the end, and that Fiona would have to go back into some form of care. They said we must tell her in advance. We told them that if we did she would run before they could get to her. They insisted.

We watched *Top of the Pops*, Fiona morose and silent. Then I asked to talk to her alone. In her little room I felt like an executioner. She heard me out in silence then she said, 'Okay, but I'll run away.' I was damned if I was going to stand guard over her. I went for a much needed drink. On my way back someone sounding young ran past me. I still have no idea whether it was Fiona, but when I reached home and checked her room she had gone. No one else in the house had heard her leave.

At midnight the phone rang. It was Fiona. She said she was with friends and we weren't to worry. For the first time in months I felt a sliver of hope. Maybe it was not the final break I had feared. I wished her luck and meant it.

The following morning two social workers turned up to collect Fiona. I told them with some satisfaction that their bird had flown. Another phone call came in the middle of the morning. It was Fiona's headmistress, seeking information. Apparently Fiona, with some panache, had turned up at school that morning, but when social workers arrived to collect her she made off. Now, Miss Thompson informed us, two policemen were chasing her around a field at the back of the school. She demonstrated more humour than she had mustered at any of our previous encounters over Fiona, probably as a result of the relief that she was about to be rid of her. They finally captured Fiona, but she proved difficult to hold for long. Meanwhile we had to tell the other children when they got home from school that Fiona had left, probably for good. It was an odd moment. Fiona had been with us for the past five years. For Cathy that represented an entire life. What were the children to think of the fact that one of their number could just suddenly disappear? We never knew what they really thought. For public consumption, Tony and Robin pondered for a moment and then began arguing about who should have her room.

Fiona's next two years were a mess of assessments, referrals and abscondings. No sooner did the various authorities pick up Fiona than Fiona was off again. By throwing in the towel we had, it appeared, lost all rights in the matter. As far as the authorities were concerned it was as if the last five years had never happened. It had a strange effect. After attending one assessment that seemed to be made up of pathetic wimps and hard-faced bitches and where we were all but ignored, it suddenly felt as if we and Fiona were fighting on the same side again. During one of her temporary absences from care Jo ran into her in town. She told Fiona to come to the house, promising that we just wanted to talk, that we would not be handing her over to anyone. Nevertheless canny Fiona still turned up an hour earlier than arranged, just in case. She needn't have worried. We fed her, talked, then gave her a lift back to the travelling fair where she was earning a few bob. Another small piece of trust had been reinstated.

But the whole jigsaw could not yet be put back together. In the end, Fiona did what I think she had always intended to do sooner or later. She went back to Scotland to try to link up with her mother's family and in particular her half-sister.

A year passed; very little contact. Then, one day, a letter. Things had obviously gone badly wrong. She didn't go into details or directly ask for help, but all the signs were there. We wrote back, sending a little cash for her to do with as she liked.

Late one Saturday night a few days later the doorbell rang. She had spent the money on a rail ticket.

Among all this turmoil Dad's condition started to worsen again. Astonishingly, despite an enormous loss of weight and strength and the deterioration in his general state of health he was beginning to master the art of walking with his artificial leg. It was pure willpower; pure stubbornness. White's Last Stand. If stories about willpower and cancer had any basis in fact he would have beaten it. But they don't. The pain began to return. The pain meant pills. The pills, for Dad, seemed to mean debilitation. He went in for one last exploratory operation on the day we attended Fiona's court case, not a day to forget in a hurry. Apparently they took one look and realised that cancer was back in battalions. They sent him home again. He had one last shot in his locker left for me. I, selfish pig that I was, still wanted him to talk. I'm not sure what I wanted him to say. Everything between us that needed to be said already had been covered. Nevertheless I arranged to go down and have a drink with him one evening while Mum had a much needed break. He got out the whisky bottle. I thought that might do the trick.

An hour later he was talking, but I had stopped. I was still moving my jaw all right but no sense was coming out. I couldn't imagine how I'd got so drunk so quickly. I'd simply been matching Dad drink for drink. When Mum came home they poured me into a taxi. The following day Jo rang me up at work, chuckling.

'Your dad wants to know if you've got a hangover.'

I'd just completed a programme with a splitting headache.

'I gather,' she said, 'you didn't get much talking done. Do you want to know why?'

I did.

'Because he was pouring you four for every one of his. He said you were too greedy to notice.'

The old bugger had had the last laugh on me by exploiting my blindness. A nice touch I thought.

Two weeks later he was dead. He died, appropriately enough, at closing time on a Saturday night, almost to the second. He had survived just long enough to see my mum through the funeral of her older sister, who also had had cancer.

He surprised us in that last year by defying every preconception we had about him. An impatient man, he bore uncertainties, indignities and towards the end great pain with enormous dignity. A hater of illness and the smells and mess that surround it, he managed to adapt to using a colostomy bag, learning to walk on a false limb and finally to wait for death with calm. In some ways a selfish man, at the time when he was enduring the most he devoted most attention to other people, those looking after him, and those who were just waiting, powerless to do anything. Although it was in some ways the most untypical time of his life, it summed up his greatest talent: adaptability. I think it's the part of his nature from which I gained the most. On having two blind children, he adhered to no rule book, but pulled off the balancing act of making allowances for our blindness while still taking account of our personalities, so that we turned out as confident and unapologetic about our blindness as we are. I believe he could have achieved many things, with more luck and different circumstances. I think it's my good fortune that, deprived of those opportunities, he put so much of his energy, enthusiasm and inventiveness into being my father.

14

The Box Beckons

Within months of my father's death, I was enjoying easily the most successful period of my career to date.

The Whites had emerged pretty battered from the end of 1982. We were exhausted from my father's long illness. Fiona had gone – probably for good we thought. Many of my certainties seemed to have departed too. But in terms of work, everything I touched seemed to turn to gold.

I can't explain this. Perhaps, like quite a lot of people, I reacted to loss by working more frenetically. I didn't do it consciously, but suddenly it seemed that from being a work-to-live person, I was piling all my energies into working and giving the living a miss.

The results were immediate. Having pottered along at Radio Solent for over twelve years, picking up steady enough employment but not uprooting any trees, I was invited to present their mid-morning current affairs and phone-in programme. Although I had presented plenty of prerecorded programmes such as *In Touch*, going live with a control panel while interviewing guests, cueing records and orchestrating irate, libellous or barmy callers is pretty demanding. Nevertheless I'd always known instinctively that I would be able to handle that kind of programme. For whatever reason – fear, idleness, lack of genuine ambition – I'd never pushed for it. Solent, so I have been told since, were nowhere near as confident of my ability to cope. In fact, they were terrified at this bold, unconventional step. On the day I presented my first edition of *View Point* the station manager, who had ultimately authorised it but who was on holiday in France, rang up at fifteen-minute intervals to ensure that no disasters had befallen me or the station. I've no idea what they were expecting. Presumably at the very least I would blow up the studios. In the event, though, paralysed with fear and managing to miss my cue as the signature tune faded at the start of the programme, things progressed moderately well. I wrapped up the last item at the end of the first hour and we went into the midday news.

I threw up my hands in elation. 'Wow, we did it,' I yelled.

My producer, with remarkable forbearance, murmured gently in my ear, 'We did. By the way, before you say any more, do you think you could close your microphone?'

Whoops!

I took to it like a duck to water. I loved being live, having to think on my feet, enjoying the risk and the challenge of callers who had given only the briefest account of their views to our switchboard and might say absolutely anything and frequently did.

Within three months I had a contract to do the programme daily, which meant a considerable hike in my earnings and in my sense of security. Within six months Neil Kinnock, Arthur Scargill, Douglas Hurd and Kenneth Clarke had all appeared on the programme. I'd also presided over some memorable on-air punch-ups. I particularly remember a confrontation between the novelist and animal rights campaigner Richard Adams and a Southampton furrier. As they squared up to each other to debate the fur trade it was deliciously clear that there was going to be trouble. The table where we were sitting was vibrating like a bowstring as a result of their both shaking, Mr Adams with anger, the furrier I suspect with fear.

At one point Richard Adams, almost exploding the microphone yelled, 'You're a horrible little man.'

The furrier paused, gulped and then with commendable pluckiness and self-knowledge said, 'I'm not little.'

Mr Adams rose to his feet. How should I cope? Just in time, my mother's words from childhood came back to me. I heard myself say, 'If you're going to fight you can go outside.'

It did the trick. They clearly remembered their mothers too. The interview continued with moderate decorum.

This was reinforced by two new series on Radio 4, the area where ultimately I longed to succeed. I had been approached to do a documentary series on new trends in nursing; the other a series on sport in literature which I had gone out and sold myself. This was unheard of. For years I had simply snapped up what crumbs had fallen from the table. Quite suddenly I had my nose in the trough with the rest of them.

By the end of the year my position had been transformed. I was better known, better paid and better motivated. My mother said, and still says, 'If only your Dad had lived to see it, he would have been so proud.' Indeed he would, and I wish he had. But I have an odd superstitious belief that in the end his death was what enabled me – freed me, if you like – to do it. I had always been so desperate to succeed to repay some of what I felt he had given me that it led me to fear failure. When I screwed up university I was far more mortified on his behalf than I was for myself. Once in broadcasting I knew I was in the right career, but along with my quest for success was mixed a large dollop of fear of failure. As a result I aimed relatively low and therefore always managed to avoid failing. I genuinely believed that I didn't climb the broadcasting ladder more quickly not because I was discriminated against but because I lacked the conviction that I could really make it. Solent and others took me at my own valuation. When the fear of falling flat on my face was removed and I felt prepared to take more risks, the opportunities instantly opened up. It does seem one of life's blacker ironies, though, that the man who in all the world I would most have wished to impress had to be off the scene before I could fully achieve what he would have wanted.

In the meantime the family was doing its best to get back to normal. Throughout Dad's illness Jo had been an absolute tower of strength, not only supporting me but also keeping both Mum and Dad as fully informed as she could when the medical profession was being less than forthcoming. She now felt she needed a break of her own. She'd gone back to nursing as an auxiliary when Cathy was three, having originally abandoned her training to have Tony. She swiftly decided to train as a SEN (State Enrolled Nurse), the compromise between skivvying and full qualifications. But by 1983 she was becoming restless again. She decided to take a look around, gave up the two-nights-a-week job she had been doing and as a temporary measure took a part-time job at the local ambulance station. After two days she knew she wanted to be an ambulance driver.

It seemed the perfect solution. Jo likes action and though a late starter adapted to driving like a natural. She saw ambulance work as a way of continuing to use her medical experience without the drudgery of nursing at the bottom of the ladder. She cake-walked the entrance exam and everything was set fair. I was excited too. She wasn't going to earn a fortune but then we didn't need her to. It seemed like the right person for the right job.

But the whole project crashlanded. Sometime within your first nine months of service you have to take the special driving course, a somewhat macho affair based on the police drivers' model. Jo was summoned for her fortnight's course within weeks of her appointment. I sensed her apprehension. It was too early. She wanted a bit longer to absorb the culture of the place, but you weren't offered a choice.

Although the course was close enough for her to have come home at night she chose to stay on site, but it quickly became clear from her phone calls that something wasn't quite right. When she finally came back for the evening towards the end of the first week, it all came tumbling out. The guy running the course was the kind who couldn't see anyone aspiring to do his job without regarding it as a challenge for a put-down. The other women on the course rose to this challenge; Jo did not. Quietly competent when left to herself, she tends to freeze when put under critical scrutiny. It was clear we were on a collision course with disaster.

It came on the skid pan during the second week. It's a hairy session at the best of times. Jo, though in no way a nervous driver, lost her bottle under the eagle eye of Action Man. Having lost it, for the rest of the course she could hardly put the car into gear without making a mistake.

She was called in on the last day and told her driving wouldn't make the grade. She was devastated; I was devastated for her. It wasn't that it was so vital in career or financial terms. It was more the feeling that the attitude of one oik had carelessly crushed her potential before it had the chance to bloom.

For the best part of a year she brooded, doing various jobs but not really taking an interest. She took and passed her advanced driving test with an instructor who'd trained many ambulance drivers, then presented herself back at Hampshire ambulance service, asking them to reconsider. They declined. Reluctantly she let it go. All was moving forward. She went back to college to get some more qualifications so that she could take the new conversion course to become a registered general nurse.

For differing reasons, the boys were having their scholastic problems too. Tony had just passed the exam to King Edward's, the high flyers' direct-grant school in Southampton. He had won one of the Conservative government's new assisted places. Originally I hadn't wanted him to sit for it. I believed in the comprehensive system and would have preferred him to have gone to the local school up the road. Jo persuaded me that it would be unfair to deny him better teaching in smaller classes if he was bright enough to pass. I yielded, one of the few big arguments over the children which I lost, and I was mightily proud when he won his place. But it had created another problem. On the night we went to look around the school we took Robin along as well. Rob, even at nine enormously class-conscious, saw this as his birthright (I suspect he saw the posh parents and their big cars as much as the superior laboratory facilities). I realised we had a potential problem. There was no way at that stage that we could afford full fees, and no way did I believe that Rob, full of chutzpah but much less academic than Tony, would win an assisted place.

Sadly I was right. On the morning the results were expected he set off for school before the post had arrived. When he got there children who had passed had already received their letters. Rob remained convinced throughout the day that his letter would be there when he came home. It was, but it carried the wrong message. Another devastated White family member.

Cathy trotted on as usual largely unregarded. She has always indignantly asserted that no one ever tells her anything about what's happening in the family. I think myself she takes a certain pride in not wanting to know. She suffered one educational indignity. As matters improved financially we finally – having eventually taken advantage of Mrs Thatcher's 'bargain of the century' – moved from the council house we had bought to a more upmarket part of the city. This meant a change of school for Cathy for the final two terms before secondary school (no talk of direct grants and assisted places for her!). In total contrast to Robin, Cathy is the archetypal inverted snob. She liked and was comfortable at her free-wheeling school on the council estate, and was mightily miffed at the rather pretentious little neighbourhood school in Oliver's Battery, the new neighbourhood. They presented her with weekly maths and spelling tests. They didn't like her and she didn't like them. They parted in the summer without regret.

As for the prodigal foster daughter, Fiona's return, when it eventually occurred in 1985, turned out to be permanent. We never delved too deeply into what had gone wrong in Glasgow. Once back, our relationship with her became easier than it had ever been before. It was as if both sides had discovered how far they could push each other and had no need or desire to repeat the experience. In the end, Fiona turned into a model citizen. She gave up the fags, stopped drinking, even seemed to lose her taste for beating up policemen. Never work-shy she tried an assortment of jobs: instructor at a holiday sports centre, serving in a DIY store, care assistant to disabled people. Badly paid and usually the fall girl, she nevertheless stuck at them until something better came along. Eventually she got the kind of job she'd always wanted; working with disturbed teenage boys in a residential school. She had always wanted to show that she could improve on the treatment she had received when she'd been in trouble. Fiona should take most of the credit for turning a lousy start into a satisfying life, but if I thought I'd had anything to do with it, I would be prouder of that than of any of my other so-called achievements.

For one obvious person life after Dad could never slip back into even a semblance of normality. Quite apart from her loss Mum hated living alone. Any hopes that, released from his fairly demanding personality, she might start thinking about her own needs and make a life outside the home were soon dashed. She threw herself even more into tending the garden they had both loved. That was fine during the daytime, but when night drew in down that rather gloomy cul-de-sac we knew that she felt gloomy and isolated too. Jo did her best to keep an eye on her. Colin bought her a dog. But in the end she came up with her own rather more dramatic and surprising solution. She acquired another husband.

Mum and Dad had both known Alan for many years. He had just returned to Winchester after running a pub in Wales. He, too, had recently lost his wife. Both lonely, they embarked on what turned out to be a remarkably brisk courtship. I think Mum expected Colin and I to object, perhaps, particularly, me. In fact I was delighted. If I had ever doubted my firmly stated belief that there is no afterlife, this incident confirmed for me that it was genuine. I had no sense, even a darkly lurking one that Dad, so jealous in his lifetime, would either know or care. He had asked me to look after her. This seemed to me by far the surest way for her to achieve some kind of contentment again.

As for Colin, the bosom pal of my youth, we had, like many brothers, grown apart as we got older and became involved with our own families. For a while Dad's death brought us together again as we used our very different skills to sort out family problems. As when we were kids the demarcation lines were clear. Colin dealt with the practicalities, while I looked after the people. When it was over we drifted back to the former pattern of only contacting each other when there was something specific to discuss. We live only six miles apart, but sometimes it might as well be six hundred.

Nevertheless without all the fanfares that I've enjoyed he continues to be particularly successful at what he does. I suspect other physiotherapists envy Colin his almost guru-like status. While their manipulations might be regarded as a lot of pushing and pulling, Colin's laying-on of hands in conjunction with his blindness appears to inspire an almost religious enthusiasm among his patients. It goes down particularly well with women of a certain age. My endless chatter on the radio appears to strike a similar chord with the same type of woman. Some people are firmly convinced that we are the same person, buzzing dementedly between the hospital and the radio station, plying an unlikely dual career. We may think we are very different, but all they seem to see is a blind man called White.

Suddenly I realised life needed kick starting again. I had been hugely enjoying the *View Point* programme on Solent. For the first time in my career, not only was I getting a regular daily dose of the adrenaline provided by live radio but the proportion of my work which dealt with my disability was far outweighed by general broadcasting. I had a feisty producer whose bellowed commands through my headphones – 'Shut that woman up' or 'For Christ's sake move on before I die of boredom' – enlivened my weekday mornings. We dealt with every subject under the sun, and often seemed to be at the cutting edge of the news agenda. On the Thursday morning in 1986 when Michael Heseltine flounced out of Mrs Thatcher's weekly cabinet meeting we were scheduled to be interviewing his parliamentary private secretary, Michael Mates, who represented Hampshire East. Mr Mates honoured his commitment to us, gave us the first informed reaction to Tarzan's resignation and in the process enabled us to upstage *The World at One*.

The period also contained the year-long miners' strike. Throughout 1984 the well-heeled burghers of Hampshire and West Sussex freely and generously dispensed advice to the miners of South Wales and the Yorkshire coal fields on our phone-ins. In the end this provoked a bright idea. We managed to persuade the chairwoman of one of the Winchester branches of the Women's Institute to accompany me to spend a week with a miner's family in the Cynon Valley. It seemed a ridiculous notion when we first came up with it but to our amazement Mrs Janet Arnold consented, and Dane and Jennifer Hartwell of Hirwaun agreed to indulge us. The results made compelling radio. I sat quietly with a tape recorder while Janet argued and listened by turns. She attended her first soup kitchen, joined a picket line, heard the hatred of the miners' wives for Mrs Thatcher, for whom the spat pronoun 'She' was especially reserved. She visited a blackleg to hear the other side of the story. And we were in Dane's front room when we heard that a taxi driver transporting miners who ignored the strike had been killed by a concrete block dropped from a bridge. I recall his mixture of horror and outrage and his realisation of what this would do to his cause, and his generosity in talking about it, even though it wasn't the face of the strike he had wanted to show.

Janet arrived in South Wales full of smug stories of her father's willingness to move about to get work and exasperation that miners didn't do the same. She returned with a clearer understanding of the dearth of opportunity to do any thing else in the valleys and the fact that these people owned houses which no one would want to buy, even if they had been prepared to up sticks and move away from their community. I was privileged to see that rarest of sights: a mind being changed.

Those were the good days. There were also times when we seemed to talk about nothing for weeks but dogs fouling the pavement, the need for regular doses of public floggings and why the latest bypass must or must not be built. On the whole I had a great rapport with our regular callers but sometimes Sheila from Swaythling and Michael from Maybush could be a total pain.

I needed another stimulus, another challenge, although when it finally came along I almost failed to spot it.

When he called me, towards the end of 1985, Martin Davison said he'd like us to meet to talk about some ideas he had about disability broadcasting. This was not a particularly unusual call. Disability was just beginning to get trendy in the Britain of the mid-eighties. A combination of tentative legislation, a few gobby disabled people and whispers from across the Atlantic were beginning to put the subject on the agenda. In addition to *In Touch*, I'd opened up my own programme on Solent to include all disabilities and had made a few contributions to the Radio 4 programme on disability *Does He Take Sugar?* It meant that I had become quite used to people asking me for my ill-informed views on a range of issues. I never hesitated to give them an answer but on this occasion Martin, typically as I was to discover later, gave very little clue about what he had in mind. I arranged to meet him after a recording of *In Touch* in London.

It was a particularly hairy programme that day. In the flurry of activity I forgot all about the appointment. It was only at three o'clock when I emerged a little frazzled from the studio that I received the message that a man had been waiting patiently in reception for the past hour.

Flustered and on the wrong foot, I rustled up a sandwich for him and his assistant and he told me the story.

He was running a self-help organisation cum wannabe television company called Contact TV. It was the kind of animal I had never heard of before. I was already puzzled. It seemed Martin's abiding ambition had been to produce a television magazine programme on disability for Channel 4.

He had all the buzz words: radical, challenging, pro-active. I yawned inwardly and it emerged that someone else had been yawning too. Channel 4 had already turned down a couple of pilot programmes. After the latest rejection they'd told him to go out and find a competent disabled presenter before he came back to them. In Martin's master plan I was to be the presenter.

My pulse was still not racing. These were very early days. His ideas were sketchy, Channel 4 had given no guarantees and at that stage no money to make a pilot. A number of others among the new breed of independent TV companies were sniffing around the same tree. But my objections ran much deeper than that. I knew very little about the subject of disabilities other than my own. Admittedly I'd gone to *In Touch* with equal ignorance, but I was older now – I knew what ignorance was.

Martin brushed this aside. He didn't know much about it either, he said (not surprisingly I'd already twigged this). That was the purpose of research. The important thing was that I had an empathy with the subject.

At a much deeper level I was just not sure I wanted to do it. It would be *In Touch* all over again, but on a bigger, much more visible scale. I would be doing a job in which it could be thought that my biggest qualification was not my talent but my disability. By this time I was much more comfortable being blind. I certainly no longer felt any sense of having to apologise for it but that didn't mean I'd yet reached the stage where I'd want to flaunt it. Whatever they may say, most disabled people would bite your hand off for the chance not to be disabled, not because of embarrassment or shame but out of the sheer boredom of having to continually explain the role. For the past three years, very little of my work had been connected with disability and I'd enjoyed the break. I felt like a normal broadcaster. This admission may outrage those people who have embraced the trendy concept of 'disability pride', but I can only tell you how I felt. And indeed it was the growth of the trendier aspects of disability politics which was also giving me pause for thought.

I have no problem with direct action as a means of protest. Wheelchairs handcuffed to buses and red paint signifying blood on the cobbles of Downing Street cause me no concern. There's enough evidence that peaceful protest achieves results when righting wrongs, and God knows there are enough wrongs. From the little I knew of disability politics, what worried me was the growth of an attitude which seemed to want to drive a wedge between disabled people and everybody else. There seemed to be a belief, borrowed from the black and women's movements, that somebody ought to pay for centuries of oppression. I recognise that revenge is a natural and enjoyable human emotion, but it's one I've never much cared for when it's aimed at whole classes of people. I don't blame every German for the Second World War; I don't see why I should take the blame for the behaviour of every male bully. By the same token I'm not smitten with the idea that the best way for disabled people to assert their independence is to make non-disabled people uncomfortable at every turn. The most blatant example of this is all the tortuous debate about correct terminology. As this process adds absolutely nothing to the sum of people's understanding it can only have one aim: joyously to wrong-foot people who use the wrong words by changing them as rapidly and regularly as possible.

I really wasn't sure I wanted to get involved in such a

game and I left Martin that day secretly hoping his scheme would go the way of so many projects dreamed up by small independents – straight down the pan!

But life's not like that. A few weeks later when I was least expecting it I got a phone call. Channel 4 had come up with the princely sum of £20,000 for us to do a pilot with me as presenter. Was I in?

I didn't know. I did what I always do in these situations – the next thing. In this case the next thing was to do as good a job on the pilot as possible, then see what happened.

By now I had a number of good contacts in the States and it was here that anything worth reporting about disability was happening. I suggested we demonstrate our initiative by blagging a couple of flights to Washington and reporting on their brand new accessible transport system – a subway with level access for wheelchair users, winking lights in the well of the platforms to alert deaf people to oncoming trains and clear, and detailed and informative announcements for blind people. Within weeks we had shot the film and it had gone like a dream. On my thirty-ninth birthday we went into a studio and recorded the pilot.

It was not an agonising wait because I still wasn't sure if I was doing the right thing. I resolved to let fate take its course. Finally, we received the all-clear. I broke the news to a gratifyingly disappointed BBC Radio Solent and prepared for the unknown.

On Wednesday 1 April 1987 I sat in my front room frozen with fear. I was supposed to be catching a train to London to start the first day's work on the programme, which was to be called *Same Difference*. Within three months, having never worked in TV before, having not the faintest idea about the techniques needed to make or script a film report or the restrictions my blindness would place on me, I was committed to producing eight half-hour programmes of riveting television.

Martin, a former cameraman, knew more about television but less about the subject. What had I done? There was no help for it. Nearly £300,000 of Channel 4 money said we were committed. I went to the station as I had hundreds of times before, and headed for London. It was time, so it seemed, to play the blind card yet again.

Warner Books now offers an exciting range of quality titles by both established and new authors. All of the books in this series are available from:

Little, Brown and Company (UK),
P.O. Box 11,
Falmouth,
Cornwall TR10 9EN.

Fax No: 01326 569555
Telephone No: 01326 569777
E-mail: books@barni.avel.co.uk

Payments can be made as follows: cheque, postal order (payable to Little, Brown and Company) or by credit cards, Visa/Access. Do not send cash or currency. UK customers and B.F.P.O. please allow £1.00 for postage and packing for the first book, plus 50p for the second book, plus 30p for each additional book up to a maximum charge of £3.00 (7 books plus).

Overseas customers including Ireland, please allow £2.00 for the first book plus £1.00 for the second book, plus 50p for each additional book.

NAME (Block Letters) ....

....

ADDRESS ....

....

....

☐ I enclose my remittance for ....

☐ I wish to pay by Access/Visa Card

Number ⬜⬜⬜⬜⬜⬜⬜⬜⬜⬜⬜⬜⬜⬜⬜⬜

Card Expiry Date ⬜⬜⬜⬜